The Jeshua Channelings

Christ consciousness in a new era

Pamela Kribbe

Booklocker.com, Inc.
2008

This book can be ordered at www.jeshua.net/book

Cover by Herbert Stam www.crea-tis.nl

Mandala drawings by Sonja Jordens www.newenergypainting.nl

Contents

Preface

This book contains a collection of inspired messages or "channelings" which I received from my spiritual teacher Jeshua over the course of four years. The channelings in this book have been published before on our website www.jeshua.net and are freely available there. Nevertheless, we felt a book might satisfy the need for a more convenient way to read the material. Also, all of the material in this book has been edited and "updated" in 2007, meaning that I have rewritten some parts that I felt – in close association with Jeshua – needed to be put differently.

Jeshua is short for "Jeshua ben Joseph" – the Aramaic name for Jesus. By choosing the name Jeshua to present himself, Jeshua stresses his humanness and his kinship to us. It is his aim to reach out to us like a friend, an elder brother perhaps, but not as the kind of deified master that has become associated with the name "Jesus Christ."

The book starts with an introductory channeling from Jeshua about who he is and what his mission was on earth 2000 years ago. Then we start with the first body of channelings, "the Lightworker series," which my husband and I received from Jeshua in the beginning years when there was no live audience present yet. These messages are about what it means to be a lightworker and about the history and destination of this group of souls. They contain a thorough description of the transformation from ego based consciousness to heart based consciousness.

In the second part of this book, we present a series of eleven messages from Jeshua received in the presence of a live audience. The issues dealt with in this series are often quite practical, referring to everyday aspects of life such as relationships, emotions, work and health. Through it all runs the thread of self healing and inner peace as the common theme that holds the messages together.

In the final chapter of the book there is more information on my own background as a channeler and some notes on the phenomenon of channeling in general.

I am very thankful to a number of people for their help and support. First of all, there is my husband, Gerrit, without whom this book would not have been written. From the start, he has accompanied me on my voyage of discovery in the field of channeling. He was and he is always by my side when I channel Jeshua, helping me feel safe and focused. Also, by his patience and trust, he has helped me get through moments of fear, resistance and doubt, which were also invoked by the channeling process. Finally, Gerrit has also contributed a lot to the technical side of the publication process.

The Jeshua channelings were originally received and written down in Dutch. I am thankful to Hedwig de Beer for typing all the audio material, and to Wendy Gillissen and Tineke Levendig for helping me translate parts of the material into English. I am much indebted to Joe Meboe for his meticulous editorial assistance, getting the whole manuscript into proper English shape. Finally, I much appreciated the presence of a number of friends and clients who regularly attended our channeling meetings and who helped create an open and loving atmosphere for the messages to be received.

Throughout the years we have met many people, at meetings, workshops or through the Internet, who were deeply moved by the messages of Jeshua. This has inspired us to go on with this work and to gradually release our own doubt and insecurity about it. We feel that by publishing the Jeshua material, we have been reconnected to our soul family, souls who feel called by the same deep longing for spiritual transformation, growth and healing. We are deeply thankful for this.

Pamela Kribbe

September 2007

Who is Jeshua?

I am the one who has been among you and who you have come to know as Jesus. I am not the Jesus of your church tradition or the Jesus of your religious writings. I am *Jeshua-ben-Joseph*; I have lived as a man of flesh and blood. I did reach Christ consciousness before you, but I was supported in this by powers which are beyond your imagination at present. My coming was a cosmic event – I made myself available for this.

It wasn't easy. I did not succeed in my endeavors to pass on to people the immensity of God's love. There was much misunderstanding. I came too early, but someone had to come. My coming was like throwing a stone in a large fishpond. All the fish flee and the stone sinks into the deep. There are ripples noticeable long afterwards, though. One might say that the kind of consciousness I wished to convey did its work underground after that. On the surface of the pool there were constant ruffles; well-intended but misguided interpretations rose to meet and fight each other in my name. The ones who were touched by my energy, moved by the impulse of the Christ energy, could not really integrate it with their psychological and physical reality.

It has taken a long time before Christ consciousness could really set foot on earth. But now the time has come. And I have returned and speak through many, through all and to everyone who wants to hear me and who has come to understand me from the quietness of their hearts. I do not preach and I do not judge. My sincerest hope is to speak to you of the vast and unfailing presence of Love, accessible to you at any time.

I am part of a much larger consciousness, a greater entity, but I, Jeshua, am the incarnated part of that entity (or field of consciousness). I do not like the name Jesus much, for it has become so caught up with a distorted version of what I stand for. "Jesus" is owned by the church traditions and authorities. He has been molded to fit the interests of the church patriarchs for centuries, so much so that the prevailing image of Jesus is now so far removed from what I represent that it would truly please me if you could just let it go and release me from that heritage.

I am Jeshua, man of flesh and blood.

I am your friend and brother.

I am familiar with being human in every way.

I am teacher and friend.

Do not fear me. Embrace me like you'd embrace one of your kin.

We are family.

Jeshua, Jesus and Christ

The Christ energy that I came to offer you stems from a collective energy that has gone beyond the world of duality. This means that it recognizes the opposites of good and bad, light and dark, giving and taking as *the aspects of one and the same energy.* Living from the reality of Christ consciousness means that *there is no struggle with anything.* There is a complete acceptance of reality. This absence of struggle or resistance is its main characteristic. Since Christ (or the Christ energy) recognizes the extremes of all thoughts, feelings and actions as the manifestation of the one divine energy, there can be no duality, no judgment in the way "he" (the Christed energy) experiences reality.

Let's give an example here. When the Christ in you watches an armed conflict between people, her heart weeps for the fate of the beaten one, but she does not judge. She feels the pain and humiliation with each blow and her heart is filled with compassion, but she does not judge. She watches the offender, the one with the gun, who has power, who inflicts pain, and she feels the hatred and bitterness inside of him, and her heart grieves, but she does not judge. The heart of Christ embraces the whole spectacle with deeply felt compassion but without judgment, for she recognizes all aspects as experiences she has gone through herself. She herself has lived out all of these roles, of offender and victim, of master and slave, and she has come to the understanding that *she is neither of them,* but *that which underlies both.*

The Christ energy has passed through all the energies of duality. It identified itself now with the dark, then with the light, but through it all, something remained the same. And when she realized this "sameness" underlying all her experiences, her consciousness obtained a new kind of unity: it was "Christed." The Christed energy was the energy I came to offer you.

Who I was is quite difficult to explain. I will try to do so by distinguishing between three identities: Jeshua, Jesus and Christ.

I, the one who is now speaking, am *Jeshua.* I was the human being who carried the Christ energy in my incarnation on Earth. This energy may also be called *Christ.*

Jesus – in my terminology – is the name for the Godlike man who was *the result of the infusion of Christ energy into the physical and psychological reality of Jeshua.*

This *Christ* energy was poured into Jeshua from spheres of Light which are – from your standpoint – located in your future. Jesus was the man who performed miracles and brought forth prophesies. Jesus was an emissary from the spheres of Light, incarnated in me. In fact, he was my future self. Jesus was, from my perspective as the man Jeshua living on earth, my future self, who had become one with the Christ energy. Because the Christ in him was clearly present and visible to many people around him, he appeared to them as divine.

I, Jeshua, was a man of flesh and blood. The unique and to some extent *artificial* aspect of the "Jesus-construction" was that I received his/my Christed self from the future. I did not become Christed on the basis of my past or the experiences of my past. I did not achieve enlightenment in a natural way, but by means of an intervention from outside, so to speak, by an infusion of Christ energy from the future. I had agreed to play this role before I began this lifetime. I agreed to be "overshadowed" by the Jesus presence as an act of service, and also because of a deeply felt longing to get to know the reality of my deepest potential.

Jesus, my future self from the spheres of light, had become one with the Christ energy. Yet he did not represent the *entire* energy of Christ here on earth, for this energy encompasses more than Jesus. He is one part or cell of it.

Christ, or the Christ energy (it is more like an energy field than a personal entity), is a collective energy which has many aspects or "cells" which are cooperating in such a way that they function as one organism. All cells make a unique contribution to the whole and experience themselves as individuals while being part of the whole as well. One might call these several aspects of the Christ energy *angels* or *archangels*. It is the hallmark of angels that they have a sense of individuality as well as a high degree of *selflessness*, which allows them to feel one with collective energies and be joyfully in their service. The notion of (arch) angels is elucidated in the last chapter of the Lightworker series ("Your Light Self").

Jesus' mission on earth

Jesus was an energy from the future who came to earth to bring illumination and knowledge to humanity. He came from another world or even dimension, and he brought with him the elevated energy of this reality. His awareness of his own Greater Self remained intact while he incarnated on earth. Because of his presence in me, Jeshua, I could easily realize the flexibility of material laws and "perform miracles."

The reason why the Jesus/Jeshua personality came to earth was to create an opening or doorway to a different state of consciousness. I wanted to set an example of the possibilities that are available to each human being.

In the spheres of Light where Jesus came from, it was felt that the earth was going in a direction that would end up in great darkness and self-alienation for the souls involved in the earth experiment. It was decided that a powerful impetus for change was going to be given which would clearly show human beings the *choices available to them.* By sending the energy personality of Jesus, we wanted to hold up a mirror to human beings and remind them of their own divine origin and the dormant potentials they carried within: the potentials for peace, freedom and mastership over yourself.

Every human being is the master of their own reality. You are creating your own reality all the time. You are able to let go of a miserable or unsatisfying reality and allow Light to enter and transform your creation. You are your own master, but you tend to give your power away to outside authorities who claim to know the truth and to want the best for you. This happens in politics, medicine, education, etc. Also, your "entertainment industry" is full of false images about happiness, success and beauty, which serve no one except the ones who construct them. Have you ever thought about how much money is spent just *creating images?* In the media, in newspapers, in movies, on radio and television and on the Internet, images are spread all the time. Where do these images come from? Why are they there? Who designs them?

Images are a means of exerting power over people. Images can make people subservient to and disconnected from their true needs, without the use of physical force or violence. Images can make people voluntarily give away their own power and self-worth. They delude you in such a way that you need not be violently forced into anything; you will accept the values portrayed by the image as your own and act accordingly. This is what we would call *invisible mind control* and it is rampant among your "free" western societies.

The function of Light is primarily to bring clarity, awareness and transparency to the invisible structures of thought and feeling that shape your life. Light is the opposite of mind control. Where Light enters a reality, it breaks bonds of mere power and authority and it breaks down the hierarchies based on them. It holds misuse of power up to the Light and it frees people from delusions and illusions that take away their power for self determination.

Jesus was a threat to the ruling order at the time he lived. By what he told people and simply by what he radiated, he caused structures of power to be seen for what they truly were. This was unbearable and unacceptable for the existing hierarchy.

The role of lightworker, which Jesus took upon him, was heavy, especially for me, Jeshua, the human being who agreed to carry this intense, bright energy in my lifetime. I, Jeshua, was almost overshadowed by the force of Jesus' presence, the presence of my future self! Although it filled me with great insights, love and inspiration, it was quite a challenge physically to carry or "hold" his energy. I could not really integrate his energy into my physical being – the cells in my body were not yet ready for it – so on a physical level my body got exhausted from carrying these intense energies of Light.

Apart from the physical aspect, there was also a psychological burden to carrying the Christ energy. I found it very hard to watch the nature of the Christ energy being frequently misunderstood, even by my closest friends or "disciples." As the human being that I was, I sometimes became desperate and doubted the value of the journey I undertook. I felt that the world was not ready for the Christ energy. I felt that its essence was not recognized. Jesus was truly a pioneer in his time.

Results of Jesus' coming to earth

By the coming of Jesus to earth, a seed was planted. It was the seed of the Christ energy. People were moved by what I said and did, and unconsciously, at the soul level, they did recognize the Christ energy. Deep within their souls, a memory was stirred. Something was touched and set in motion.

At the surface, on the level of what can be seen and felt in the physical world, my coming created much commotion. By virtue of the law of duality, the powerful infusion of light creates a powerful reaction from the dark. This is just a matter of logic. Light is confronting. It wants to break structures of power and set the imprisoned energies free. Darkness is the energy that wants to suppress and control. So these two energies have opposing interests. Where one gains in power, the other will strike back to defend itself and regain balance. Thus my coming to earth also initiated much struggle and violence, as a counter reaction to the light I came to spread.

The persecution of my followers, the early Christians, is one example of this violent counter reaction. But the Christians themselves, the founders of the Church, did not shun violence either in their eagerness to spread my teachings. Think of the crusades and the Inquisition. In the name of Christ, the most barbaric deeds of darkness have been performed, by Christians as well as by non-Christians.

The masters of Light, who decided to send me as an emissary to earth, were aware of the fact that the intense and unprecedented energy of Jesus might invoke strong reactions of darkness. Jesus penetrated the reality of earth like a comet. It was a kind of emergency measure from the spheres of Light, from energies which were deeply concerned with earth and its inhabitants. It was an ultimate attempt to divert the direction in which the earth was heading, a way of interrupting cycles of ignorance and destruction which kept on repeating themselves.

The results were ambiguous. On the one hand, the light of Jesus invoked much darkness by way of counter reaction. On the other hand, the seed of the Christ consciousness was planted in the hearts of a number of people. An important reason for my coming was to awaken the *lightworker* souls on earth. (See the first part of this book for an explanation of the notion of lightworker). They would be most sensitive and receptive of my energy, although many had become lost in the density and darkness of the earth plane as well. Lightworkers are in fact emissaries of light with the same mission as Jesus. The difference is that in their incarnation in a physical body, they are less connected to their wider divine Self than I was. They are more subject to the karmic burdens and illusions of the earth plane. They are more bound to the past. With the incarnation of Jesus, something special was occurring. Jesus did not carry any karmic burdens from the past and he could therefore more easily keep in touch with his divinity. He was here in a somewhat artificial way, a presence from the future, being here and there at the same time.

The consciousness of the beings of light, which jointly decided to insert the energy of Jesus into earth reality at that time, was not perfect and all-knowing. Every conscious being is in the process of developing and understanding itself all the time. Among humans, there is a persistent belief that everything is predestined by some divine plan; behind this belief is the notion of a dominant, omniscient God. This notion is false. There is no predestination by an outside force. There are only probabilities which are the result of inner choices you yourself make. My coming to earth was based on a decision made by a collective energy of light, of which Jesus was a part. It was a choice that involved risks and an unpredictable outcome.

The collective energy of light I am speaking of is an angelic realm that is deeply connected to humanity and earth because it helped to *create* humans and the earth. Actually, you are *part of them* and not separate from them at all, but we are now speaking *multidimensionally*, i.e. on a level of consciousness that is outside of your linear framework of time. In another dimension or framework of time, you *are* these angels that make up the spheres of light, from which Jesus descended to earth. (See the last chapter of the Lightworker series ("Your Light Self") for an in-depth explanation of multidimensionality and your angelic nature.) You – lightworkers – are much more interconnected with "the Jesus event," this infusion of Christ energy on earth, than you suppose. It was to some extent a collective endeavor to which you all contributed and of which I, Jeshua, was the visible physical representative.

My message was that the Christ energy is present in all human beings as a seed. When you look up to me as some kind of authority, you have misunderstood my message.

I wished and still wish to *invite you to believe in yourself,* to find the truth within your own heart and not to believe in any authority outside of you.

Ironically, the official Christian religion has placed *me* outside of your reality as an authority figure to worship and obey. This is quite the opposite of what I intended. I intended to show you that you can be a living Christ yourself.

I now ask you to recognize the Christ within, and to return my humanness to me.

I am Jeshua, man of flesh and blood, and truly a friend and brother to you all.

Part I

The Lightworker Series

The New Earth I

In this day and age, a transition is taking place on earth. A new consciousness is dawning which will take material shape sooner or later. How exactly this transition will come about, what form it will take, is not fixed. The future is always indeterminate. The only thing that is really given is this moment: the Now. From the well of the Now, countless possible roads are springing, an infinite web of possible futures.

On the basis of the past, we can predict that one particular future is more probable than another, *but the choice is always yours*. It is you who decide whether you let the past determine your future! Predictions are always based on probabilities. Probabilities are related to the past. It is in your power as a human being to break with the past, to set out a different course. You are endowed with free will. You have the power to change, to *recreate* yourself. In this power rests your divinity. It is the power to *create from nothing* (to create *ex nihilo*). This divine power belongs to the very essence of who you are.

In speaking of this day and age as an age of transition, never forget that you are the master of your own reality. There is no such thing as a predestined Plan or a Cosmic Power which overrules your individual soul's path or your individual power to create your own reality. It doesn't work that way. Every soul on earth will experience this transition in a way that fits their inner propensities. There are many realities. The reality you choose will answer your inner needs and desires.

What makes this time (1950 – 2070 approximately) special is that there are two different cycles of consciousness coming to an end: a *personal cycle* (or a set of personal cycles) and a *planetary cycle*. The completion of these cycles coincides, so that one reinforces the other.

For a part of humanity, the completion of their personal cycle of earth lives is near. Most of the souls involved in this completion are lightworkers. We will speak in much more detail about this group of lightworker souls. Here we would like to explain the nature of this personal cycle: what it means to go through it and what is the purpose of living all these quite complicated lives on earth.

The personal karmic cycle

The earth lives you experience are part of a greater cycle of your soul. This cycle was designed to enable you to fully experience duality. You have within this cycle experienced what it is like to be male and female, to be healthy and ill, to be rich or poor, to be "good" and "bad." In some lives you were intensely involved with the material world, being a farmer, worker or craftsman. There have been more spiritually oriented lives, in which you carried within you a strong awareness of your spiritual origins. In those lives you were often drawn to religious callings. Also there have been lives in which you explored the worldly domain of power, politics etc. There may have been lives devoted to an artistic expression of yourself.

Often souls tend to specialize somewhat in the course of all these lives. This can clearly be recognized in people who possess a natural gift in a certain area. It seems they have a potential there, even as a child, which only needs to be awakened at the right time and which is then easily developed.

Lightworker souls are often drawn to religious lives and have lived numerous lives as monks, nuns, priests, shamans, witches, psychics etc. They were drawn to be intermediaries between the material, physical world and the spiritual realms. And so they developed an expertise in this field. When you feel this calling, this strong urge to be involved with spirituality, even if it does not fit in with your normal daily life, you may very well be part of this family of lightworkers.

Living on earth provides you with an opportunity to fully experience *what it is like to be a human.* Now you may ask: what's so special about being human? Why would I want to experience that?

The human experience is both diverse and intense. When you live a human life, you are temporarily immersed within an overwhelming field of physical sensations, thoughts and feelings. Because of the duality inherent in this field, there is great contrast and intensity in your experiences, much greater than when you are in the astral planes, as you call it. (These are the planes you enter after you die and where you remain between lives.) It may be hard to imagine for you, but many entities on our side would love to be in your shoes. They would love to be human, to gain human experience. The human experience has a kind of *realness* to it which is invaluable to them. Although they can create countless realities by the power of their imagination, it gives them less satisfaction than the creation of one "real" reality on earth.

On earth, the creation process is often a struggle. You typically meet a lot of resistance in making your dreams come true. The mental type of creation in the astral world is much easier. There is no time lag between the thought of something and the actual creation of it. Moreover you can create any reality you want or can think of. There are no limits. The moment you picture a lovely garden, it is there for you to enter.

To give birth to an idea on earth, to make it a reality in the material world, is a great endeavor. It demands a strong intention, perseverance, clarity of mind and a trusting heart. On earth, you have to deal with the slowness and stubbornness of the material world. You have to deal with contradictory impulses in yourself: with doubt, despair, lack of knowledge, loss of faith, etc. The creation process may be obstructed or even fail because of any of these elements. Yet these potential problems, even the failures, are the very reasons that make the experience of earthly life so valuable. In this process, the challenges you meet are your greatest teachers. They give earth experience a profundity that is so much deeper and broader than the effortless creation process on the astral planes. This effortlessness breeds meaninglessness. The astral entities which have not yet experienced lives on earth know and understand this.

You often get discouraged and even desperate by the non-compliant nature of your reality. So often, reality does not answer your wishes and hopes. So often, your creative intentions seem to end up in pain and disillusion. However you will find that key to peace and happiness at some point. You *will* find that key *within your own heart.* And when you do, the joy that will befall you will not be matched by anything created in the astral planes. It will be the birth of your mastership, your divinity.

The ecstasy you will experience when your divinity awakens will provide you with the power to heal yourself. This divine love will help you recover from the deep hurts you have suffered throughout your lives on earth.

After that, you will be able to help cure others who have been through the same trials and sorrows. You will recognize their pain. You will see it in their eyes. And you will be able to guide them on their path to divinity.

The purpose of going through duality

Please do not underestimate the meaning of your lives on earth. You belong to the most creative, advanced and courageous part of God (All-That-Is). You are explorers of the unknown and creators of the new. Your explorations through the realm of duality have served a purpose far beyond your imagination. It is hard to explain to you the deepest meaning of your travels, but we can say that you have created a new type of consciousness, one that did not exist previously.

This consciousness was first displayed by Christ when he walked the earth. This consciousness, which I call the Christ consciousness, results from a *spiritual alchemy.* Physical alchemy is the art of transforming lead into gold. Spiritual alchemy is the art of transforming dark energy into "the third energy," the spiritual gold present in the Christ energy.

Please note that we do not say that the purpose is to transform dark into light, or evil into good. Dark and light, evil and good are natural opposites; they exist by the grace of one another.

True spiritual alchemy introduces a "third energy," a type of consciousness which embraces both polarities through the energies of love and understanding. The true purpose of your journey is not to have Light conquer

Dark, but to go beyond these opposites and to create a new type of consciousness which can maintain unity in the presence of both light and dark.

We will explain this rather difficult point by means of a metaphor. Imagine you are deep-sea divers in search of a pearl. Time and again you dive into the ocean to find this particular pearl which everyone talks about but nobody has actually seen. Rumors go that even God, the Chief Diver, has never touched the pearl.

Diving into the ocean is full of perils, since you can get lost or go too deep to catch your breath in time. Still you persist and you dive into this ocean time and again, for you are determined and inspired. Are you insane?

No, you are explorers of the new.

The secret is: *in the process of finding the pearl, you are creating it.* The pearl is the spiritual gold of the Christ consciousness. *The pearl is you, transformed by the experience of duality.*

What we have here is a true paradox: in exploring the New, you are creating it. *You have become the pearl of God's creation.*

God had no other way of doing it, for what you were attempting to find did not exist yet; it had to be created by you. Why was God so interested in creating something new? Let us state this in as simply a way possible.

First, God was entirely GOOD. There was goodness everywhere and all around. In fact because there was nothing else, things were kind of static. His creation lacked aliveness; it lacked the possibility of growth and expansion. You might say it was stuck.

To create change, to create an opportunity for movement and expansion, God had to introduce an Element in his creation that was different from the Goodness that pervaded everything. This was very hard for God, for how can you create something that is not-you? How can Goodness create Badness? It can't. So, God had to come up with a trick, so to speak. This trick is called *ignorance.*

Ignorance is the element that opposes Goodness. It creates the illusion of being outside Goodness, of being separated from God. "Not knowing who you are" is the incentive behind change, growth and expansion in your universe. Ignorance breeds fear, fear breeds the need to control, the need to control breeds the struggle for power and there you have all the conditions for "Evil" to flourish. The stage has been set for the battle between Good and Bad.

God needed the dynamics of opposites to get his creation "un-stuck." It may be very hard for you to comprehend in view of all the suffering caused by ignorance and fear, but God put great value on these energies, since they provided him with a way to go beyond *Him/Herself.*

God asked you, the ones that belong to the most creative, advanced and courageous part of herself, to take the veil of Ignorance. In order to experience the dynamics of opposites as thoroughly as possible, you were temporarily soaked in forgetfulness about your true nature. You consented to take this plunge into ignorance, but this fact was overlaid by the veil of forgetfulness as well. So now you often curse God for being in the situation you're in: the hardships, the ignorance – and we understand. In essence though: *you are God, God is you.*

Despite of all the troubles and sorrows, deep down within you there is still a sense of wonder and excitement about living in duality, about experiencing and creating the New. This is God's original excitement, the reason God started with his journey through You in the first place.

When you started out on your journey, you faced Evil (fear, ignorance) with only a vague memory of the Good (Home) in your mind. You started to battle fear and ignorance, while longing for Home. However you will not return Home in the sense of returning to a state in your past. For creation has changed because of your journey.

The end of your journey will be that you have become larger than good and evil, light and dark. You will have created a third energy, the Christ energy, which embraces and transcends both. You will have expanded God's creation. You will be the New Creation of God. God will have gone beyond Him/Herself when the Christ consciousness is fully born on earth.

The Christ consciousness did not exist before the "human experience." The Christ consciousness is the consciousness of one who has gone through the multilayered experience of duality, has come to terms with it and emerges "on the other side." He will be the inhabitant of the New Earth. This one will have let go of duality. She will have recognized and embraced her own divinity. He will have become one with his divine Self. But his divine Self will be different than before. It will be deeper and richer than the consciousness from which it was born. Or one could say: God will have enriched Him/Herself by having gone through the experience of duality.

This story is simplified and distorted as anything we say is distorted by the illusions of time and separation. These illusions have served a valuable purpose. But the time has come to go beyond them. Please try to feel the energy behind our words, stories and metaphors. This energy is in a sense *your own*. It is the energy of your future *Christed* selves that is speaking through me, Jeshua. We are waiting for you to join us.

How to overcome duality – the completion of the karmic cycle

Your earthly cycle of lives ends when the game of duality no longer has a hold on you. It is essential to the dualistic game that you identify yourself with a particular position in the playfield of polarities. You identify yourself with being poor or rich, famous or humble, man or woman, hero or villain. It really doesn't matter that much which part you are playing. As long as you feel one with the actor on the stage, duality still has a firm grip on you.

This is not wrong of course. In a sense it was meant to be that way. You were meant to forget about your true self. To experience all the aspects of duality, you were meant to narrow your consciousness down to a particular role in the drama of earth life.

And you played it well. You got so caught up with your roles that you totally forgot about the aim and purpose of going through this cycle of lives to begin with. You were so forgetful about yourself that you took the games and dramas of duality to be the only reality there is. In the end this made you very lonely and full of fear, which is not surprising since the very game of duality, as noted in the previous section, is based on the elements of ignorance and fear.

To understand the workings of duality in your everyday life, we would like to mention a few typical hallmarks of the duality game.

Characteristics of the duality game

1) Your emotional life is essentially unstable.

There is no emotional anchor present, since you are always in the "up" or "down" side of a particular mood. You are angry or forgiving, narrow-minded or generous, depressed or enthusiastic, happy or sad. Your emotions perpetually fluctuate between extremes. You seem to have only limited control over these fluctuations.

2) You are intensely involved with the outer world.

It is very important to you how other people judge you. Your self-esteem depends on what the outer world (society or your loved ones) mirrors back to you about who you are. You are trying to live up to their standards of right and wrong. You are doing your very best.

3) You have strong opinions about what's good and what's bad. Being judgmental gives you a sense of security. Life is so well organized when one divides actions, thoughts or people into right and wrong.

Common to all these characteristics is that in all you do or feel, you are *not really there.* Your consciousness resides in the outer layers of your being where it is driven by fear-oriented patterns of thought and behavior.

Let us give an example. If you're used to being nice and agreeable all the time, you are displaying a pattern of behavior that does not spring from your inner being. You are in fact suppressing signals from the inner part of you. You are trying to live up to someone else's expectations in order not to lose their love, admiration or care. You are reacting from fear. You are limiting yourself in your expression. The part of you that is not expressed will however live a hidden life of its own, creating dissatisfaction and tiredness in your being. There may be anger and irritation present in you which no one is aware of, not even you!

The way out of this state of self-denial is to make contact with the suppressed and hidden parts within you.

Making contact with the suppressed and hidden parts within you is not difficult in the sense that it requires particular skills or knowledge to do so. Don't make "going within" a difficult process that others have to teach you or do for you. You can do it yourself and you will find your own ways of doing it. Motive and intent are far more important than skills and methods. If you really intend to know yourself, if you are determined to go deep within and change the fearful thoughts and emotions that block your way to a happy and fulfilled life, you *will* do it through any method that comes along.

Having said that, we'd like to offer one simple meditation which may help you get in touch with your emotions.

Take a moment to relax the muscles in your shoulders and neck, sit straight up and put your feet flat on the floor. Take a deep breath.

Picture yourself walking on a country road under a wide open blue sky. You take in the sounds of nature and you feel the wind through your hair. You are free and happy. Further down the road, you suddenly see some children running toward you. They are getting closer to you. How does your heart respond to this sight?

Then the children are in front of you. How many are they? How do they look? Are they boys, girls or both?

You say hello to all of them. Tell them how happy you are to see them. Then you make contact with one child in particular who is looking you in the eye. She or he has a message for you. It is written in the child's eyes. Can you read it? What does it want to tell you? It is bringing you an energy that you need right now. Name the energy that this inner child has come to bring you and don't judge it. Simply thank her or him and then release the image.

Feel the earth firmly under your feet again and breathe deeply for a while. You have just contacted a hidden part of yourself.

You can go back to this scene anytime you want and perhaps talk to the other children there as well.

By going within and making contact with the hidden, suppressed parts of yourself, you are becoming *more present*. Your consciousness is rising above the fear-motivated patterns of thought and behavior that you have taken for granted for such a long time. It is taking responsibility for itself. It takes care of the sorrow, anger and hurt inside, like a parent takes care of its children. We will describe this process in much more detail elsewhere. (See Lightworker III).

Characteristics of releasing duality

1) You listen to the language of your soul which speaks to you through your feelings.

2) You act upon this language and create the changes your soul wishes you to make.

3) You value quiet time alone, for only in silence can you hear the whispers of your soul.

4) You question the authority of thought patterns or rules of behavior which block the free expression of your true inspiration and aspirations.

The turning point in letting go of duality

Your earthly cycle of lives draws to a close when your consciousness is able to hold all the experiences of duality in its hand, while remaining centered and fully present. As long as you identify with one aspect of duality rather than another (with light as opposed to dark, with rich as opposed to poor etc.), your consciousness is on a swing. Karma is nothing but the natural harmonizer for the swings in which your consciousness engages. You release your ties to the karmic cycle when your consciousness finds its anchor point in the motionless center of the seesaw.

This center is the exit point for the karmic cycle. The predominant feeling tones in this center are stillness, compassion and quiet joy. Greek philosophers had premonitions of this state which they called *ataraxia:* imperturbability.

Judgment and fear are the energies that most take you off-center. As you release these energies more and more, you become more quiet and open inside. You truly enter another world, another plane of consciousness.

This will be manifested in your outer world. It will often be a time of change and saying goodbye to aspects in your life that do not reflect YOU anymore. Great upheavals may occur in the area of relationships and work. More often that not, your whole lifestyle turns topsy-turvy. This is only natural, from our perspective, since inner changes are always the forerunner of changes in your outer world. Your consciousness creates the material reality you dwell in. It is always that way.

Releasing the grip of duality takes time. Unraveling all the layers of darkness (un-consciousness) is a gradual process. Yet once you embark upon this road, the road to the inner Self, you are slowly distancing yourself from the game of duality. When you have tasted the true meaning of *ataraxia*, the turning point is taken. When you have felt the silent yet all-pervading joy of simply *being with yourself,* you will know that that is what you've been looking for all along. You will go inward time and again to experience this peace inside.

You will not shy away from worldly enjoyment. But you will have found an anchor of divinity within yourself, and you will experience the world and all its beauty from that state of bliss. Bliss never resided in material things to begin with. It resides in the way you experience them. When there is peace and joy in your heart, the things and people you meet will give you peace and joy.

In this day and age, a certain group of souls is preparing itself to step off the karmic cycle. We will speak in depth about this group in the next chapters. However it is not just a group of human souls that is now reaching the end of a transformative personal cycle. The very earth on which you live is undergoing a deep and thoroughgoing transformation. A planetary cycle is coming to an end as well. This era is so special because of these two cycles coinciding. We will now speak about the planetary cycle.

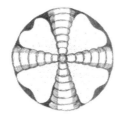

The New Earth II

The planetary cycle

Everything that is evolves in cycles, planets as well as humans. It is not exceptional for an individual or groups of individual souls to step off the karmic cycle at some point in time. What makes this era special however is that the earth herself is completing a major karmic cycle. The earth is involved in an inner transformation which will result in a new type of consciousness in her being as a planet. At whatever point individual souls are within their own cycle, the earth's transformation process will affect them.

The earth is your house. Compare it to the house you live in. Imagine that it is being rebuilt. This will greatly affect your daily life. Depending on your state of mind, you will experience it as a welcome change or a disrupting and upsetting event. If you were planning and looking forward to rebuilding your house anyway, you are in sync with the changes and you can go with the flow. The earth's transformation process will support and enhance your personal transformation process.

If you did not want to have your house rebuilt at all, you will feel frustrated by the chaos surrounding you. The inner earth changes will throw you off balance.

For the ones who are welcoming the inner changes of your planet earth, these will be extremely empowering times. You will be lifted by the wave of Light that is presently flooding your universe.

At present, the earth is almost cracking beneath the karmic burden of humanity. The negativity and violence which spring from this karmic burden form a kind of energetic waste that the earth is hardly able to process, to neutralize or integrate.

Focus your consciousness for a moment on the heart of the earth. Relax and focus... can you feel something there? Can you feel how the earth is being torn apart, how there is so much violence upon her?

The earth is feeling powerlessness and resistance at the same time. She is on the verge of creating a new foundation for her being. The earth is going to release the energies of struggle, competition and drama, on inner and outer levels. The new foundation that is dawning within her is the energy of the heart, the energy of balance and connectedness: the living Christ energy.

The earth, just like humanity, is involved in a learning experience. Just like humanity, her consciousness is evolving and transforming itself. As with humanity, her journey started from a certain type of ignorance or unconsciousness about her own being.

The earth once was a "dark planet" which absorbed or swallowed the energies surrounding her. She took in energies or beings that she encountered and she assimilated them completely; she took away their uniqueness and in a sense killed them. This sprang from a desire for expansion. The earth somehow sensed a lack or inadequacy within her which she interpreted as a need to conquer and assimilate other energies. Since the earth did not give anything back to these energies, there was not really an interaction between them. It was a deadly and deathlike process.

At a certain time, the earth became aware that this process did not satisfy her. She felt something lacking in this way of feeding herself. Her sense of inadequacy was not relieved by it. Her urge towards expansion was not satisfied by making energy dead.

At this moment within earth consciousness the desire was born for liveliness, for Life. Not that the earth was fully aware of it. She just knew she wanted something else, something new, a kind of interaction with other energies which would not end in the reduction of those energies to earth energy.

Within earth consciousness a space was created for the *experience of something different than herself.*

Energetically this meant the beginning of life on earth.

It is a cosmic law that all deeply felt desires will ultimately create the means for their realization. Desires, which are essentially a mixture of thought and feeling, are *creative* energies. This holds for planets as well as for people. Within earth as a planet a longing had arisen, a longing to experience life, a longing to preserve and cherish life, instead of destroying it.

And so it happened.

When life came to earth, the earth herself started to bloom and blossom. She entered a new domain of experience which filled her with a sense of surprise and satisfaction. She was surprised that such a simple longing, such a vaguely felt need, would bring about such grand and novel developments.

On earth, a grand experiment of life forms unfolded. Many life forms were drawn to manifest themselves on earth and to experiment with the energies present. The earth became a breeding place for novelty. There was freedom to explore new roads, new possibilities. There was and still is free will for all creatures.

With the creation of life, the earth and all living creatures upon it started to pursue a certain line of inner development. This path of experience had as its central theme *the balance between giving and taking.*

At the inner level of consciousness, the earth has been striving for eons to find the right balance between giving and taking. As a planet, earth gives and takes life. In earth's "dark period," the stage in which she absorbed and liquidated energies, the accent strongly was on "taking."

At present she has wound up at the other extreme: giving to the limit of what she can give.

The earth has long tolerated violence and exploitation by humanity, for this was karmically fitting in a sense. The earth had to explore the other side of power and oppression. Her actions as an offender incited the opposite experience of being a victim, like a boomerang. That is how karma works; it's not a matter of punishment. To really understand and come to terms with the issue of power, you have to experience both sides to it. Anything you struggle with or want to assert power over, you will meet again as victim or offender, until you recognize that you are both ONE, both part of the one divine energy.

The ruthless exploitation of earth in current times, then, is to some extent karmically adequate, since it has provided the earth with an opportunity to come to a full understanding of the balance between giving and taking.

However the limits to which disrespect and exploitation are karmically adequate are within sight. The earth has reached its understanding of the balance and is completing her karmic cycle of consciousness. She has attained a level of love and awareness now that will not tolerate human abuse for much longer. This level of consciousness will cause her to attract like-minded energies which savor harmony and respect, and to repel energies with destructive intent.

The time has come for a new balance between giving and taking. On the New Earth, there will be peace and harmony between planet earth and all that lives upon her: human, plant and animal. The harmony and heartfelt connectedness between all beings will be a source of great joy and creativity.

The transition from old earth to new earth is a process that is not fixed in time and character. Much depends upon the choices made by humanity, the choices made by all of you as individuals right now.

A lot of predictions have been and are being made about this time of transition. Making such predictions is always a dubious affair. The point is: your visible material reality is a manifestation of inner, collective states of consciousness. Consciousness is, as we put it at the start, *free and creative.* At any time, you can decide to change your future by thinking and feeling differently. You have power over your thoughts and feelings. At any time, you can say no to limiting, destructive thoughts or feelings. This counts for you as an individual but it also goes for larger groups of people.

When a substantial group of individuals chooses freedom and love over self-hate and destruction, then this will manifest itself in material reality. The earth will react to it. She is sensitive to what takes place inside of people. She responds to your inner movements.

By this we would like point out that no one, not even on our side, is able to make accurate predictions as to the way in which the New Earth will be birthed. It is clear however that the group of souls now completing their karmic cycle is closely connected energetically to the New Earth. These people, who often feel deeply connected to the ideals embodied in the New Earth, will have beautiful opportunities to grow and release because of the planetary and personal cycle coinciding.

In the following chapters, I will speak about this group of souls in particular. They are often called lightworkers and I will use that name also. Their reason for incarnating during this age of transition is not coincidental. They are deeply connected with the history of earth. I will describe the psychological traits that most lightworkers possess. I will speak about their history, their galactic roots and their mission on earth. I will discuss in detail the stages of inner growth that are involved in releasing oneself from the karmic cycle.

Lightworker I

The Lightworker's identity

Lightworkers are souls who carry the strong inner desire to spread Light – knowledge, freedom and self-love – on earth. They sense this as their mission. They are often attracted to spirituality and to therapeutic work of some kind.

Because of their deeply felt mission, lightworkers often feel different from other people. By experiencing different kinds of obstacles on their way, life provokes them to find their own unique path. Lightworkers are nearly always solitary individuals, not fitting into fixed societal structures.

A note on the notion of "lightworker"

The word "lightworker" may evoke misunderstanding, since it lifts out a particular group of souls from the rest. It may be taken to suggest that this particular group is somehow superior to the others, i.e. those "not working for the light." This whole line of thought is at odds with the very nature and intent of lightwork. Let us state briefly what is wrong with it.

First, claims of superiority are generally unenlightened. They block your growth toward a free and loving consciousness. Second, lightworkers are not "better" or "higher" than anyone else. They simply have a *different history* than the ones not belonging to this group. Because of this particular history, which we will discuss below, they have certain psychological characteristics which distinguish them as a group. Third, every soul becomes a lightworker at some stage of its unfolding, so the label "lightworker" is not reserved to a limited number of souls.

The reason we use the word "lightworker" despite possible misunderstandings is because it carries associations and stirs memories within you that *help you remember*. There is a practical convenience to it as well, since the term is frequently used in your current spiritual literature.

Historical roots of lightworkers

Lightworkers carry within them the ability to attain spiritual awakening faster than other people. They carry inner seeds for a rapid spiritual awakening. With regard to this, they seem to be on a faster track than most people, if they choose it. This again is not because lightworkers are in any way "better" or "higher" souls. They are, however, *older* than most souls presently incarnate on earth. This older age should preferably be understood in terms of experience rather than time.

Lightworkers have reached a particular stage of enlightenment before they incarnate on earth and start their mission. They consciously choose to become entrenched in the "karmic wheel of life" and to experience all forms of confusion and illusion that go with it.

They do this in order to fully understand "earth experience." This will enable them to fulfill their mission. Only by going through all stages of ignorance and illusion themselves will they eventually own the tools to help others achieve a state of true happiness and enlightenment.

Why do lightworkers pursue this heartfelt mission to help humanity, thereby running the risk of losing themselves for ages in the heaviness and confusion of earth life? This is a question we will deal with extensively below. For now we will say that it has to do with a *galactic type of karma.* Lightworkers stood on the eve of humanity's birth on earth. They took part in the creation of man.

They were co-creators of humanity. In the process of creation, they made choices and acted in ways which they came to regret deeply afterwards. They are here now to make up for their decisions back then.

Before we go into this particular history, we will name a few characteristics of lightworker souls which generally distinguish them from other people. These psychological traits do not uniquely belong to lightworkers and not all lightworkers will recognize all of them as theirs. By drawing up this list, we simply want to give an outline of the lightworker's psychological identity. With regard to the characteristics, outer behavior is of less importance than inner motivation or felt intent. What you feel inside is more important than what you show outside.

Psychological characteristics of lightworkers:

- From early on in their life, they feel they are *different*. More often than not they feel isolated from others, lonely and misunderstood. They will often become *individualists* who will have to find their own unique ways in life.

- They have trouble feeling at home within traditional jobs and/or organization structures. Lightworkers are naturally *anti-authoritarian* which means that they naturally resist decisions or values based solely on power or hierarchy. This anti-authoritarian trait is present even if they seem timid and shy. It is connected to the very essence of their mission here on earth.

- Lightworkers feel *drawn to helping people* as a therapist or as a teacher. They may be psychologists, healers, teachers, nurses, etc. Even if their profession is not about helping people in a direct manner, the intent to contribute to the higher good of humanity is clearly present.

- Their vision of life is colored by a *spiritual sense* of how all things are related together. They consciously or subconsciously carry memories within them of non-earthly spheres of light. They may occasionally feel homesick for these spheres and feel like a stranger on earth.

- They deeply *honor and respect life* which often manifests as a fondness for animals and a concern for the environment. The destruction of parts of the animal and vegetable kingdoms on earth by human doing invokes deep feelings of loss and grief in them.

- They are *kind-hearted, sensitive and empathic.* They may have trouble dealing with aggressive behavior and they generally experience difficulties in standing up for themselves. They can be dreamy, naive or highly idealistic, as well as insufficiently grounded, i.e. down-to-earth. Because they easily pick up negative feelings and moods of people around them, it is important for them to spend time alone on a regular basis. This enables them to distinguish between their own feelings and those of others. They need solitary time to touch base with themselves and with mother earth.

- They have lived many lives on earth in which they were deeply involved with *spirituality and/or religion.* They were present in overwhelming numbers in the old religious orders of your past as monks, nuns, hermits, psychics, witches, shamans, priests, priestesses, etc. They were the ones providing a bridge between the visible and the invisible, between the daily context of earth life and the mysterious realms of the afterlife, realms of God and the spirits of good and evil. For fulfilling this role, they were often rejected and persecuted. Many of you were sentenced to the stake for the gifts you possessed. The traumas of persecution left deep traces within your soul's memory. This may presently manifest as a fear of being fully grounded, i.e. a fear to be really present, because you remember being brutally attacked for who you were.

Getting lost: the lightworker's pitfall

Lightworkers can be caught up in the same states of ignorance and illusion as anyone else. Although they start from a different point of departure, their capacity to break through fear and illusion in order to attain enlightenment may be blocked by many factors. (By enlightenment, we mean the state of being in which you realize that you are essentially of the Light, capable of choosing light at any time.)

One of the factors blocking the road to enlightenment for lightworkers is the fact that they carry a heavy karmic burden which may lead them astray for quite some time. As we stated before, this karmic burden is related to decisions they once made with regard to humanity in its infant stages. These decisions were essentially disrespectful of life (we will speak of this later in this chapter). All lightworkers now living wish to set right some of their past mistakes and to restore and cherish what was destroyed because of those mistakes.

When lightworkers have made their way through the karmic burden, which means to *release the need for power in any way*, they will realize that they are essentially beings of light. This will enable them to help others in finding their own true selves. But first they have to go through that process themselves. This generally demands great determination and perseverance on the inner level. Because society feeds them values and judgments which often go against their own natural impulses, many lightworkers have gotten lost, ending up in states of self-doubt, self-denial and even depression and hopelessness. This is because they cannot fit into the established order of things and they conclude there must be something terribly wrong with them.

What lightworkers have to do at this point is to stop looking for validation from the outside – from parents, friends or society. At some point in time, you who are reading this will have to take the momentous leap to true empowerment, which means to really believe in yourself and to truly honor and act upon your natural inclinations and your inner knowing.

We invite you to do so and we assure you that we will be with you every step of the way – just like you will be there for others on their way in the not too distant future.

Lightworker II

The galactic history of lightworkers

The birth of the soul

Lightworker souls were born long before the earth and humanity came into being.

Souls are birthed in waves. There is a sense in which souls are eternal with no beginning and no end. But in another sense, they are born at some point. It is at this point that their consciousness reaches a *sense of individual self*. Before this point, they are already there as a *possibility*. However there is no consciousness yet of me and other.

The consciousness of "me" arises when somehow a demarcation line is drawn between groups of energies. We have to revert to metaphors in order to explain this.

Think of the ocean for a moment and imagine it to be a huge field of flowing energies, streams that constantly mingle and part. Imagine that a diffuse consciousness pervades the entire ocean. Call it the ocean spirit if you want. After a while, concentrations of consciousness arise at certain places in the ocean. Consciousness here is more focused, less diffuse than in its direct surroundings. All over the ocean there is an ongoing differentiation which leads to the development of transparent forms within the ocean. These forms, which are focused points of consciousness, move independently from their environment. They experience themselves as different from the ocean (spirit). What occurs here is the birth of a rudimentary sense of self or self-consciousness.

Why did focused points of consciousness arise in some parts of the ocean rather than in others? This is very hard to explain. Can you feel, however, that there is something very natural about this proceeding? When you throw seeds on a bed of earth, you notice that the little plants that sprout will each grow in their own time and rhythm. One will not grow as large or as easily as the others. Some will not grow at all. There is differentiation across the field. Why? The energy of the ocean (the ocean spirit) intuitively seeks the best expression possible for all its multiple streams or layers of consciousness.

During the formation of individual points of consciousness within the ocean, there is a power that works on the ocean from the outside, or so it seems. This is the power of divine inspiration, which can be conceived as the male aspect of That which created you. Whereas the ocean represents the female, receptive side, the male aspect may be visualized as light beams pouring into the ocean, which enhance the process of differentiation and the separation into individual lumps of consciousness. They are like the rays of the sun that warm the seedbed.

The ocean and the light beams together form an entity or being that may be referred to as an archangel. It is an *archetypical* energy with both a male and a female aspect and it is an *angelic* energy that manifests or expresses itself to you. We will come back to the notion of an archangel in more detail in the last chapter of Part I, called "Your Light Self."

After the soul is born as an individual unit of consciousness, it slowly leaves the oceanic state of oneness that had been its home for a long time. The soul increasingly becomes aware of being separate and on its own.

With this awareness, a sense of loss or lack arises in the soul for the first time. When the soul embarks upon its road of exploration as an individual entity, the soul will carry with it a certain longing for wholeness, a desire to belong to something bigger than itself. Deep within itself, the soul will keep the memory of a state of consciousness in which everything is one, in which there is no "me" and "other." This is what it considers "home" to be: a state of ecstatic oneness, a place of complete safety and fluidity.

With this memory in the back of its mind, the soul starts its travels throughout reality, throughout countless fields of experience and inner exploration. The newborn soul is driven by curiosity and has a great need for *experience*. This was the element that was absent in the oceanic state of oneness. The soul now is able to freely explore anything it wishes to explore. It is free to search for wholeness in all sorts of ways.

Within the universe, there are countless planes of reality to explore. The earth is simply one of them and one that came into being relatively late, speaking on a cosmic scale. Planes of reality or dimensions always originate from inner needs or desires. Like all creations, they are the manifestation of inner visions and ponderings. Earth was created from an inner desire to bring together elements from different realities that clashed with each other. Earth was intended to be a melting pot for a great array of influences. We will explain this further below. For now suffice it to say that the earth was a relative late-comer on the cosmic stage and that many souls lived many lives of exploration and development on other planes of reality (planets, dimensions, star systems, etc.), long before the earth was even born.

Lightworkers are souls who lived many, many lives on these other planes before they ever incarnated on earth. This is what distinguishes them from "earth souls" as we will call them for the sake of convenience. Earth souls are souls who incarnated in physical bodies on earth relatively early in their development as individualized units of consciousness. One might say that they started their cycle of earth lives when their souls were in their infant stage. At that time, the lightworker souls were "grown-ups." They had been through many experiences already and the type of relationship they bore with earth souls may be likened to that of parent and child.

The development of life and consciousness on earth

On earth, the evolution of life forms was closely intertwined with the inner development of the earth souls. Although no soul is bound to a particular planet, the earth souls could well be said to be the natives of your planet. This is because their growth and expansion roughly coincides with the proliferation of life forms on earth.

When individual units of consciousness are born, they are somewhat similar to single physical cells as regards structure and possibility. Just like individual cells have a relatively simple structure, the inner movements of a newborn consciousness are transparent. Not much differentiation has set in yet. There is a world of possibilities at their feet, both physical and spiritual. The development from a newborn unit of consciousness to a type of consciousness that is self-reflective and able to observe and react to its environment may roughly be compared to the development of a single-celled organism to a complex living organism interacting with its environment in multiple ways.

We are here comparing the development of soul consciousness with the biological development of life and we do so not just by way of metaphor. In fact the biological development of life as it took place on earth should be seen against the background of a spiritual need for exploration and experience on the part of the earth souls. This need or desire for exploration called into being the rich variety of life forms on earth. As we said, creation is always the result of an inner movement of consciousness. Although the evolution theory, as presently embraced by your science, correctly describes the development of life forms on your planet to some extent, it completely misses the inner drive, the "hidden" motive behind this deeply creative process. The proliferation of life forms on earth was due to inner movements on the soul level. As always, spirit precedes and creates matter.

At first, earth souls incarnated in physical forms which best fitted their still rudimentary sense of self: single-celled organisms. After a period of gaining experience and integrating this within their consciousness, the need arose for more complex means of physical expression. That is how more complex life forms were propelled into being. Consciousness created physical forms to answer the inner needs and desires of the earth souls whose collective consciousness primarily inhabited the earth.

The formation of new species and the incarnation of earth souls into individual members of those species represent a great experiment of life and consciousness. Although evolution is consciousness-driven, not driven by accident or incident, it does not follow a predetermined line of development. This is because consciousness itself is free and unpredictable.

The earth souls experimented with all kinds of animal life forms. They inhabited several types of physical bodies in the animal kingdom but they did not all experience the same line of development. The soul's path of development is much more fanciful and adventurous than you assume. There are no laws above or outside of you. You are the law for you. So for instance, if you desire to experience life from the standpoint of a monkey, you may at some point in time find yourself living in a monkey's body, from birth onward or as a temporary visitor. The soul, especially the young soul, craves experience and expression. This urge to explore accounts for the diversity of life forms that flourished on earth.

Within this great experiment of life, the rise of the human life form marked the beginning of an important stage within the development of soul consciousness on earth. Before explaining this in greater detail, we will first discuss the stages of inner soul development in general.

Consciousness evolving: infant stage, maturity, old age

If we look at the development of soul consciousness after it is born as an individual unit, it roughly goes through three inner stages. These stages are there independent of the particular plane of reality (planet, dimension, star system) that consciousness chooses to inhabit or experience.

1) The stage of innocence (paradise)

2) The stage of ego ("sin")

3) The stage of "second innocence" (enlightenment)

One may compare these stages metaphorically with infancy, maturity and old age.

After souls are born as individual units of consciousness, they leave the oceanic state of oneness which they remember as blissful and totally safe.

They then go on to explore reality in a whole new way. They slowly grow more aware of themselves and the way in which they are unique in comparison with their fellow travelers. They are very receptive and sensitive at this stage, like a young child who looks at the world with wide open eyes, expressing curiosity and innocence.

This stage may be called paradisiacal, since the experience of oneness and safety is still fresh in the memory of the newborn souls. They are still close to home; they do not yet question their right to be who they are.

As their journey continues, the memory of home fades while they immerse themselves in different types of experiences. Everything is new in the beginning and everything is uncritically absorbed at the infant stage. A new stage sets in when the young soul *starts to experience itself as the focal point of its world*. It then truly starts to realize that there is such a thing as "me" and "other." It starts to experiment with how it can influence its environments by acting upon this realization. The very notion of doing something that stems from your own consciousness is new. Before there was a more or less passive taking in of what flows by. Now there is a growing sense within the soul of its power to exert influence on what it experiences.

This is the start of the ego stage.

The ego originally represents the ability to use your will to affect the outer world. Please note that the original function of the ego is simply *that which enables the soul to experience itself fully as a separate entity*. This is a natural and positive development within the evolution of the soul. The ego is not "bad" in and of itself. It does however tend to be expansive or aggressive. When the newborn soul discovers its ability to influence its environment, it falls in love with the ego. Deep down, there still is a painful memory within the now maturing soul; it remembers home, it remembers paradise lost. The ego seems to hold an answer to this pain, this homesickness. It seems to enable the soul to actively get a grip on reality. It intoxicates the still young soul with the illusion of power.

If there ever was a fall from grace or a fall from paradise, it was this: the young soul consciousness becoming entranced by the possibilities of the ego, by the promise of power. However the very purpose of consciousness being born as individual souls is to explore, *to experience everything there is*:

paradise as well as hell, innocence as well as "sin." So the fall from paradise was not a "wrong turn." There is no guilt attached to it, unless you believe it to be. No one blames you, apart from you.

When the young soul becomes mature, there is a shift to a "me centered" way of observing and experiencing things. The illusion of power enhances separation between souls instead of connectedness. Because of this, loneliness and a sense of alienation set in within the soul. Although it is not really aware of it, the soul becomes a fighter, a warrior for power. Power seems to be the only thing that puts the mind at ease – for a while.

We distinguished a third stage in the development of soul consciousness above: the stage of enlightenment, "second innocence" or old age. We will have a lot to say about this stage and in particular about the transition from the second to the third stage later on in this series. Now we will return to our tale of the earth souls and we will clarify how the awakening of the ego stage fit in with the appearance of human beings on earth.

The earth souls entering the ego stage; the appearance of human beings on earth

The stage in which the earth souls explored plant and animal life coincided with the stage of innocence or paradise on the inner level. Life flourished on earth under the guidance and protection of spiritual beings from the angelic and devic realms. (Devas work on the etheric level, i.e. closer to the physical world than angels do.) The etheric bodies of plants and animals were uncritically receptive to the caring and nurturing mother energies of the angelic and devic realm. They had no inclination to "break free" or go off and find their own way of doing things. There still was a great sense of oneness and harmony among all living things.

The rise of the man-ape, however, marked a transformation point in the development of consciousness. Essentially, by walking upright and through the development of the brain, the consciousness that resided in the human ape got a better grip on its environment. Consciousness as incarnated in the anthropoid started to experience what it was like to have more control over its direct surroundings. It started to discover its own power, its own ability to influence its environment. It started to explore *free will.*

This development was not coincidental. It was a response to an inner need felt by the earth souls, a need to explore individuality on deeper levels than before. The growing self-awareness of the earth souls set the stage for the appearance in biological terms of man, the human being we know.

When the earth souls were ready to enter the ego stage, the creation of man enabled these souls to experience a life form with *free will*. It also endowed the incarnated consciousness with a greater awareness of "me" as opposed to "other." With this, the stage was set for possible conflicts between "my interest" and "your interest," "my desire" and "your desire." The individual was breaking away from the self-evident oneness, the natural order of "giving and taking," to find out what other roads were available. This marked the "end of paradise" on earth, but we ask you to conceive of this not as a tragic event but as a natural process, like the seasons in your year. It was a natural turn of events that would ultimately enable you in this day and age to balance divinity and individuality within your being.

When earth soul consciousness entered the ego stage and started out to explore "being human," the devic and angelic influences slowly receded into the background. It is in the very nature of these forces to respect the free will of all energies they encounter. They will never exert their influence uninvited. So ego consciousness got free reign and the earth souls got acquainted with all the privileges and drawbacks of power. This also affected the plant and animal kingdom. One might say that the emerging warrior energy was partly absorbed by these non-human realms which created a sense of turmoil within them. This is still present today.

When the earth souls craved new venues of experience, this made them receptive to new outer influences as well. Here we want to draw attention especially to types of extraterrestrial galactic influences which greatly affected the maturing but still young earth souls. It is at this point of our history also that the souls which we have called lightworker souls entered the stage.

Galactic influences on man and earth

By galactic or extraterrestrial influences, we mean influences from collective energies associated with certain star systems, stars or planets. In the universe, there are many levels or dimensions of existence. One planet or star may exist in various dimensions, ranging from the material to the more ethereal dimensions. In general, the galactic communities that influenced the earth souls existed in a less "dense" or material reality than you exist in on earth.

The galactic realms were inhabited by mature souls who were born long before the earth souls and who were in the prime of their ego stage. When the earth came to be inhabited by all kinds of life forms and ultimately by human beings, the extraterrestrial realms watched this development with great interest. The diversity and abundance of life forms drew their attention. They felt something special was going on here.

Between the different galactic communities, a lot of fighting and battling had been going on for a long time. This was a natural phenomenon, in a sense, since the consciousness of the souls involved *needed battle* to find out all about me-centeredness and power. They were exploring the workings of the ego and as they "progressed," they became very adept at manipulating consciousness. They became experts in subordinating other souls or communities of souls to their rule by means of subtle and less subtle psychic tools.

The interest that the galactic communities took in earth was mainly egocentric. They felt an opportunity there for exerting their influence in new and powerful ways. You might say that at that point, the intergalactic battles had reached deadlock. When you fight one another over and over again you reach a type of balance after a while, a division of power zones, so to speak. You know each other so well that you know where there is room to act and where there is not. The situation reached an impasse in this way and the galactic enemies hoped for new opportunities on earth. They thought earth might provide the stage for renewing the battle and overcoming the impasse.

The way in which the galactic communities sought to exert their influence on earth was by manipulating the consciousness of earth souls. The earth souls were particularly receptive to their influence when they entered the ego stage. Before they did so, they were immune to any power motivated outside force, because they had no inclination to exert power themselves. You are immune to aggression and power when there is nothing inside you that these energies can attach to. So the galactic energies could not access earth soul consciousness before these souls decided to explore the energy of power themselves.

The transition to the ego stage made the earth souls vulnerable because, apart from their intention to explore ego-consciousness, they were still largely innocent and naive. So it was not difficult for the galactic powers to impose their energies upon the consciousness of earth souls. The way they operated is by means of consciousness manipulation or mind control. Their technologies were very sophisticated. They had psychic tools mostly, not unlike brainwashing through subconscious hypnotic suggestions. They operated on psychic and astral levels but they influenced human beings up to the material/physical level of the body. They influenced the development of the human brain, narrowing down the range of experiences available to human beings. They essentially stimulated fear-related patterns of thought and emotion. Fear was already present in the earth soul's consciousness as a result of the pain and homesickness any young soul carries inside. The galactic powers took this existing fear as their starting point to greatly enlarge the energies of fear and subservience in the earth souls' minds and emotions. This enabled them to control human consciousness.

The galactic warriors subsequently tried to battle their previous galactic enemies through the human being. The struggle of power over humanity was a struggle between old galactic enemies that used human beings as their straw men.

The earth soul's tender sense of individuality and autonomy was cut in its prime by this violent intervention, this war for the heart of humanity. However the galactic interveners could not truly take their freedom away. However massive the extraterrestrial influence was, the divine essence within each individual soul-consciousness remained indestructible. The soul cannot be destroyed, although its free and divine nature may be veiled for a long time. This relates to the fact that power is not, in the end, real. Power always achieves its ends through the illusions of fear and ignorance. It can only hide and veil things; it cannot truly create or destroy anything.

Moreover this very attack on the earth souls did not only bring darkness to earth. It would unintentionally initiate a profound change in the consciousness of the galactic warriors, a turn toward the next stage of consciousness: enlightenment or "second innocence."

Galactic roots of lightworker souls

How does the notion of lightworker souls tie in with this history? Before they came to earth to incarnate in human bodies, lightworker souls inhabited several star systems for a long time. In terms of the three-staged development of consciousness, they spent a large part of their maturity there. It is in this stage that they explored the ego-consciousness and all the power issues related to it. It was the stage in which they explored darkness and in which they greatly misused their power.

In this galactic stage, lightworkers were co-creators of the human being as it developed. Just like other galactic forces, they had the intention of using man as a straw puppet to win dominance in other parts of the universe. It is hard to explain the techniques that the galactic powers used in their battles because they do not match anything in your world, at least not to the extent to which they perfected it. Essentially, galactic war technology was based on a non-materialist science of energy. They knew the power of the psyche and they knew that consciousness creates physical reality. Their metaphysics were more adequate than the materialist views your current scientists embrace. Because your established science conceives of consciousness as a result of material processes instead of the other way around, it cannot fathom the creative and causal powers of the mind.

At the age of the Cro-Magnon, the lightworker souls interfered with the natural development of man at a genetic level. You should conceive of this genetic interference as a top-down process of manipulation; they imprinted the human brain/consciousness with particular thought forms that affected the physical, cellular layer of the organism. The effect of these mental imprints was that a robotic, mechanical element was installed in the human brain which took away part of the natural strength and self awareness of the human being. There was an artificial implant that made man more suitable as an instrument for the extraterrestrials' strategic goals.

By interfering in this way with the development of life on earth, the lightworker souls violated the natural course of things. They did not respect the integrity of the earth souls who inhabited the evolving human species. In a way they robbed them of their newly gained free will.

There is a sense in which no one can rob any soul's free will, as we indicated at the end of the last paragraph. However in practical terms, because of the extraterrestrial superiority at all levels, the earth souls lost their sense of self-determination to an important extent. The lightworkers looked upon the human beings as tools, as *things* essentially, which helped them realize their goal. At that stage they were not ready to respect life as valuable in itself. They did not recognize in "the other" (their enemies or their slaves) a living soul like themselves.

Now there is no sense in placing any judgment on this, since it is all part of a grand and profound development in consciousness. At the deepest level there is no guilt, only free choice. There are no victims, no offenders; ultimately there is only experience.

You, the lightworker souls who once employed these dark means of oppression, judged yourself very severely for your deeds afterwards. Even now you carry a deep sense of guilt inside, which you are partly aware of as the feeling that *you are not good enough* in whatever you do. This feeling originates from a misunderstanding.

It is important to understand that "lightworker" is not something you simply are or aren't. It is something you *become*, when you go through the journey of experience: experiencing *light and dark. Being* light and dark. If we had to name you, we would call you the Christed souls instead of lightworkers.

Have you ever had the experience that a bad mistake you made eventually changed things in positive and unexpected ways? Something similar happened as a result of the galactic interference with earth and humanity. In the process of imprinting the earth souls with their energies, the galactic forces actually created a big melting pot of influences on earth. You might say that the battling elements within the different galactic souls were implanted within humanity as a race, thereby forcing the human being to find a way of uniting them or bringing them to peaceful coexistence. Although this severely complicated the journey of the earth souls, it would ultimately create the best chance for a positive breakthrough, a way out of the stalemate situation the galactic conflicts had reached.

Remember, all things are interconnected. There is a level at which the earth souls and the galactic souls were and are driven by the same intent. This is the angelic level. Every soul is in an angel in the deepest core. (See chapter *Time, multidimensionality and your light self*, p.103). At the angelic level, both the galactic warriors and the earth souls consented to take part in the cosmic drama sketched above.

The galactic interference not only "helped" earth become the melting pot it was intended to be, it also marked the beginning of a new type of consciousness within the galactic warriors. In unforeseen ways it marked the end of the ego stage, the end of maturity for them, and the beginning of something new.

The end of the ego stage for lightworkers

The intergalactic wars had reached deadlock before earth came into play. When the battle was renewed on earth, it was *actually transposed to earth.* With this transposition, something started to change within galactic consciousness. The time of the galactic wars was over.

Although they remained actively involved with humanity and earth, the galactic souls slowly retreated into the role of observer. In this role, they started to become aware of a particular kind of *tiredness* within their being. They sensed emptiness within. Although the fighting and battling went on, it did not fascinate them as much as it once did. They started to ask philosophical questions such as: what is the meaning of my life; why am I fighting all the time; does power really make me happy? By raising these questions, their war weariness grew stronger.

The galactic warriors were gradually reaching the end of their ego stage. They had unknowingly transferred the energy of ego and power struggle to earth, a place that was energetically open to this energy. The human souls were at that time just starting to explore the ego stage of consciousness.

Within the consciousness of the galactic warriors, a certain space was created: a space for doubt, a space for reflection. They entered a transformation phase, which we will describe by distinguishing the following steps:

1. Being unsatisfied by what ego based consciousness has to offer you, longing for "something else:" *the beginning of the end.*

2. Becoming aware of your ties to ego based consciousness, recognizing and releasing the emotions and thoughts that go with it: *the middle of the end.*

3. Letting the old ego based energies inside you die, throwing off the cocoon, becoming your new self: the *end of the end.*

4. The awakening of a heart based consciousness within you, motivated by love and freedom; helping others making the transition.

These four steps mark the transition from ego based to heart based consciousness. Please remember that both the earth and humanity and the galactic realms go through this phase, only not simultaneously.

Planet earth is now taking step 3. Many of you lightworkers are also taking step 3, in tune with the earth's inner process. Some of you are still struggling with step 2, and there are some who have arrived at step 4, tasting the delights of heartfelt joy and inspiration.

Large parts of humanity, however, do not desire to release ego based consciousness at all. They have not entered step 1 of the transition phase yet. This is not something to judge or criticize or grieve over. Try to view it as a natural process such as the growth of a plant. You do not judge a flower for being a bud instead of being in full bloom. Try to see it in this light. Making moral judgments about the destructive effects of ego based consciousness in your world is based on lack of insight into spiritual dynamics. Moreover it weakens your own strength, since the anger and frustration you sometimes feel by watching the news or reading your newspapers cannot be transformed into something constructive. It merely depletes you and lowers your own level of vibration. Try to see things from a distance, from an attitude of trust. Try to intuitively sense the undercurrents in collective consciousness, the things you hardly read or hear about in the media.

It makes no sense to try and change souls who are still caught up in the reality of ego based consciousness. They do not want your "help," since they are not yet open to the heart based energies hat you – lightworkers – wish to share with them. Even though to you they seem to need help, as long as they don't want it, they don't need it. It's as simple as that.

Lightworkers are quite fond of giving and helping but they often lose their power of discernment in this area. This leads to a waste of energy and may result in self-doubt and disappointment on the lightworker's part. Please use your power of discernment here, as the desire to help can tragically become a pitfall to lightworkers which prevents them from really completing step 3 of the transition. (The notion of "helping" is discussed further in "Pitfalls on the way to becoming a healer," part II).

We will now finish our description of the lightworkers at the end of their ego stage. As we said, at that time you, among other galactic empires, interfered with humanity when the modern human being took form. When you started more and more to play the role of observer, you got tired of fighting.

The power you had been after for such a long time resulted in a type of dominance which annihilated the unique and individual qualities of that which you dominated. So nothing new could enter your reality. You killed everything that was "other." This way of proceeding made your reality static and predictable after a while. When you became aware of the emptiness within the struggle for power, your consciousness opened up to new possibilities. A longing arose for "something else."

You had completed step 1 of the transition to a heart based consciousness. The energies of the ego, which had had free reign for eons, settled down and allowed a space for "something else." In your hearts a new energy awakened, like a tender flower. A subtle and quiet voice began to speak to you of "home," a place you had once known but had lost track of along your way. You sensed a homesickness within you.

Just like the earth souls, you had once experienced the oceanic state of oneness from which every soul is born. You gradually evolved from this ocean as individual units of consciousness. As these "little souls," you had a great zest for exploration, while at the same time carrying the painful memory inside of a paradise you had had to leave behind.

Once you entered the ego stage of consciousness later on, this pain was still inside you. What you essentially tried to do was to fill this empty spot in your heart with power. You sought to fulfill yourselves by playing the game of fighting and conquering.

Power is the energy that most opposes oneness. By exerting power, you isolate yourself from "the other." By struggling for power, you distance yourself even more from home: the consciousness of unity. The fact that power leads you away from home instead of bringing you closer to it was hidden from you for a long time, since power is strongly interwoven with *illusion*. Power can easily hide its true face to a naive and inexperienced soul. Power creates the illusion of abundance, fulfillment, recognition and even love. The ego stage is an unrestricted exploration of the area of power: of winning, losing, struggling, dominating, manipulating, of being the offender and being the victim.

On the inner level, the soul gets torn apart during this stage. The ego stage entails an attack on the soul's integrity. By integrity we mean the natural unity and wholeness of the soul. With the entrance of ego based consciousness, the soul gets into a state of schizophrenia. It loses its innocence. On the one hand, the soul battles and conquers; on the other hand, it realizes that it is wrong to damage or destroy other living beings. It is not so much wrong according to some objective law or judge. But the soul subconsciously realizes that it is doing something that opposes its own divine nature. It is in the nature of its own divine essence to *create and give life*. When the soul operates from a desire for personal power, deep within a sense of *guilt* arises. Again there is no external verdict on the soul which proclaims it to be guilty. The soul itself realizes it is losing its innocence and purity. While the soul pursues power on the outside, a growing sense of *unworthiness* is eating at it from the inside.

The stage of ego based consciousness is a natural stage in the journey of the soul. Actually it involves the full exploration of one aspect of the soul's being: the will. Your will constitutes the bridge between the inner and the outer world. The will is that part of you that focuses your soul's energy into the material world. The will may be inspired by the desire for power or by the desire for oneness. This depends on the state of your inner awareness. When a soul reaches the end of the ego stage, the will becomes more and more an extension of the heart. The ego or the personal will is not destroyed but it is flowing in accordance with the heart's wisdom and inspiration. At this point the ego joyfully accepts the heart as its spiritual guide. The natural wholeness of the soul is restored.

When you, the lightworker souls, arrived in step 2 of the transition from ego to heart based consciousness, you felt the sincere desire to make right what you had done wrong on earth. You realized that you had ill treated the living human beings on earth and that you had hindered the free expression and development of the earth souls. You realized that you had violated life itself by trying to manipulate and control it according to your needs. You wanted to release human beings from the bonds of fear and limitation which had brought much darkness into their lives, and you felt you could accomplish most in this respect by incarnating into human bodies yourself. *So you incarnated into human bodies, whose genetic make-up was partly created by yourself, in order to transform your creations from the inside.* The souls who went to earth with this mission intended to spread Light into their own manipulated creations.

Hence they are called lightworkers. You made the decision to do this – and to become entangled in a whole series of earth lives – from a newborn sense of responsibility and also from the heartfelt urge to take this karmic burden upon you, so that you would be able to fully let go of the past.

Lightworker III

Lightworkers incarnating on earth

When you incarnated on earth, you had just started the transition from an ego based to a heart based consciousness. We have sketched this transition as consisting of four steps. You took the first step when you became aware of your longing for "something else," something different from the struggle for power that filled your lives before.

That struggle provided your lives with purpose and meaning for a substantial period of time. Your fascination with power led you to use the human being as a straw puppet in your galactic battles. All galactic empires were part of this. But when the warring energies were transposed to earth with man as their playground, you became more of an observer and you withdrew from direct battles. You watched what took place on earth. You saw the human being develop into something, a state of being you had reached long before. You had become sophisticated warriors with refined methods of psychic manipulation and warfare. Man was to become the same, with your genetic implants in place.

These genetic implants caused a high level of *mental* development within the human being. The functions of natural instinct and feeling were more or less suppressed in favor of the function of thinking and reasoning.

We mentioned that the galactic influences caused a high level of fear within the developing human. In fact this element of fear was closely connected with the overemphasis on thinking. In a balanced situation, fear is overcome or put into perspective by your natural *intuitive* skills and your ability to *feel* what is right or appropriate to do. However when the faculty of thinking gets the upper hand, fear tends to be reinforced, since thinking relies on a mechanical logical process that does not allow intuition or feeling to enter the process. When the mental faculty is fed by the emotions of fear, it tends to run wild and produce delusional ideas, ideas about controlling everything and everyone. Dictatorial regimes are an example of this mental faculty running wild.

The answer to fear is never to *think more*. It is to *think less* and to trust the flow of life. It is to fall back into the state of grace that is your birthright. It is to *release* instead of to grab hold.

When the stage of ego rule ended within the lightworker souls, they opened up to a new way of being. You intuitively reached out for the energy of the heart. You were in fact looking for a kind of creativity that transcended the mere play with power. You sensed that the struggle for power was destructive and could not create anything new, since it killed and assimilated everything that was "other."

By trying to control and dominate life, whether inside you or outside you, you actually tried to make reality static and predictable. Ultimately, power is incredibly boring.

When you became aware of this, you realized that your true desire was not to have power but to be truly creative. To be truly creative is to be in touch with your own divinity.

Since you are divine beings, whatever you do or don't do, you are always creating some kind of reality. Creativity is your very nature. In the ego phase, you explored the possibility of *denying* your true nature. Indeed this is a creative act at some level, in a twisted kind of way. To be truly creative however is to create according to life, not according to death.

When this realization dawned upon you, the memory of "home" awoke. The vague remembrance of a state of pure and blissful oneness entered your consciousness again and you knew that this was somehow the key to your happiness. But you felt helpless and ignorant, as you had no idea how to go about it. You knew that the ego did not hold the answer but you had not really entered the realm of heart based consciousness yet.

At the same time, a growing sense of remorse and guilt rose within you about what you had done to human beings on earth.

Especially on earth, there were splendid opportunities for consciousness to freely express itself in many different ways. Earth was meant to be a unifier of different energies, a melting pot in which differing and even opposing energies could reach a way of coexisting in harmony. The energetic playground of earth was created to house a very heterogeneous set of energies.

The difference between living on earth and living in other places in the universe, whether on physical or on astral levels, is the enormous variety of energies present on earth. Moreover this variety is not just present as a vast array of life forms or species. It is actually present within one single being, the human being. The human being is able to contain a spectrum of energies that has a wider range than any other being is capable of. You have within you the energy of the murderer and the saint, the energy of the child, the grown-up and the old, the energy of male and female, the energy of active and passive, the energy of the rational and the emotional, the energy of water, air, fire and earth, etc. This may seem trivial or simply natural to you as a human being, but to any other being in the universe it is quite a feat. It is quite a feat *to be human at all*, without having done anything special.

But the most unique quality of the human being is the ability to *meld energies* which seemed incompatible before. Man was designed to not just hold all these different energies, but to be a mediator, a builder of bridges between them.

The reason why Spirit or God or All-That-Is came up with the concept of the human being is that the universe had wound up in a situation of stasis. Consciousness, as it explored life outside of oneness, tended to try out different life forms, on different planes and places in the universe. When a soul had experienced all there was to a particular life form, it left – in the sense of not incarnating in there anymore – and went on to other life forms which answered its particular needs. *There was no need to transform energy while living in a particular life form.* When you wanted a change, you switched bodies. This was not because souls were lazy or shallow. Most bodies, ranging in density from physical to astral, offered limited ranges of experience and therefore limited opportunities to grow or transform while in the body. The body could not hold so many different energies. For example, if you lived on a water planet where you incarnated as a water being, this enabled you to experience the nature of water in all kinds of ways. The "feel" of being liquid, not fixed, flowing, moving, is indeed wonderful. But when you wanted the experience of being fixed and unmovable, you needed to leave that body and live inside of a mountain for a while. Also when you lived as galactic beings in search of power, you could not really change your consciousness within that body.

The consequence of this limited or specialized range of experience within a certain body was that the created world of life forms got stuck. It could not grow or expand and it got sort of locked into a sort of stasis.

The unique power of the human being is the power to hold a wide array of energies and to bring them into a state of creative, not static, balance. Actually this power is equal to the ability to transform darkness into light, i.e. the power of spiritual alchemy. That which brings the formerly opposing energies into a state of dynamic harmony is the *Christed energy*, the energy that maintains oneness in the face of duality. This is the same energy that transforms darkness, by accepting it and thereby allowing the fear to transform into joy. The Christed energy is the "third energy" which unites by accepting. Its alchemic force lies in its quality of being all-embracing, all-accepting and fearless.

You as human beings are the *only* being that has this ability for spiritual alchemy. Neither the plants, nor the animals, nor the angels, nor the "dark lords" have this power.

All souls can experience what it is like to be light, what it is like to be dark, what it is like to be all the different kinds of beings that live in the universe, but they cannot experience what it is like to transform darkness into light while remaining in your present life form. They cannot imagine what it is like to change on inner levels in such a way that you create a different physical and spiritual reality for yourself as you go along.

Souls which are incarnate in other than human life forms also "create their reality" and have free will, but they have less possibility to span highly different and even opposing states of consciousness while remaining in the same body, in the same (human) form. You, as humans, are bridge builders, or spiritual alchemists, and that is what makes earth and the human being unique.

We now return to our tale of the lightworker souls who felt anguished and regretful about their interference with the human being. They realized that on earth a whole new game was being set up, a game full of promise, which they had done their best to smother for their own sake. They felt pain because of this. At some level, they also realized they had blocked their own spiritual journey towards light and true joy by their acts of selfishness.

Also when you awoke from your ego slumber, you saw that earth was such a beautiful place, a green planet teeming with life. This stirred deep memories within you. You were present at the very beginning of life on earth. Earth had not lost its innocence then. In those distant times before your fall into warrior consciousness, you were part of paradise on earth, as the angelic beings that nurtured and looked after life. You were angels in the Garden of Eden. Even if later on you acted out your dark side as galactic warriors, you also had with regard to earth acted out a light and pure aspect of yourselves in ancient times, when you prepared the planet for the coming of the earth souls. You contributed to the blossoming of the green planet and at some level, you knew this when you came out of your "warrior" stage of consciousness. You knew you had been destroying that which you had nurtured and helped to create.

When you realized the promise and the beauty of earth, you felt the inner urge to go down there and restore what had been damaged. You incarnated into human bodies with the intention of bringing light and creating heart based values in an environment that was essentially dominated by egotistical values. We want to expand a little on this motive of bringing light, because there is something to it that frequently causes confusion and misunderstanding within you.

When you lightworkers incarnated on earth, you actually started an inner transformation process in which you would complete your own transition from ego based to heart based consciousness. You were on the road to fully release ego based consciousness, and life on earth provided you with the opportunity to deal with what was left of the ego based energy within you. The energies you wished to come clean with you would meet in the very being you had manipulated and would now dwell in: within the human being, within yourselves.

Your deepest motive for coming to earth was to come to terms with your own inner darkness, and you agreed to meet this darkness within yourself as human beings. Although you often think you are here to help others or to help mother earth, *the most fundamental reason you are here is to heal yourself.* This is your true lightwork. All else is secondary.

At the deepest level your souls wished to take responsibility for the darkness they had spread. However to take responsibility for your dark side is a *solitary* venture in principle. It does not involve others you need to help or cure. It involves only you. You *will* help others in the process, but this is a secondary effect. It is important to realize the right order of things here, you know, since you have a tendency to be too diligent in helping others. This enthusiasm to help others often becomes a pitfall, since your energy gets entangled with the other person and more often than not, you feel depleted and disappointed afterwards. Please remember: *to give more than to receive is not noble or heart based, it is simply a mistake.* The mistake is that you think that you are in part responsible for someone else's situation or state of mind. This is not true. Everyone is responsible for their own happiness or misfortune. And this is indeed a blessing, as it provides everyone with the power to create and therefore to change their own reality.

You are not here to "fix" other people or mother earth. You are here to heal the deep wounds within your own being. Please tend to this task and all else will fall into place without any effort on your part.

When you came to earth and incarnated into human bodies, you were inclined to *fight* the energies you wished to overcome. At that stage, you were in a paradoxical situation. On the one hand, you knew you wanted "something other" than power and you hated yourselves for what you had done wrong before. But you were not free of that which you hated in yourselves. You were not free of ego dominance yet. When you came to earth, you had the tendency to get upset by darkness, to get angry about it, and your reaction was to *fight* it. The paradox is that you wanted to battle egotistical energies through struggle, the very energy that you wished to let go of.

You were as yet not aware of the true implications of a heart based consciousness. When you observe from the heart, there is no battle between Good and Bad. The reality of the heart transcends both. The heart does not oppose darkness. Heart based consciousness is founded upon acceptance of everything, of all that is. It is a type of consciousness that releases the idea that struggle will solve anything.

Although you longed for a peaceful, non-struggling way of dealing with reality, you had no experience with actually living out this ideal. You were really in an "in between-zone," a piece of no man's land before you enter a new realm of consciousness.

So you started to make all kinds of "mistakes" in the sense of falling back into ways of being that you wanted to let go of. You were anxious to change or convert anyone or any group who displayed ego like behavior or embraced ego based values. They however responded aggressively to you, oftentimes not even understanding what you were trying to convey to them. Lightworkers have been persecuted for centuries as witches, heathens or political agitators. They seemed to be driven by ideals for which the world was not ready. They seemed different and would not fit in. They typically met with a lot of resistance.

What happened here is that you switched into the role of victim after having played the role of offender for quite some time in the galactic realms. Your "spiritual anger" evoked angry responses from your environment and you became the victim, experiencing humiliation, deep pain and disempowerment. The trauma of being rejected and/or cast out repeatedly in several lives has left scars on your soul. You ended up feeling disempowered and unwelcome. Many of you in this lifetime feel tired and homesick for a more loving and meaningful world.

It is very important for you to realize that the victim role is just that: a role you play. It is one possible interpretation of the facts, but it is a narrow and distorted one. You are neither victim nor offender. You are the soul consciousness that has created roles for yourself to play for a while.

You are not really the victim of a materially minded, selfish world.

In fact, the encounters you had with aggressive, non-cooperative energies in many of your lifetimes simply mirrored back to you *your own ties to ego based consciousness*, your own dependence upon it. If you seek results through struggle, you will receive the energy of struggle back to you. This is/was your own energy coming back to you! And that is the *only* meaning of karma.

The tendency to fight "evil" is based upon the belief that evil is outside of you and must be banished from reality. The spiritual invitation to you lightworkers during all of your incarnations has always been to recognize and accept your own dark side and to understand its role and purpose.

The deepest invitation is to *forgive yourselves and find back your innocence.* You are innocent and have always been so. Can you truly understand that? If you do, you will not want to change the world or fight injustice any more. You will want to play, to have fun and enjoy every moment of your life and simply *be who you are and share that with others.*

When you lightworkers release the idea that you have to struggle for anything or anyone, you will no longer be opposed by "the outer world," by society or other people in general, for being different. You will not want to change anything and therefore you will not encounter resistance. You will know that you are welcome, that your contribution to this reality is valuable and that you are valued by others.

When you have fully released ego based consciousness, you will know you are exempt from persecution or outside threats. You will have gone beyond the roles of victim and persecutor; your journey will have come full circle. You will have released your karmic burdens and you will be totally free to create whatever you want.

You are on the verge of birthing a new consciousness. This is a type of consciousness that has fully released the need to control or possess anything. It is free of fear. It is the Christ consciousness.

When I, Jeshua, lived on earth, I wanted to tell you that spirituality is not about a war between light and dark. It is about finding a level of awareness that goes beyond good and bad, a place from which you can understand and accept all things. "The kingdom of God is within." Everything you need is on the inside. Peace, joy and tranquillity are yours when you truly realize who you are: a divine being in physical expression.

It is only when you realize that you are here to transform and heal *yourself* that things really start to change for you, and as a side effect, for other people surrounding you. The world is what it is and the highest thing you can do for it is simply to love it for what it is. Love and see the beauty of every single being that is traveling through this plane of reality.

Many of you are moved by my energy, the energy of Jeshua or Jesus. This is because I am your kin. I was simply a lightworker unburdened by karmic ties, a lightworker in possession of a high level of self-understanding. You are touched by my energy because you know this is the energy you are moving toward. The energy of Christ is the energy of your own future self.

From ego to heart I

Four stages in the transformation of consciousness

In the previous chapters, we have described the historical background of the lightworker's journey from ego based to heart based consciousness. This part will be dedicated entirely to the psychological characteristics of this transformation. We have divided up this process into four steps or stages, which we sum up again for the sake of clarity:

1. Being unsatisfied by what ego based consciousness has to offer you, longing for "something else:" the *beginning of the end.*

2. Becoming aware of your ties to ego based consciousness, recognizing and releasing the emotions and thoughts that go with it: *the middle of the end.*

3. Letting the old ego based energies inside you die, throwing off the cocoon, becoming your new self: *the end of the end.*

4. The awakening of a heart based consciousness within you, motivated by love and freedom; helping others making the transition.

ʼ

Stage one: the ego does not fulfill anymore

The transition from ego based consciousness to heart based consciousness starts with the experience of an *inner void*. Things that used to draw your full attention or situations that you got completely caught up in now leave you empty or uninspired. Somehow things seem to have lost their usual meaning and purpose.

Before this void is experienced, consciousness is in the grip of fear and the ensuing need to constantly reaffirm itself. It is continually looking for outside validation because it is unwilling to face the underlying fear of rejection and loneliness. This deep fear and the need for outside validation may long be hidden as the true motive for many of your actions. Your whole life may be built upon them without you being consciously aware of it. Perhaps you are aware of a vague restlessness or tension within. But often a major event such as the break up of a relationship, the passing of a loved one or the loss of a job has to come along to invite you to truly examine what this tension or unrest is about.

When the ego is the center of your being, your consciousness and your emotional life are in a state of *cramp*. You cringe in fear and from that position you are constantly on the defensive. When you're in the ego stage, you always experience *lack*, a need for *more*. The foundation of your thoughts, feelings and actions is a black hole, a void which can never be filled completely. It is a hole of fear, a place covered in shadows, since you turn your consciousness away from it. In the shadows, there is a void which you are vaguely aware of, but you don't want to go there.

In this stage, your relationship with God or All-That-Is is marked by feelings of separation. Deep within you feel alone and abandoned. You feel like you are a broken, meaningless fragment with no purpose. And as you cover up your fear of this, you only experience it indirectly, as a shadow.

People are terrified of facing the inner void with full awareness. They are terrified of meeting their inner darkness head on and investigating it. However if you don't face it, it is still there, and you will need to develop "coping strategies" to make life bearable. The ego's strategy is always to deal with the problem at the periphery, instead of at the center. The ego seeks to solve the problem by turning your consciousness outward. It tries to alleviate the inner pain by *feeding you with outside energies.* The energies it is particularly fond of are acknowledgement, admiration, power, attention etc. In this way, the ego seemingly creates an answer to the soul's deep longing for oneness, safety and love.

This longing in itself is entirely valid and genuine. It is God calling you. It is your own nature calling out to you. You are God! God is the energy of oneness, safety and love. Everyone longs for the unconditional love and embrace of the Energy you call God. In essence, this longing is the longing for being totally aware of, and therefore one with, your own divine Self. Your own divinity is your entrance to unconditional love. You can only find it by going through the fear and darkness surrounding it, and this you do *by turning inward,* instead of outward. You do it by using your consciousness as a light that chases the shadows away. Consciousness *is* light. Therefore it does not need to fight darkness; its mere presence dissolves it. By turning your consciousness inward, miracles will indeed befall you.

The ego, however, proceeds in exactly the opposite way. It registers the need for love and safety but it aims at answering this need without facing inner darkness and fear. To accomplish this, it applies a certain "trick:" it transforms the need for love into the need for approval and recognition from other people. It transforms the need for oneness and harmony into the need for excelling and being better than others. Once you think that to be loved is to be admired for your achievements, you don't need to go inside for love anymore; you simply have to work harder! In this way, the ego strives to keep the lid on the pan of fear.

Your original longing for love and blissful unity has now become distorted into the desire for recognition. You are constantly looking for outside validation which provides for some temporary reassurance. Your consciousness is essentially focused on the outer world. You rely on other people's judgments and you are very edgy about what people think of you. This is highly important to you, since your self-esteem depends on it. In fact, your sense of self-worth sinks lower and lower, since you are giving your power away to outside forces who judge you for your outside performances, not for your true being.

Meanwhile the deep-seated sense of abandonment and loneliness is not alleviated. It actually gets worse, since you refuse to look at it. That which you don't want to look at becomes your "shadow side." Fear, anger and negativity can roam there and influence you, intensified by the refusal to go within. The ego can be very stubborn when it comes to suppressing certain doubts, hunches and feelings; it will not release control easily.

What you perceive as "evil" in your world is always the result of clinging to personal power. It is the refusal to give up control and accept inner fear and darkness.

The first step to enlightenment is surrendering to "what is." Enlightenment means that you *allow* all aspects of your being into the light of your consciousness. Enlightenment does not mean you are fully conscious of everything within you, but that you are *willing* to face every aspect consciously.

Enlightenment equals love. Love means that you accept yourself as you are.

The inner darkness, that sense of abandonment in the depths of your soul that you all fear so much, is temporary. This ego stage is just one step in a large development and unfolding of consciousness. In this stage, the first leap is taken towards an *individualized divine consciousness.*

The birth of individual consciousness, the birth of you as a "separate soul," goes together with the experience of being left alone, of being separated from your Mother/Father. It is comparable to the trauma of birth in your physical world. In the womb, the baby experiences an oceanic sense of oneness with the mother. When it is born, it becomes a unity unto itself.

Because of this birth trauma – speaking now of the birth of the soul – the soul takes with it a sense of being torn apart; it had to part with everything it took for granted.

The newborn soul longs for a return to the semi-consciousness state of oneness from which it came and which it considers to be its Home. Because this is impossible, the soul experiences great fear and feelings of desolation and doubt. This inner pain and disorientation will gradually form the breeding ground for the ego's seizure of power. The soul has to deal with the fear and the pain, and the ego promises to provide a solution. The ego holds up the prospect of power and control to the soul consciousness. The soul, feeling powerless and lost, gives in and puts the ego in command.

The ego is that part of the soul which is oriented towards the material, external world. In essence, the ego is the soul's instrument for manifesting itself as a physical being within time and space. The ego provides consciousness with *focus*. It makes consciousness specific instead of oceanic, "here and now" instead of "all over the place." The ego translates inner impulses into specific material form. It is that part of you which bridges the gap between the non-physical spiritual part of you and the physical part.

For the soul as a non-physical spiritual being, it is quite unnatural to be fixated in time and space. The soul is essentially independent of any material form. When you have dreams of flying around, you are contacting this independent and free part of yourself. The ego, on the other hand, *binds and fixates*. It enables you to function in physical reality. As such, the ego plays a very valuable role that has nothing to do with "good" or "bad." When it operates in a balanced situation, the ego is a neutral and indispensable tool for the soul who dwells on earth in a physical body.

However when the ego starts to *rule* soul consciousness, instead of functioning as its tool, the soul gets out of balance. When the ego dictates to the soul (that is the hallmark of ego based consciousness), the ego will not simply translate inner impulses into material form, but it will *control and selectively suppress* those impulses. The ego then presents you with a distorted image of reality. The unbalanced ego is always in pursuit of power and control and it will interpret all facts as positive or negative in this light.

It is quite instructive to uncover your own power based and control based motives in your daily goings about. Try to notice how often you want to bend things or people to your will, even if it is for a noble cause. How often do you get annoyed by things not going your way? It is important to realize that beneath the need for control is always a fear of losing control. So ask yourself: what is the risk of releasing control, of letting go of the need for predictability? What is my deepest fear?

The price you are now paying for keeping things "under control" is that your attitude to life is tense and restrained.

When you dare to live from inner inspiration and only do what brings you joy, this will create a natural and true order in your life. You will feel relaxed and happy without the need to mold the flow of life. This is living without fear: living with full trust in what life will bring to you. Can you do that?

For a young soul, the pitfall of ego based consciousness is nearly inevitable. The ego offers a way out of the problem of fear and abandonment; it shifts your attention from "what there is on the inside" to "what you can get from the outside world." This is not a real solution to the problem but it does seem to bring relief for a while. Exerting power and control over your surroundings may give you a temporary satisfaction or "kick." There is a brief sense of being loved, admired and respected. This soothes your pain for a while. But it is short lived and you have to exert yourself again to stand out, to be even better, nicer or more helpful.

Please be aware that under the flag of the ego, you can be both sweet and nasty, both giving and taking, both dominant and subservient. Much that is given seemingly unselfishly is an unconscious call for attention, love and recognition from the receiver of the gift. When you are always caring for and giving to others, you are simply hiding from yourself. So to understand what ego domination means, you do not necessarily have to think of cruel tyrants such as Hitler or Saddam Hussein. Keep it simple; watch yourself in your daily life. The presence of ego domination can be recognized by the need to control things. An example is that you want certain people to behave in particular ways. To make this happen, you display certain patterns of behavior. You are compliant and sweet for example, and you try not to hurt someone's feelings ever. There is a need for control behind this behavior. "Because I want you to love me, I will not go against you." This line of thinking is based on fear. It is fear of standing on your own, fear of being rejected and abandoned. What appears to be sweet and nice is in fact a form of self-denial. This is the ego at work.

As long as the ego governs your soul, you will need to feed yourself with the energy of others in order to feel good. You seem to have to deserve acceptance from other people, from some authority outside of you. However the world around you is not fixed or stable. You can never rely on the permanent adherence of whatever it is you rely on, be it spouse, boss or parents. That is why you have to "work" all the time, being always on the look-out for "portions of approval" coming your way. This explains the tense and nervous state of mind that anyone stuck in the ego stage is permanently in.

The ego cannot provide you with true love and self-esteem. The solution it offers for the trauma of abandonment is in fact a bottomless pit. The true mission of the young soul consciousness is *to become the parent it has lost.*

Please be aware that the structure of earth life, meaning the process of starting out as a helpless baby and growing up to be a self-contained adult, often invites you to do precisely that. How often the key to real happiness in your lives lies in this: that you become your own father and mother, and give to yourself the love and understanding you have missed and are missing from others. On the larger, metaphysical level we have been speaking of, this means: come to the understanding that you are God, not one of his little lost sheep. This is the realization that will bring you home. This is the realization that will bring you to the heart of who you are, which is love and divine power.

The end of the ego stage comes within sight when the soul realizes that it is repeating the same cycle of actions and thoughts over and over again. The ego loses its dominance when the soul grows tired and weary of struggling all the time for an ever elusive treasure. The soul then starts to suspect that the promises of the game it is in are false and that there is really nothing there for it to win. When the soul grows tired of trying and being on top of it all the time, it *lets go of control* a little.

With less energy going out to controlling thoughts and behavior, an energetic space opens up which allows for new and different experiences. At first when you enter this stage, you may just feel very tired and empty inside. Things you deemed important before may appear entirely meaningless now. Also fears may surface that have no clear or immediate causes. It may be vague fears of death or of losing your loved ones. Also anger may come up with regard to situations in your job or your marriage. Everything that seemed self-evident is now in doubt. That which ego based consciousness set out to prevent happens at last.

Gradually the lid is lifted from the pan, and all kinds of uncontrollable emotions and fears pop out and enter your consciousness, seeding doubt and confusion in your life. Until that moment, you were functioning largely on autopilot. Many thought and feeling patterns within you happened automatically; you let them pass by unquestioned. This gave unity and stability to your consciousness. However when your consciousness grows and expands, your personality gets split in two. One part of you wants to hold on to the old ways; the other part of you questions these ways and confronts you with uncomfortable feelings such as anger, fear and doubt.

The expansion of consciousness that occurs at the end of the ego stage is therefore often experienced as a spoil-sport, an unwelcome intruder which spoils the game. This new awareness unsettles everything that seemed obvious before and it awakens emotions within you that you don't know how to deal with. When you start to doubt ego based patterns of thinking and doing, a whole new side of you enters your consciousness. It is a part of you that loves truth instead of power.

Living according to the dictates of the ego is very repressive. You are serving a little fearful dictator that aims at power and control, not just over your environment but especially over you. Your spontaneous flow of feeling and intuiting is restrained by this dictator. The ego does not like spontaneity so much. It holds you back from freely expressing your feelings, since feelings and emotions are uncontrollable and unpredictable, which is dangerous to the ego. The ego works with masks.

If your ego dictates to you, "be sweet and considerate, to win people's sympathy," you will systematically suppress feelings of displeasure and anger within you. If you start to doubt the viability of this dictate, these suppressed emotions come up again at once. Feelings are not eliminated by being suppressed. They live on and gain in intensity the longer you suppress them.

Once the soul experiences the emptiness and the doubt that is so characteristic of the ending ego stage, it is possible to meet and face all the feelings and emotions that were hidden in the dark before. These pent up emotions and feelings are the entrance gate to your greater Self. By exploring what you truly feel instead of what you are supposed to feel, you restore your spontaneity and integrity, that part of you which is also called your "inner child." Getting in touch with your true feelings and emotions sets you on the road to liberation. The transition to a heart based consciousness has then begun.

From ego to heart II

Exploring your inner wounds

We distinguished four steps in the transformation from ego based to heart based consciousness.

1. Being unsatisfied by what ego based consciousness has to offer you, longing for "something else:" *the beginning of the end.*

2. Becoming aware of your ties to ego based consciousness, recognizing and releasing the emotions and thoughts that go with it: *the middle of the end.*

3. Letting the old ego based energies inside you die, throwing off the cocoon, becoming your new self: *the end of the end.*

4. The awakening of a heart based consciousness within you, motivated by love and freedom; helping others making the transition.

In this chapter, we will discuss step two.

When you stop identifying yourself with the ego, you first get into a state of confusion as to who you are. This confusion can be profound and very philosophical in nature. You get to ask questions about the meaning of life, about good and bad, about what you really feel and think as opposed to what others have taught you to feel and think. These questions are suddenly very real to you and they have a direct bearing on the life choices you make. You look at yourself and you think: is this me? Is this what I want? It is hard to make choices now, since nothing is self-evident anymore.

In fact, you are now taking a step *backwards*, a step into the deep, a step inward. You become aware of deeper parts of yourself, parts that are less conditioned by your upbringing and by society. You receive glimpses of who you truly are: your uniqueness, your individuality. You remember that there is a part to you that is not dependent upon anything around you, your parents, your work, your relationships, not even your body. This is when you - vaguely - sense your divinity, the part of you that is completely unbound and eternal.

In fact, you are all multidimensional beings; you can and do manifest yourselves in several different realities at the same time. You are not bound to a linear timeframe. Your current personality is only one aspect of the multidimensional entity you are. Whenever you realize that your current expression as a physical human being is simply one aspect of you, you go beyond it and you can get in touch with the greater Self that you are.

But before you get there, you need to heal the wounded parts within you.

Living according to the dictates and demands of the ego has created psychological wounds within you. Letting go of ego based consciousness initially creates confusion, doubt and disorientation. After this first step, you enter a new stage: it is the stage of observing, understanding and healing your inner wounds. We will speak of this stage now.

With the ego in control, your actions and thoughts have been based on fear for a long time. In a sense, you have ruthlessly pursued your desire for power, recognition and control. In this, you have belied your own nature. Your behavior has been based on outer standards instead of on your own true needs. Also you have not been able to really love someone else, since love is completely opposite to the need to control or dominate. This whole state of consciousness formed an attack on the integrity of your soul. The soul suffered under the reign of the ego.

When you disentangle yourself from the grip and the hold of the ego, this inner pain gets more visible to you. It is exposed to you, naked and raw, bereft of masks. You do not, however, know how to deal with this pain yet, since you still are in a state of confusion and disorientation. More often than not, you go through a stage of judging your inner wounds, because they seem to lead you to negative patterns of behavior: addiction, depression, uncontrollable mood swings, problems with communication, difficulties with intimate relationships.

This judgment of yourself inflicts more pain on the soul, which has just begun to turn toward the Light. The soul is letting go of the need for power and control, it is growing more sensitive... and then it gets caught up in self-judgment.

Many people are wandering in this no man's land in between the ego and the heart. They are searching for a more loving reality, but they are still within reach of the ego's whip.

In fact, it is not your inner hurt that makes you fall prey to what you consider "negative traits" in yourself. It is your *judgment of the hurt* that causes the negativity. If you look at yourself with an attitude of acceptance, you do not see an addicted, or depressed, or failing persona. You just see inner pain that needs to be tended and cared for in the gentlest and kindest way possible.

The most important step in stage two of the transition from ego to heart is that *you are willing to understand your inner pain*: accept it, understand its origins and allow it *to be*.

If you can perceive the core of fear that is inherent in all expressions of ego centered consciousness, you have entered the reality of heart based consciousness. However reprehensible someone's behavior is, if you recognize the pain, the loneliness and the need for self-protection beneath, you get in touch with *the soul* displaying the negative behavior. As soon as you perceive the soul in fear, you are able to *forgive*. This applies first and foremost with regard to yourself.

Take something in yourself that you truly detest, something that really annoys you that you think you should have gotten rid of long ago. It may be insecurity, or laziness, or impatience, or an addiction: anything you feel *should not be there*. Now try to understand the real motive behind this trait or tendency. What compels you to feel or do this thing over and over? Can you perceive an element of fear within your motivation?

Do you notice that as soon as you realize there is fear, you grow mellow inside, feeling something like: "Oh gosh, I didn't know you were so afraid! I will help you." There is tolerance in your attitude now. There is love and forgiveness.

As long as you judge fear-based behavior such as aggression, addiction, subservience, vanity, etc. as "bad," "sinful" or "dumb," you are judging. But judging itself is a fear-based activity. Have you noticed that when you judge, you grow harsh inside. Something tightens, like lips pressing to each other and eyes growing cold. Why do we need to judge things? What is this urge to narrow things down to right and wrong? What is the fear beneath our need to judge? It is a fear of facing our own inner darkness. It is, essentially, a fear of *living*.

In letting go of ego based consciousness, you will want to develop a whole new way of looking at things. This way of looking may be best described as neutral, meaning that it just takes notes of *what is*, and has no interest in how things "should be." The causes and effects of ego based behavior are observed, the core of fear within is recognized and so the ego truly becomes transparent to you. Whatever is transparent to you, you can let go of if you want to.

Every human being knows fear. Every one of you knows the darkness and loneliness of being caught in fear. When fear is shown openly in the face of a child, most people react instantaneously by reaching out their hands. But when fear is shown indirectly, through masks of violence and brutality, it seems unforgivable. The more destructive and cruel the behavior is, the more difficult it is to perceive the fear and desolation behind it.

Still, you are able to do so.

From the depths of your own experience of fear and desolation, you can get in touch with the deep fear in the souls of murderers, rapists and criminals.

It is possible for you to *understand* their actions. And if you do so based on your own intimate experience with darkness, you can let go of it. You can *let it be* without the need to judge any of it. If you truly understand fear as a power that is and that you are thoroughly acquainted with through your living experiences, you can let go of judging. Fear is neither good nor bad. Fear IS and has a certain role to play.

In ways that are very hard to express in human concepts, fear is a blessing as well as a torture. In any case, the choice to allow fear in your reality was not made *for* you. You were the Gods, so to speak, who allowed fear to play a constitutive role in your reality. You did so not to torture yourselves but *to create*, to create a reality that has more substance, more "fullness" to it than a world solely based on love. I realize this may sound unbelievable, but perhaps you can intuitively grasp what I am trying to say here.

Fear is a viable part of creation. Where fear is, love is not. Where love is not, love can be *found* in new and unpredictable ways. A whole range of emotions can be explored, even created by the absence of love. The absence of love can be *felt* in a variety of ways. The presence of love can only be felt against the background of fear. Otherwise it would be all pervading and you would not notice it as such.

So by creating fear, by catapulting yourself outside of the ocean of love that surrounded you, you allowed yourself to *experience love for the first time.*

Do you understand?

You did not create love, but you created the *experience* of love. You needed an opposite, something other than love, to do this and you used fear as an instrument. We on the other side of the veil can clearly see the spiritual role that fear plays in your reality. Therefore we plead with you, again and again, to not *judge*. Please do not judge fear and the darkness it brings, either in yourselves or in any other being. You are all created from love and to love you shall return.

When you enter stage two of the transformation process from ego to heart, you are confronted with your inner hurt, your fear and you are invited to look at it with understanding and acceptance.

After becoming aware of your inner hurt and fear, you may go through a period of self-judgment at first, in which you may display destructive behavior. It may seem that you are going backwards instead of forwards. At that point, you are in the danger zone, the no man's land in between ego and heart. You know you want to get rid of the old but you cannot yet really embrace the new, so you get caught up in self-doubt and self-judgment. The turning point is when you stop judging yourself - at least for a while.

It is only when you are prepared to look at yourself with an attitude of interest and openness that you enter the reality of heart based consciousness. Before that, you are merely comparing yourself to an artificial standard or ideal that, most of the time, you fall short of. You beat yourself up for this and then you try again to force yourself into the mold that you created for yourself in your head.

This kind of perfectionism, I tell you, is a murderous weapon. It is quite the opposite of love. Love truly does not compare and, more importantly, it never wants to force you into anything or change you in any way. Love has no eye for what *should* be. The very category of "should" is absent from the consciousness of the heart. Seen from the heart, moral categories are simply ways of interpreting or "dividing up" reality. They are ideas in your head and as you know, they may differ greatly from head to head. The very need to set standards and define the good is the forerunner to human conflict and war. It is not so much the ideas as the underlying need to control and fixate that causes aggression and conflict.

Political, personal or spiritual ideals, standards of health, beauty and sanity, all provide you with standards of how things should be, of how you should behave. They all try to fixate and define what is Good.

But Love is not interested in defining the Good. It is not interested in ideas, but in reality. Love turns to what is real.

The heart is interested in all that is, in every actual expression of you, the destructive and the constructive ones. It simply takes note; it simply is there, encircling you with its presence, if you let it.

If you open up to the reality of love, the reality of the heart, you let go of judgment. You accept who you are at this moment. You realize that you are who you are because of a multitude of reasons, which you are now going to investigate and explore.

When this moment arrives, it is a great blessing for the soul. You are now able to heal yourself. You will fall back into self-judgment from time to time, but you now have a conscious memory of how love feels. And as soon as you have that, you will return to find it anew, for you have tasted the sweet perfume of Home again.

In the second stage of the transition from ego to heart, you get into closer contact with yourself. You are taking a closer look at your baggage from the past. You are reliving painful memories again, memories from this life, perhaps memories of past lives. The psychological baggage you carry from all your lifetimes, up to the present, makes up your current identity. You may look upon this baggage as a suitcase full of clothes. You have played many roles in the past, assumed many identities, just like pieces of garment. You so strongly believed in some roles that you came to look upon them as part of your identity. "This is me," you think of such roles or "clothes."

When you truly investigate what these roles have to do with you, however, you will find out that *you are not them.* You are not the psychological roles or identities you assume. You are not your clothes. You have *used* these roles, from a soul-felt need for experience.

The soul takes delight in all experiences, because they are part of the learning process the soul committed itself to. All experiences are helpful and valuable in this respect.

When you take a closer look at your own roles or identities, you soon notice there have been painful, even traumatic experiences in your past, which still "stick" to you. You seem unable to let go of them. They have become like a "second skin," skin instead of mere garment.

Those are the difficult elements in your past, the pieces that now keep you from truly living and enjoying life. You have identified so much with these parts that you think you *are* them. Because of this you feel that you are a *victim* and you draw negative conclusion from this about life. But these conclusions do not hold for life as such; they just hold for the traumatized parts in your soul consciousness.

It is these parts that need healing now. You do so by entering the past again, but with a consciousness that is more loving and wise than you ever had before. In the second stage of the transformation process from ego to heart, you heal episodes from the past by encircling them with your present consciousness. Through reexperiencing them in the present, from a heart centered focus, you will let go of the traumatic parts in your past.

Trauma occurs when you experience a great loss or pain or evil and you cannot understand why it happens. You have all experienced trauma in many of your lives. In fact, the soul's consciousness during the ego stage is traumatized from the outset: there is the loss of Oneness or Home that it remembers and does not understand.

When you go back to the original traumatic event through imagination and you encircle it with the consciousness of the heart, *you are changing your original* response to the event. You change it from horror and disbelief, to simply taking note of what happens. In the regression, you *simply take note* of what happened and this very act creates *room for understanding*, room for a spiritual understanding of what actually took place in this event. When this room is present, you are becoming master of your reality again. You are now able to come to an acceptance of the whole episode, since you understand from the heart that there is meaning and purpose to every thing that happens. You can sense from the heart that there is an element of free choice present in everything that occurs, and so you grow towards an acceptance of your own responsibility for the event. When you accept your own responsibility, you are free to move on.

It is only when you relate to your own past identities as actors do to their roles that you are free to go wherever you want. You are then free to enter heart based consciousness. You no longer hold on to any aspect of what you have been in the past: victim or aggressor, male or female, black or white, poor or rich, etc. When you can be playful about the aspects of duality and simply use them whenever it brings you joy and creativity, you have grasped the meaning of life on earth. You will experience great happiness and a sort of homecoming. This is because you are getting in touch with the consciousness underlying your different roles and identities. You touch base with your own divine consciousness again, the realization that everything is one: in short, the reality of love.

We will close this chapter by giving you two meditations which may help you get in touch with the stream of oneness, that stream of divine consciousness that is the undercurrent of all your experiences.

Meditation 1

- *Which psychological characteristics that you consider very much a part of you cause you the most problems in your life? Name two such characteristics.*

- *Focus on the opposites of those characteristics. So if you picked "impatience" or "insecurity," you now focus on their counterparts: patience and self-confidence. Feel the energy of these characteristics for a moment.*

- *Go within and look for these energies inside you. Name three examples from your own life in which you displayed these positive characteristics.*

- *Now that you are in touch with these positive characteristics, let their energy flow through you and feel how they balance you.*

Meditation 2

- *Relax and let your imagination travel back to a moment in which you felt very happy. Take the first thing that enters your mind. Feel the happiness again.*

- *Now go to a moment in which you felt extremely unhappy. Feel the essence of what you felt back then.*

- *Capture what is common to both experiences. Feel what is the same in both moments.*

Both meditations are meant to make you aware of the underlying consciousness, the ever present "you-ness" in all of your experiences. This ever-present vessel of consciousness, the carrier of your experiences, is the divine You. It is your entrance to a reality beyond duality: the reality of the heart.

From ego to heart III

Letting go of the old you

The transition from ego based to heart based consciousness progresses along a number of stages:

1. Being unsatisfied by what ego based consciousness has to offer you, longing for "something else:" *the beginning of the end.*

2. Becoming aware of your ties to ego based consciousness, recognizing and releasing the emotions and thoughts that go with it: *the middle of the end.*

3. Letting the old ego based energies inside you die, throwing off the cocoon, becoming your new self: *the end of the end.*

4. The awakening of a heart based consciousness within you, motivated by love and freedom; helping others making the transition.

We will now speak of stage three. But before we do, we wish to point out that the transition does not take place along a straight and linear pathway. There are moments in which you may fall back to a stage you had already left behind. But such a fallback may later on lead you to a big step forward. So detours may turn out to be shortcuts. Also, every soul's spiritual path is unique and individual. So this scheme we are providing you with, of four different stages, should be conceived of as simply a way of highlighting some of the turning points in the process. Schemes and categories are merely instruments that make visible a reality that cannot be captured by the mind, the mental part of you.

After you have accepted your inner wounds and you have healed the traumatized parts of your consciousness as we have described in the previous chapter, your energy shifts. You are letting go of an older you. You are making room for a totally different way of being and experiencing. In this chapter, we would like to explain what happens *energetically* when you release ego centered consciousness. What happens energetically when you move from ego domination to heart based consciousness is that *the heart chakra takes precedence over the will or the third chakra.*

Chakras are spinning wheels of energy located along your spine. These energy centers are all related to particular life-themes, for example "spirituality" (crown chakra), "communication" (throat chakra), or "the emotions" (navel chakra). The chakras are to some extent part of material reality, since they are related to specific places in your body. But they are not visible to the physical eye, so you might say they linger in between spirit and matter; they bridge the gap. They form the point of entrance for spirit (your soul consciousness), enabling it to take physical form and create the things that are happening in your life.

The heart chakra, located in the middle of your chest, is very much the seat of the energy of love and oneness. The heart carries energies that unify and harmonize. When you draw your attention to this center for a while, you may feel warmth or something opening up. If you do not feel anything, simply let go and perhaps try some other time.

The chakra below the heart is called "the solar plexus" and it is located near your stomach. It is the seat of the will. It is the center that focuses your energy into physical reality. Therefore it is the chakra that is connected to issues of creativity, vitality, ambition and personal power.

The ego and the will are closely related to each other. The faculty of the will enables you to focus on something, either without or within. Your perceptions of reality, of both yourself and others, are greatly influenced by what you want, by your desires. Your desires are often intermingled with fear. You often want something because you feel you are in need of it; there is a sense of lack or neediness beneath. Because of the fears that are present in many of your desires, the solar plexus is often driven by the energy of the ego. The ego especially expresses itself through the solar plexus.

Through the faculty of the will, the ego literally puts a pressure on reality. Reality has to be squeezed into what the ego wants you to believe. The ego works from a set of basic assumptions about how reality works, which are all fear-based. It presents you with a highly selective picture of reality, since its way of looking is prejudiced towards its own needs and fears. Also it has to place judgments on everything it notices. There is no room for simply taking note of things. Everything has to be divided in categories, to be labeled right or wrong.

When you live from the heart, there is no firm set of beliefs by which you interpret or value facts. You do not hold strong convictions on anything anymore. You have become more of an observer. You postpone moral judgments on any issue, since you feel you may not have understood all there is to understand about the situation. Judgments always have something definitive about them, but the heart is not interested in definitions. It always tries to go beyond what seems definite and defined. The heart is open, exploring, and ready to re-examine, ready to forgive.

When you use ego centered will power, you can sense something pulling on your solar plexus chakra. Using your will in this way is an energetic happening that you can be consciously aware of, if you want to. Whenever you feel this pull, accompanied by a strong desire to have things your way, you are trying to mold reality to your wishes. You are trying to force your beliefs upon reality.

When you act from the heart, you go along with the flow of things as it presents itself; you are not pushing or forcing.

If you work very hard to achieve something and you fail to reach your goals time after time, please ask yourself from what chakra, from what energetic center, you are doing it. Also you can tune into your heart and ask why this thing is not working or why you have to put so much energy into it.

Often you try to realize certain goals without having truly gone within and checked with your heart whether this is what really serves you on your inner path to wisdom and creativity. Also, even if your goals do represent your deepest heart-felt desires, you may have unrealistic expectations about the timeframe in which things will happen. You may be on a timeline that is not of the heart but of the personal will.

There is a natural rhythm to all things, and it does not necessarily have the pace that you think is desirable. The realization of your goals requires energy to be shifted. Energy shifts often take more time than you expect or wish for. In fact, energy shifts are nothing else but *you changing.*

When you will have reached your goals, *you* will not be you anymore. You will have become an expanded version of your current self, filled with more wisdom, more love and more inner power. The time it takes to fulfill your goals is the time it takes to change your consciousness in such a way that your desired reality may enter your actual reality. So if you want to speed up things, focus on you and not so much on reality.

Often you even need to *let go of your goal,* in order to be open to receive. This sounds paradoxical. But in fact we are saying only that you need to fully accept your current reality, before you can step forward into a new one. If you do not accept your current reality and you are holding onto your goals in a tense way, you are not moving forward.

Nothing will leave your reality, unless you love it. Loving it is equal to "setting it free."

Unless you truly embrace your current reality and accept it as *your* creation, it cannot leave you, for you are denying part of yourself. You are saying "no" to the part of you that has created this reality for you. You would like to cut this unwanted part from you and move forward.

But you cannot create a more loving reality from self-hate. You cannot "will yourself" into a new reality by pushing unwanted parts aside. Will power does not serve you here.

What you need is to get in touch with your heart. The energies of understanding and acceptance are the true building blocks of a new and more fulfilling reality.

When you interact with reality from the heart, *you let reality be.* You do not try to change it; you simply and carefully take note of what is.

When the heart becomes the steward of your being, the center of the will (the solar plexus) will go along with it. The ego, the faculty of the will, will not be eliminated, since it naturally serves the role of translating energy from the level of consciousness to the level of physical reality. When this translation or manifestation is guided by the heart, the energy of the will creates and flows effortlessly. No pushing or forcing is involved. This is when *synchronicity* occurs: a remarkable coincidence of happenings which greatly enhances the realization of your goals. It seems miraculous to you when things work together in such a way. But in fact this is what happens all the time when you create from the heart. Effortlessness is the hallmark of creating from the heart.

Creating your reality from the heart

True creativity is not based on determination and strong will but on an open heart. Being open and receptive to the new and unknown is vital to being a true creator.

One key to true creativity, then, is the capacity *to do nothing:* to withhold from doing, fixing, focusing. It is the ability to place your consciousness in a purely *receptive but alert mode.*

Only by not knowing, by keeping things open, can you create room for something new to enter your reality.

This runs contrary to what much new age literature says about "creating your own reality." It is true that you create your reality all the time. Your consciousness is creative whether you are aware of it or not. But when you want to create your reality *consciously,* as many books and therapy teach you, it is essential to understand that the most powerful form of creating is not based on *the will* (being active) but on *self-awareness* (being receptive).

All change in the material world, for example in the areas of work, relationships or your material surroundings, is a reflection of changes at the inner level. It is only when inner transformation processes are completed that material reality can respond by mirroring it back to you through changing circumstances in your life.

When you try to create from the will, for example by focusing on or visualising your goals all the time, you ignore the inner transformation that is the real prerequisite for change. You are creating in an artificial way and you are bound to be disappointed. You are not creating from the depths of your soul.

The soul speaks to you in moments of silence. You truly listen to its voice when you *don't know* anymore. Often the soul speaks very clearly at times when you give up and throw in the towel. What happens when you *give up* and despair is that you open up *to the new.* You release all your expectations and you are truly receptive to *what is.*

The despair is caused by the strong beliefs that you had about *what should happen* in your life. When reality fails to answer these beliefs, you get disappointed and even desperate at some point.

However, if you give up strong expectations and dare to be open to the new, you do not have to reach that point of despair before you get in touch with your soul again. You can become still, receptive and open to what it tells you, without having to be disappointed first.

As long as you "know exactly what you want," you are often limiting the possibilities that are energetically available to you. This new reality you are looking for, whether a job or a relationship or better health, contains many elements that are unknown to you. Often you think that what you desire is *something you know* (a nice job, a loving partner) *projected into the future.* But that is not so. What you are really doing by creating a new reality is going outside of your own psychological borders. And you *cannot* know now what lies beyond those borders.

You can sense very clearly that there is something very desirable there, but you need not narrow it down by focusing or visualizing it. You can simply look forward to it with a sense of openness and curiosity.

Really, to create the most desirable reality for yourself, self-acceptance is much more important than focusing your thoughts or your will. You cannot create something that you are not. You may recite mantras a thousand times and create a lot of positive images in your mind, but as long as they do not reflect what you truly feel (for example anger, depression, unrest), they create nothing but confusion and doubt. ("I'm working so hard but nothing happens".)

Self-acceptance is a form of love. Love is the biggest magnet for positive changes in your life. If you love and accept yourself for who you are, you will attract circumstances and people that reflect your self-love. It's as simple as that.

Feel your own energy, all of your feelings. Feel how beautiful and sincere you are right now, in all of your struggles and sorrow. You *are* beautiful, with all your "imperfections" and "faults." And that is the only realization that counts.

Embrace who you are, get relaxed with yourself, perhaps look at "your many flaws" with a sense of humor. Perfection is not an option, you know. It is just an illusion.

Creating your reality from the heart is to recognize your Light, here and now. By recognizing it, by becoming aware of it, you are sowing a seed that will grow and take shape at the physical level.

When God created you as individual souls, she did not exert her will. She was simply being Herself and at some point she sensed that there was something "out there" worth exploring. She didn't know exactly what it was, but it did make her feel a little like *falling in love.* And she assumed without further ado that she was worthy of experiencing this new and inviting reality. She was also a little in love with herself!

And so you took shape as individual souls and God started to experience life through you. How this all came about – the details of the creation process – God did not really bother about. She just loved herself and she was open to change. And those are really the only elements required for you to create your own perfect reality: self-love and a willingness to venture into the new.

Adjusting to living from the heart

Creating from the heart is more powerful and requires less effort than creating from the ego. You do not have to bother about the details; you just need to be open to *all there is*, both inside and outside.

From this openness, you may now and then sense a certain pull. You may feel *drawn* towards certain things. This pull is actually the quiet whisper of your heart; it is your intuition. When you act from intuition, you are being *pulled* instead of *pushing*. You do not act until you sense on the inner level that it is appropriate to act.

Since you are very much used to *pushing*, i.e. using your will to create things, the energetic shift from ego to heart is quite challenging for you. The shift requires a tremendous "slow down." To really get in touch with the flow of your intuition, you consciously have to make an effort to "not do," to *let everything be*. This runs counterintuitive to much that you are taught and are used to. You are very much in the habit of basing your actions upon thought and willpower. You let your thinking determine your goals and you use your will to realize them. This is quite opposite to heart centered creating.

When you live from the heart, you *listen* to your heart and then act accordingly. You do not think, you listen with an alert and open awareness to what your heart is telling you. The heart speaks through your feelings, not through your mind. The voice of the heart can best be heard when you feel quiet, relaxed and grounded.

The heart shows you the way to the most loving and joyful reality for you right now. Its whispers and suggestions are not based on rational thinking. You can recognize the voice of your heart by its lightness and the note of joy in it. The lightness is there because the heart does not impose; there are no strings attached to its suggestions. Your "heart-self" is not attached to your decisions and it loves you whatever you do.

Living from the heart does not mean you become passive or lethargic. Letting things be without labeling them right or wrong, without pushing them in one way rather than another, requires a lot of strength. It is the strength to be *totally present,* to face everything there is and *just look at it.* You may feel empty, or depressed, or nervous, but you do not try to drive these things away. All you do is *surround them with your consciousness.*

You do not understand the true power of your consciousness. Your consciousness is made of Light. When you hold something in your consciousness, it changes because of that. Your consciousness is a healing force, if you do not bind it by your thinking and your addiction to "doing."

Your lives are filled with the dictatorship of the mind and the will, the primacy of thinking and doing.

Note that both the mind and the will work with general rules. There are general rules of logical thinking; they are the rules of logic. There are general strategies for putting thought into matter; they are the rules of "project management."

But these are all general tenets. General guidelines and rules always have a *mechanical* component. They are applicable to all or most individual cases; otherwise they would be of little use.

Now intuition works very differently. Intuition is always tailored to one person, at one particular moment. It is *highly individualistic.* Therefore it cannot be subjected to rational analysis or to general rules.

To live and act according to your intuition therefore asks for a high level of *trust,* for your choices are then purely based on what *you* feel is right, instead of what other people's rules say is right.

To live from the heart thus asks you not just to release the habit of overusing your mind and your will-power; it also challenges you to truly trust yourself.

It will take time to learn to listen to your heart, to trust its messages and act upon them. But the more you do so, the more you will understand that it is only by surrendering your worries and doubts to the wisdom of your own heart that you will find inner peace.

When you proceed along this path and you enter the third stage of the transformation from ego to heart, you will find inner peace for the first time.

You will realize that it is the urge to control reality through thinking and willing that makes you restless and anxious.

When you release control, you allow the magic of life to unfold. All you have to do is *listen*. Be alert to what is happening in your life, to what your feelings are towards other people, to what your dreams and desires are. When you are alert to what is happening inside you, reality will provide you with all the information you need to act appropriately.

For example, you may be aware of a desire in your heart for a loving relationship in which you truly communicate with another. If you just *notice and accept* this longing, without trying to do something about it, you will be amazed about how the universe will respond to it. By not drawing any conclusions, but just holding the longing in the Light of your consciousness, your call will be heard and answered.

It may take longer than your expect, for there are energy shifts that have to take place before certain longings can be fulfilled. But you are the master, the creator of your energetic reality. If you create it from fear, reality will respond accordingly. If you create it from trust and surrender, you will receive everything you desire and more.

From ego to heart IV

Opening up to Spirit

We have distinguished four stages in the transition from ego based to heart based consciousness:

1. Being unsatisfied by what ego based consciousness has to offer you, longing for "something else:" *the beginning of the end.*

2. Becoming aware of your ties to ego based consciousness, recognizing and releasing the emotions and thoughts that go with it: *the middle of the end.*

3. Letting the old ego based energies inside you die, throwing off the cocoon, becoming your new self: the *end of the end.*

4. The awakening of a heart based consciousness within you, motivated by love and freedom; helping others making the transition.

We will now speak of the last stage, which is stage four: opening up to Spirit.

When you have entered stage four, you have found a place of peace and quiet inside you. You frequently make contact with a silence in your heart that you know is of the eternal. Everything you experience is relative compared to this unlimited and all-embracing Being.

This place of peace and silence inside you has also been called Spirit.

In your esoteric traditions, a distinction is made between spirit, soul and body.

The body is the physical dwelling place of the soul for a limited amount of time.

The soul is the non-physical, psychological anchor of experience. It carries the experiences of many lifetimes. The soul develops over time and slowly grows into a many-faceted stone of beauty, every facet reflecting a different type of experience and the knowledge based on it.

The spirit does not change or grow in time.

Spirit is outside of time and space. The spirit in you is the eternal, timeless part of you that is One with the God that created you. It is the divine consciousness that is the foundation of your expression in space and time. You were born from a realm of pure consciousness and you carried part of that consciousness within you throughout all your manifestations in material form.

The soul partakes of duality. It is affected and transformed by its experiences in duality. The spirit is outside of duality. It is the background against which everything develops and evolves. It is the Alpha and Omega, which you might simply call Being or Source.

Silence, outer but especially inner, is the best entrance to experiencing this ever present energy, which is You in your deepest core. In silence, you can get in touch with the most miraculous and self-evident thing there is: Spirit, God, Source, Being.

The soul carries memories of many incarnations. It knows and understands much more than your earthly personality. The soul is connected to extrasensory sources of knowledge, such as your past life personalities and guides or acquaintances on the astral planes. Despite this connection, the soul can be in a state of confusion, ignorant of its true nature. The soul can be traumatized by certain experiences and therefore remain in a place of darkness for some time. The soul is continually evolving and gaining understanding of the duality inherent in life on earth.

The spirit is the immovable point within this development. The soul can be in a state of darkness or enlightenment. Not so the spirit. Spirit is pure Being, pure consciousness. It is in the dark as well as in the light. It is the oneness underlying all duality. When you have arrived at stage four of the transformation from ego to heart, you connect with Spirit. You connect with your Divinity.

Connecting with the God inside you is like being taken out of duality while remaining fully present and grounded. In this state, your consciousness is filled with a deep but quiet ecstasy: a mixture of peace and joy.

You realize that you are not dependent on anything outside of you. You are free. You are truly in the world but not of it.

Connecting with the spirit inside you is not something that happens once and for all. It is a slow and gradual process, in which you connect, disconnect, reconnect... Gradually the focus of your consciousness moves from duality to oneness. It re-orients itself, finding that eventually it is drawn to silence rather than to thoughts and emotions. By silence we mean being fully centered and present, in a state of non-judgmental awareness.

There are no fixed methods or means to get there. The key to connecting with your Spirit is not to follow some *discipline* (like meditating, or fasting etc.), but to really *understand* – understand that it is silence that brings you home, not your thoughts or emotions.

This understanding grows slowly as you are increasingly aware of the mechanism of your thoughts and emotions. You let go of old habits and open up to the new reality of heart based consciousness. Ego based consciousness inside you withers and slowly dies.

Dying is not something you do; it is something you allow to happen. You surrender yourself to the dying process. Death is another word for change, transformation. This is always so. Death is always a releasing of the old and an opening up to the new. Within this process, there is not one single moment in which you "are not," i.e. in which you are dead by your definition. Death as you define it is an illusion. It is only your fear of change that makes you fear death.

You are afraid not only of dying physically, but also of dying emotionally and mentally during your lifetime. But without death, things would become fixed and rigid. You would become the captive of old forms: a worn out body, outdated thought patterns, limiting emotional reactions. Suffocating, isn't it? Death is a liberator. Death is a cascade of fresh water that breaks open old, rusty gateways and propels you into new areas of experience.

Do not fear death. There is no death, only change.

The passage from ego based consciousness to heart centered living is in many ways a death experience. The more you identify yourself with Spirit, with the God inside you, the more you release things that you used to worry about or that you used to put a lot of energy into. You realize on deeper and deeper levels that there is truly nothing *to do,* except *to be.* When you identify with your beingness, instead of the fleeting thoughts and emotions that pass through you, your life is affected immediately. Spirit is not something abstract. It is a reality that you can truly bring down into your life. Being in touch with this purest of sources will eventually change everything in your life. God or Source or Spirit is by its nature creative but in ways that are nearly incomprehensible to you.

Spirit is silent and perennial and yet creative. The reality of the divine cannot really be grasped by the mind. It can only be felt. If you allow it into your life and you recognize it as the whisperings of your heart, everything slowly starts to fall into place. When you are tuned into the reality of spirit, the silent awareness that is behind all of your experiences, you stop pushing or forcing your will upon reality. You allow things to fall back into their natural state of being. You become your natural, true Self. This all occurs in a harmonious, meaningful way. You experience that things come together in a way that has a natural rhythm, a natural flow to it. All you have to do is stay tuned into this divine rhythm and let go of fears and misunderstandings that make you want to intervene.

Helping others from the level of Spirit

When you have made the transition from ego based to heart based consciousness, you are more or less continually in touch with the divine flow of being inside. In this state of being, there is no need or desire to help others, but it comes naturally to you. You draw it to you but not through the will. Energetically you are now emitting certain vibrations. Something is present in your energy field which draws people to you. It is not something you do but something that you are. There is a vibration available in your energy that can help them get in touch with their own divine self.

You can be a mirror to them in which they can see a difficult problem or condition actually being released and transformed into the energy of the solution. They can sense the energy of the solution which is always founded upon contact with the divine self in your being.

You are able to teach them something, and the teaching takes place *by you being yourself.* It is not by you transmitting knowledge or using certain methods that you teach and heal. It is by allowing yourself to be just who you are and by expressing yourself as you find most joyful that your presence becomes truly helpful. It is by sharing yourself with others that you make available a space of healing for them that they may choose to enter or not. That is up to them.

As a healer or therapist, you really have only to keep in touch with the divine inner flow, with the silent awareness that is Spirit. It is really this connection that moves people and lifts them into a higher, freer state of awareness, if they choose it. If they do, it will occur in a rhythm and flow that is their own.

Being there for others in this way has a very neutral feeling tone to it. It represents a level of detachment where you release your personal desire to change or "cure" others. Such a desire, displayed by all lightworkers at some stage, does not stem from a true understanding of the inner road that people want to travel to find their own truth. Most people need to go to the bottom of certain issues before they are truly ready to release them. When they do so, they really "own" the solution to the issue and this gives them deep satisfaction. Perhaps you recognize this within your own life and the issues you struggled with. Please be aware of this and do not struggle to keep people from "hitting bottom." If they are determined to go there, they will go there in spite of all that you do or say.

It is better to not be emotionally involved with the people you help. The emotional involvement invites in the personal will to cure or transform others.

This personal desire does not help others; it may actually cause blocks in their healing process. Whenever you want people to change, you are not in a space of love and allowance. They sense this. You may think that you are observing and reading them, but they are keen readers of you as well!

In stage four of the transition from ego to heart, it is about transcending the level of the soul and rising to the level of the spirit. We do not mean to say that the soul is in any way "less" than spirit, of course. The point is: you are greater and more encompassing than your soul. The soul is a vehicle for experience. By identifying with Spirit in you, with your divine self, all the things that you have experienced in many, many lifetimes fall into place. You rise above the experiences by not identifying yourself with any one of them. This has a healing effect upon the soul.

Time, multidimensionality and your light self

In the previous chapters of the Lightworker Series, we have told a more or less chronological tale about the history and inner development of lightworker souls. This story may give you the impression that you develop in *time* from point A to point B, from dark to light, from ignorance to wisdom.

And in certain ways, this is the case.

Yet in this closing chapter, we wish to draw your attention to a different perspective, a different way of looking at yourselves, a perspective that lifts you outside of time, outside of this particular history, and acquaints you with your timeless existence, in other words your *multidimensionality*.

There is a part of you that is completely independent of space and time. This part is free at any moment to enter any dimension or area of experiences it wishes. It is free to choose dark or light at any time.

From your earthly perspective, you travel from point A to point B in a linear fashion. For example, you travel through the four stages of inner development that we discussed, step by step.

From a timeless, multidimensional perspective, however, the real you is not developing over time, it is the one who is *experiencing* the development. The real you does not *need* to develop. It allows this experience in by its own free choice. This choice is motivated by a deep knowing of the great value of experiencing duality.

From the perspective of your timeless, spiritual self, you are at any time free to experience any point on the line from A to B to Z and beyond. You can activate any reality of consciousness for yourself at any time, for the idea that you are stuck within a certain stage of inner development is ultimately just an illusion.

The reason we want to draw your attention to this perspective is that it may help you break through your inner barriers. It may help you pierce the veil of illusion and get in direct touch with your own Light Self: *the energy of the angel that you truly are.*

To grasp this as a real perspective from which to view yourself, we need to expound a little on the notion of time.

Time

At the highest level of oneness, there is no time. This is the level of Spirit, God, pure beingness. At this level, there is no *development*, no "becoming" but only "being."

At the lowest level of oneness, at which separation is experienced at its strongest, a hollow, linear notion of time is employed. By "hollow" I mean a scientific, abstract notion of time that is completely devoid of subjectivity and felt content. Time in this notion is an objective structure outside of you. Time is something laid over your experiences as an external framework.

A "curriculum vitae," for example, which you send in when you are applying for jobs, often consists of such an objective timeline of facts. In this year I did that, in that year I graduated from that school, etc. You emphasize the visible, external side of things. The inner side of things – the motivation, the meaning, the subjectivity – is left out.

On the energetic levels in between oneness and separation, time is a reality that "fluctuates" with your experience. Time is an experiential notion: a way of carving up experience. At these levels, there is time but it is not something independent of or external to your experiences.

For example, on the astral planes where you travel during sleep and also after you die, there is no "clock time." Clock time is the utmost attempt to disentangle time from subjectivity, i.e. from you and your experiences. It is a grand illusion. On the astral planes, time is the *rhythm of your experiences.* Sometimes you rest, now you meet someone, then you study for yourself, etc. The point at which one stage ends and another one begins is not determined by clock time – something external – but by your inner flow of feelings, by what seems natural to you.

This natural sense of time or rhythm can be part of earth life too. The subjectivity of time, i.e. the fact that time can be experienced differently in various circumstances, is familiar to all of you. You say that "time flies" when you are having fun, whereas time seems to come to a standstill when you are in the waiting room at the dentist or in a line at the supermarket.

Now the sceptic inside you may say: time is perceived as moving slowly when circumstances are experienced as negative, whereas time is seemingly going faster when circumstances are positive. But time itself is always the same, ticking by in the same rigid manner, however we experience things.

This is the "objective framework" notion of time, also called the linear notion of time. It stems from a rationalistic, scientific approach to time.

But imagine that there were no clocks, no night and day, no natural influences such as sun, moon and tides by which to measure time. Then you could only rely on your own subjective sense of time.

Your objective measure of time – the clock – is not really based on something external; it is the product of the human mind that wishes to divide up and classify. The human mind has abstracted a certain order of things from the natural phenomena on earth. But "time in itself," independent of the human factor, does not exist. It is an illusion that is the product of a type of consciousness that is caught in the belief in separation.

Time is essentially subjective. Time is a way of carving up experience in such a way that you can make sense of it. For example, you say of someone: "he is an old soul." Do you really mean the number of years or lifetimes when you refer to his old age? Or do you mean by "old" that he expresses certain qualities, such as wisdom, balance and serenity, rather than a certain quantity of time? The reference to *time* in the phrase "old soul" is really a reference to *experience.*

Time in the full sense of the word is the "dynamics of becoming" on the inner level. It may be a helpful concept insofar as it helps you articulate the natural rhythm or flow of things. But when conceived as something objective, standing over and above you, it tends to limit and distract you. You are not limited to a particular timeline. You are not a linear being. There are levels of your being that are outside of the framework of time that you are presently experiencing. It is to this aspect of yourself, i.e. your multidimensionality, which we wish to draw your attention to now.

Multidimensionality

According to the linear notion of time, you cannot be present in more than one place at the same time. By "you," the linear concept refers to your body, your brain and your consciousness that is somehow tied to your body/brain. (Science cannot yet explain how exactly body and consciousness are "tied," but it does maintain – generally – that consciousness cannot exist without a physical body.)

According to the "full," subjective concept of time, you are present wherever your consciousness dwells. Where you are, in time and place, is determined by the focus of your consciousness, not by the location of your body.

For example: you are at the station, waiting for your train to arrive. It will take some time yet, so you just sit and stare for a while and unnoticed you get into a slightly altered state of consciousness. You are now thinking of someone you were talking to yesterday. You recall that conversation easily and you vividly remember how it affected you. You are reliving certain aspects of that conversation, drawing it into your Now moment from the past. What you are actually doing here is that you travel to the past and you visit the energies of that moment again. Your Now energy interacts with the energy of the past, possibly creating changes in your experience of that moment and thus altering the past.

By altering the past we do not mean that you alter any physical facts, but that you overlay them with a different interpretation or perspective. By altering the felt content of a certain past event, however, you are in a sense altering the event for you.

Just think of this example.

You had a conversation with someone, who got really offended by a remark of yours which had no critical intention at all. The other person you were talking with started to scold you and then walked away. Now you in turn felt offended, feeling misunderstood, angry and shocked at the same time. After you got home you felt troubled for some hours, but then you let it go and had a good night's sleep. Next morning at the train station, you had to wait for your train and you suddenly recalled this peculiar conversation, where things went wrong so surprisingly. You now look at it from a different perspective and suddenly you realize why the man felt so offended by your remark. You remember some facts about his past that you simply had forgotten before you had that conversation. You can now see his emotional reaction in a whole different light, especially as having nothing to do with you. It wasn't you who was causing the hurt; you just triggered an old hurt inside of him. This perspective sets in motion a different emotional response inside you. You feel a sense of relief, insight and yes... forgiveness. "Oh, I see... now I understand... poor fellow."

At that moment, you are recreating the past. You are overlaying it with a different interpretation of the facts, which replaces your initial response. To be clear, this does not mean that the initial response did not take place, but that the energies of anger, shock and misunderstanding have been transformed into understanding and forgiveness. A "spiritual alchemy" has taken place by the interaction between past and present.

Really, the physical facts aren't that important. It is the felt content of a situation, your energetic reaction to it, that really shapes your life and your reality. Therefore we may rightly say that you can alter the past by traveling through time to past energies which still need resolution.

While you are sitting at the station conducting your time travel, there is some layer of your consciousness still present with your body. You may sense "in the back of your mind" that your hands are getting cold or that some youngsters behind you are talking loudly.

Consciousness is able to divide itself up. It can be in different places at the same time, meaning that consciousness can dwell in different energetic realities at the same time.

This is the meaning of multidimensionality. Your consciousness is not limited to space and time. Although you have a basic agreement during a lifetime on earth that some part of your consciousness is always connected with your earth body, your consciousness is not thereby limited to one specific point in time. You are not limited by the past or the future, for they are not fixed. They are liquid fields of experience. They are changeable and you can interact with them from the Now.

Your consciousness is multidimensional even when you think that you are imprisoned within your physical body. Do you know the expression: "She is stuck in the past?" Someone cannot let go of the past and her consciousness is filled with past experiences and with emotions such as regret, remorse or just grief. This person is "not here." She is literally in the past. She is, as in the example above, interacting with the past from the now moment, but not in a liberating, alchemical way. Her body is present in the here and now, and she is stuck in the past. Time for her stands still, while the clock is ticking and measuring the passage of weeks and months. This is because she does not move experientially.

She doesn't flow with the natural processes of life and experience. This is an example of multidimensionality. Even when you limit yourself to such a narrow focus of consciousness, you are being multidimensional. By this I mean to say that multidimensional is not something you become, it is something that you are. It is your nature; it is your natural state of being.

The real question is: how can you be multidimensional in a liberating and transforming way? How can you employ your multidimensionality in such a way that you can move freely through the dimensions and not lose touch with your divine spirit? Being multidimensional from a place of wisdom and awareness: that is your spiritual destiny. It is your destiny to become fully conscious multidimensional creators.

Being consciously multidimensional means that you release the illusion of linear time, which also means to release the notion that you are no more than your body.

Being consciously multidimensional is to identify yourself with the spirit (God) inside you that is absolutely free to enter any realm of experience, i.e. dimension, it chooses.

Being consciously multidimensional is an essential part of the reality of the New Earth.

The reason you struggle with the concept of multidimensionality is that you conceive of "being in two different places at the same time" in a physical way. Your physical body cannot be in two physical places at the same time. However dimensions are not physical places, not "chunks of matter," so to speak. Dimensions are realms of consciousness, spheres of consciousness that abide by certain energetic laws.

Your consciousness can partake of different dimensions at the same time. This happens NOW. There are realities of the past, the future, the astral planes, past lives, of the angel inside you and even more, that are intersecting and meeting inside you right here right now. You *are* multidimensional now, but are you multidimensional in a conscious manner? Do you allow the dimensions to flow in and out of you, do you accept what energies they bring you and can you recognize them as yours?

You interact with the other dimensions you are part of all the time, but if you do so in a conscious and accepting way, you are actually transforming those dimensional realities. By embracing stuck or pent-up energies from those dimensions and holding them up to the light of your consciousness, you liberate and integrate parts of your Self and you change your present.

Many realms of consciousness meet inside you and you are essentially the master who chooses to experience any of them. You are free to travel through any of them, fast or slowly, near or far. As long as you identify with the Spirit inside you, you will keep the awareness that you are free.

But when you get stuck in thoughts of limitation, holding beliefs such as "this is not possible," "that is not allowed," "this will go wrong," etc., you sink into the illusion of separation. You are caught in the illusion of linear time, the illusion that you are a body, the illusion that you are separate from God. In this way, the soul gets temporarily "bound" to certain realms of experience. The soul forgets about its true origins, its divinity and its freedom.

This being caught or "bound" is also called *karma*.

Getting "unbound" or unstuck often proceeds along a number of steps or stages of what you call "inner growth." From the human linear standpoint, you are "releasing karma" and slowly transforming yourself according to the four stages of inner development that we have described in this Lightworker series. From the standpoint of Spirit, however, you are simply bouncing back into your natural state of divine awareness. From that point of view, releasing karma is nothing else than remembering your own divinity.

Your Light Self

Many dimensions, many realms of consciousness, come together inside you. And you are really the master, the creator of the whole field of dimensions. You are a star with many rays, a soul consciousness with many manifestations. You are free to activate whatever reality you choose.

If you drop the notion of linear time or chronology, you allow yourself to believe that the past or the future do not determine you. You can then feel yourself to be at the center of a vibrating field of dimensions, all emanating from one divine, timeless source: you.

Imagine yourself at the center of all these realities, all these possibilities, and then choose the one that carries the most Light for you.

You choose the brightest, most lovely ray in the field, and now, for a moment, go inside of it and feel what it is like to BE that ray.

This is your Light Self.
This is the part of you that is most like God.

Traditionally, the beings closest to God are called archangels.
And that is what you are, in this dimension, right now.
You truly are archangels.

Archangels are beings that are very close to Spirit or God, but they are not completely one with it. They are one step removed from absolute consciousness, meaning pure Being without differentiation, becoming or individuality.

Archangels have a kind of *individuality*. There is uniqueness to all of them. An archangel may be said to have certain characteristics. One cannot say this of God or Spirit. God is All and Nothing. Because of this, archangels have entered "the realm of separation," the realm of "I" versus "Other." They are part of duality, however slightly.

An archangel is an aspect of God that has manifested itself as a particular Being, a particular Form. The Greek philosopher Plato called this an Idea, which in our terms, is a basic or "archetypical" energetic reality that transcends the physical world. Archangels are in that sense platonic Ideas. There is an archangel (Idea) of Love, of Truth, of Goodness, etc., each embodying the energy of a particular aspect of God. Archangels are not so much persons as energy fields with an individual flavor.

Why did Spirit or God externalize aspects of himself in this way?

It was from the joy of creativity that he did this.

The archangel energies are an expression of God's unending creative joy.

Archangels are not outside of God. Nothing is outside of God. God is in everything. God is present in all created energies as the "spirit aspect." This aspect is what makes all these energies *one*.

That which *separates* a being from another one, what makes it different and unique, is the "soul aspect." The soul aspect covers the individuality of a being.

All created beings that have individuality are truly a coming together of Spirit and Soul, of consciousness (spirit) and experience (soul).

Creation is a dance of Spirit and Soul.

The archangels are, so to speak, the first born children of God. Not "first" in a linear sense but in the sense of being very close to God. They carry a deep awareness inside of their divinity, the "spirit aspect." Humans perceive archangels as a bright and pure Light.

There are different archangels. Every archangel emanates energy like rays of light from a sun. By emitting these rays farther and farther away, the archangel gets in touch with unknown spaces, with realms of experience that are new to it. The archangelic energy reaches out and in this spontaneous, creative movement, it stumbles across that which is Other than it, that which is not light, but dark. Dark here just means: further removed from Oneness/Spirit, further drawn into the realm of individuality.

God or Spirit is neither dark nor light. God simply *is*. Archangels are beings of light. By creating Light, God also created Dark. This is simply because archangels are in the dimension of duality, outside of Oneness. They have a sense of individuality. The creation of the Light self (the angel) brought with it the creation of the Dark self, the part of the Self where light is absent. There is beauty in this polarity, since it constitutes the dynamics of creation.

God, pure being and consciousness, longed for *experience*, and this experience she gains through the created universe, through her presence in the light and the dark aspects of it.

What the archangels were going to experience, after they entered the realm of duality, God did not know. This is what she craved: not to *know* everything, but to *experience* something new.

In stepping outside of Oneness, the archangels entered an empty space, a space of potentiality, a space of unending possibilities.

The archangels found out that they could create many forms and live in them. Every form you inhabit as a conscious being has a certain angle or perspective to it which enables "unformed consciousness" to experience things in specific ways.

The whole process of the archangels venturing out for experiences can be portrayed as a huge waterfall of sparkling light. The energy of the archangels poured out of God/Source like a massive flow of sparkling, bright water, going in every direction. Within this huge stream of water, little streams separated themselves, dividing up into even smaller streams, until they were tiny drops of liquid light. These drops may be compared to individual units of consciousness, each with their own set of experiences.

The dance of Spirit and Soul had now truly begun!

The individual units of consciousness, which we call souls, went on with their journey. They carried deep within themselves the energy of Spirit or Source, as well as the energy of the archangel they stemmed from. But as they traveled further and farther, they came to experience that it was possible to forget about their origins, to forget about their divinity and to become lost in darkness and illusion. This polarity of dark and light could best be experienced as a human being, living on earth.

When we describe the process of archangels emanating from Source and eventually becoming human, it seems that we are telling a linear, chronological tale. But this is not so. The emanation or waterfall of energy from God is happening *right Now*. This tale tells you about the identities that are available to you Now, not about who you were in some distant past. At this very moment, there is a layer of pure archangel energy inside you, a layer of pure Light. There are also layers of confusion and fear inside you. But you can choose, at any moment, to be the Light self, the angel that you are. This is not something you need to *develop*, it is simply a part of who you are.

It is important to realize that you do not need to look up to spiritual masters, guides or angels. There is *not one authority above you*. You yourself are among the "first born," sitting next to God's throne. You yourself are God and angel.

The easiest way to get in touch with your Light self is through connecting with the layer of pure consciousness, pure Spirit inside you. This you do by becoming silent on inner and outer levels. The silence you experience then is really ever present in you; you only need to become aware of it.

When you are connected to silence, the dimension of eternity inside you, you can feel Spirit's desire *to experience*. From this desire, your Light self was born.

The soul experiences the greatest joy in the interplay between Spirit and experience, the interplay between divinity and humanness. This is the secret of the universe.

When you are purely Spirit, your reality is static. Nothing changes. Experience and movement only arise when there is a relationship with *something outside of you/Spirit.* When you sense something other than yourself, there is an invitation to explore, to feel, to find out. But to experience something other than you, you need to remove yourself out of absolute Oneness, out of God/Spirit. When you do so, you become an individual soul.

You are a unique soul: one foot in the realm of the Absolute, one foot in the realm of the Relative (i.e. duality).

In your explorations of relativity (duality), you may go so far away from Home that you lose contact with the element of Spirit inside you. Your soul then gets lost in the illusion of fear and separation.

The greatest joy possible is when you take part of the realm of Experience while staying connected with Spirit, with Home. The balanced interplay between Spirit and Soul is the source of the greatest creativity and love.

From this perspective, you are all on your way to finding the right balance between absolute Oneness and being an individual soul. The ones among you who are lightworkers are at present working towards a greater awareness of their oneness with Spirit. They have traveled into duality long and far, and they, i.e. *you*, my dear reader, are ready to come back Home. Not however to a static Home of Pure Oneness, but to a dynamic, creative reality of divine, multidimensional humans whose experiences will be filled with joy and light.

In all of you who read this, there is an intense longing for Home and a profound determination to truly know who you are. Keep your longing and determination alive and trust them, for they will bring you Home.

Part II

The Public Channelings

2003 - 2006

The power of your own consciousness

Dear friends, I have come today to speak with you all. You are so well known to me! You do not know how well I know you. I am often with you because my heart is connected to you. I see your pain; I witness your joy, your worries, your suffering. And I would so much like to tell you about the power that resides in you. The power of your own consciousness. The power of your own being. The power of your own soul.

Too often you are still searching. Ever again, you are looking for solutions from outside yourselves. But as you take these solutions into yourselves, they already start melting away. Realise that you are the center of your being, the sun of your own universe. The direction of your consciousness and what it is attuned to will decide how you feel, how you think, how you act. From deep within yourself you direct these things, like a sun directs its rays outward. If you believe that there are aspects of yourself this sun should not shine its light upon, that there are places where it shouldn't shine, that there are things it shouldn't warm with its rays, then everyone and everything you meet around you will confirm these beliefs.

In the same way, the help or advice of someone else can only be received if you allow your own sun to shine its light on the aspect with which you need help. It is always your decision to put that aspect into the light and open the door. There is no one else who can force you to do that. That is why no one can help you if you don't allow yourself to be helped. (That goes for earthly help as well as help from our side.)

Convictions are alive within you that make you think you lack the strength to find your own way, to feel your own destiny again. These convictions are linked to a past in which you lost yourselves for a very long time. I am speaking in particular about a past here on earth, a past of many earthly lives in which you have experienced much darkness.

This history has not been meaningless. It is a history in which you were confronted with much fear and in which fear overshadowed your inner sun. But now you are all slowly awakening. Parts of you are already in the light again but there also many aspects that are still in the dark, overshadowed by fear and insecurity about yourselves.

You can compare this inner darkness to a child being lost. A part of your soul is a lost child. It has lost its way in a past of pain. But the past is not a static thing. Time is to some extent an illusion. Nothing is irrevocably lost in time. There are no closed-off doors. The lost child within yourself which is fragmented in the past can be found and healed. You are its parent, you are the one who is made to cherish that child, who can warm it and bring it back to life.

And by life, I mean truly living. You have forgotten how to *live*. You are very good at surviving, but truly living is so much more sparkling and inspiring and happy.

It is precisely the part of you that is best capable of doing this, the child within, that has been lost. It got lost in the shadows of the past, in an accumulation of events that were traumatizing to your consciousness. In all the times you have been incarnating here on earth, on the level of the soul you have been developing like children do into adulthood. In that sense you came to earth as children, made many experiences your own and made many experiences you did not fully understand. Now we are coming to the end of a certain stage in your history, a certain cycle in your development, and it is time to rise above the experiences that have not been understood: to grow into the *parent*. It is now time to be the father and the mother of your own child. And that is what I am pointing out in speaking to you about the power of your consciousness: the power in you to rise above the wounded inner child.

The child in you is the victim of many experiences that have not been understood. I am telling you that your deepest inner wound can best be compared to the emotional state of an abandoned child. It's a child that has somehow become separated from the security and loving arms of Home and doesn't know why and what for. In you there's a child that feels abandoned and frightened and that doesn't have the frame of reference to be able to understand. This pain relates back to a very distant point in time, a time when you departed from the God-like state of oneness and started your journey as individual souls. (This will be elucidated in the next channeling: "Cosmic birthing pain".)

At some point you will understand that this journey was your own choice and an act of creation that was truly divine. The deep pain you felt when you commenced your journey alone, your journey of experience, this deep pain was at the same time a great act of creation. Because by disengaging yourselves as souls from the great whole, from Father-Mother-God, you were allowing yourselves to discover a great deal, to experience and feel a lot of things. At the current stage of your journey where there is still much inner pain, it is hard to see what the ultimate meaning of that long journey home is. But I want to assure you that you are wonderful beings of light, with great courage and great trust in the creator, otherwise you never would have commenced this journey. What I would like to remind you of is that spark of courage and creativity and light in yourselves. Feel that spark again in your heart, reconnect with it. Know that you have the power to let the child within you come to life again and let it sing and play. By looking upon your inner darkness as the calling of a lost child, I'm offering you a perspective that invites you to cherish and love yourselves as the parent you truly are.

At the beginning of your journey as a soul, you were entrusted with a lost and abandoned child, left alone in the dark. It was your challenge to deal with this emotional part of you. This part of you represents the most vital and "raw" aspect of you, the thrust of life itself. At the end of your journey, the end of this cycle of lifetimes, you will hold the hand of your inner child and see how it radiates joy, pleasure and inspired consciousness to you. It will feel safe again and will therefore show its true treasure: its ability to intensely feel and live life to the fullest. What it needs to get there is a grown-up who will take it by the hand and cherish it and inspire it with trust. And that is your mission: to be the guardian of the child within. This child has caused you pain, it has been the carrier of your emotional traumas, but at the same time it holds the greatest promise: to be your profoundest source of love, joy and creativity.

The time has come. At this point in your history, it is time to gather and integrate the lost parts of yourself. It is time to be the central sun that you are. In reclaiming the power of your own consciousness, you are not simply returning to "how things were before you started your journey." You are creating a new reality or level of consciousness altogether. Recognizing your own divinity feels like coming home; it awakens in you old memories of a blissful oneness and harmony you once knew. But now for the first time you will give birth to that sense of oneness purely from your own consciousness, while you are in material reality. You will embody God on earth. You are returning to your divine essence, without giving up your individuality and your material form. This is the miracle of the New Era: to be *one* and *as One*, to be a unique and individual consciousness and at the same time to be One with and connected to the whole.

Cosmic birthing pain

Dear friends, I am so happy to see you. And some of you have come from so far! I know who you are and you are so dear to me. My journey is your journey and I know your sorrows and pain from within. That is why I would like to share some of my insights into this long journey that you as souls have embarked on.

I would like to take you to the beginning of this journey, all the way back to the beginning when you were born as souls in a reality that was new and unknown to you. I would like to take you to the very moment you started your journey through time and space, through material reality. This event lies a very long way back, but the emotions that go with it, the pain of *being separated from home*, are still very present in all of you. This cosmic birthing pain, as I call it, lies behind many of your everyday feelings and behaviors.

Many of you are continually confronted with a sense of restlessness or unease within, the nagging notion that you are "in search of something." There is an internal tension that comes from *not being entirely at home with yourself.* You do not feel comfortable or at home with your own being, your own essence.

From this basic tension, the tendency arises to search for outside validation in the form of acknowledgement by others, material possessions or whatever makes you feel loved and cared for. You constantly need something outside of you to reassure you, something that relieves the tension and says: "you are all right." Look at how often you crave this reassurance and then you will know how tense you really are, how much pain there is inside you.

I would like to speak about the origin of this pain and the ensuing addiction to outside validation. The real cause is like the *center of an onion* that has many layers around it. The outer layers are formed by certain events in your life which have caused you to feel hurt, restless, not at home within yourself. In the deeper layers closer to the core of the onion, there are events from other lifetimes that have been emotionally traumatic. Still, from the perspective I am now taking, these are only trigger points. If you peel away all the layers and get to the core, you will discover an original pain, an *essential homesickness* that is connected to *the very beginning of your journey.*

Imagine yourself as part of an ocean of love, feeling safe and completely free from worry or anxiety. Imagine yourself being embraced by this all-pervading, loving consciousness and not knowing anything outside of it. This is the energy of Home, the energy you were born from. To understand the feeling tones of this ancient state, think of the consciousness you have when you drift away into sleep, when your mind releases control and your consciousness is very receptive. You also know this state in your earthly lives when you are an embryo in the motherly womb. When consciousness is in this gentle, blissful slumber, there is no clear distinction between inner and outer, no sense of *me* as opposed to *you.* In the embryonic, dreamy state of consciousness there is a boundless sense of oneness and safety.

In those ancient times, you as souls felt safe and boundless within in a huge cosmic womb. At a certain point, however, something changed. You experienced a kind of *tearing apart.* It was as though birthing contractions rippled through your oceanic awareness and awoke you from your slumber. That was the beginning of your birth as individual souls. It is when you broke loose from this ever present oneness that engulfed you that you experienced yourself *as yourself* for the first time. There was a rudimentary sense of "I" that was initiated in that very moment.

The experience of being torn apart, of being separated from the cosmic womb, left you bewildered and disoriented. You were not in a state of knowing when this happened; you were purely in a state of experiencing. You started to blindly search for something to hold onto, a way of returning back to the safety you knew. You felt lost. You felt shut out. It was a moment of darkness.

Nonetheless, the moment you tore yourselves free from prime Source and left Home was at the same time a moment of immense creativity. It was the beginning of a grand journey of experience, of life. Imagine a dark empty space, strange, vast and nameless, lying before you. You entered this space as little seedlings. It was a space full of potentiality, full of possible experiences that were as yet unknown. There was darkness, but there was also room for *something new.*

Many of the emotions you had to deal with at the start of your cosmic journey are comparable to the emotions of a *lost child* that I spoke about last time (see "The power of your own consciousness"). They are the emotions of a newborn baby who has to get used to a strange and unfamiliar reality that is utterly different from the semi-conscious slumber state it was in before. The image of the lost child, crying and bewildered, makes vividly clear the inner wounds with which you started your journey.

During this journey, you have experienced a lot. You have taken on many forms, inhabited different bodies and eventually you ended up here, on planet Earth. Earth is a place of great creativity and many possibilities. Still, despite the possibilities available to you and the richness and depth of your experience, you continue to feel homeless. There is a sense of lack deep within, as if something is missing and you do not know what it is, but it is essential for you to feel good. What is missing is the very basic sense of love and emotional safety that you once knew in the cosmic womb. This unconditional sense of belonging and safety is essential for your well being, for your self expression and your sense of self worth, and you have been looking for it ever since you left Home. You have been trying to heal your cosmic birthing pain for a long, long time.

What I would like to ask you now is whether you can recognize deep within yourself the *original wound* that was created when leaving Home. Can you find within your own psyche this sense of being *torn apart from an original whole?* It is a state of wholeness or oneness that cannot be explained by the mind but in your heart you can remember that you were part of it.

By turning your attention to this original birthing pain, by becoming aware of the deep feelings it evoked in you, the loneliness and homesickness you have felt up to this present moment, you can start the healing process. You can start to heal yourself at the deepest possible level. It is here that you can get to the core of your pain.

All of you who are present here or who are reading these words are growing towards a new level of consciousness. You are seeking to establish an inner foundation of safety and unconditional love for yourself. You are recreating the feeling tones of the cosmic womb by yourself and for yourself. This is your mission, your spiritual goal. As soon as you realize that Home is within you, that you carry a piece of that divine safety and oneness in your very core, then you can really get peaceful and relaxed about who you are. There's no need for outside validation anymore. It feels good when you are appreciated and cared for by others but you do not depend on it anymore.

The coming of the New Era depends on individuals who recognize the core of their pain and who dare to face it openly. In this stage of your development, it is time to not only look at the pains and traumas that have arisen in your present life and perhaps in the lifetimes before, but to *go beyond all of these* and to address the original wound. As soon as you consciously recognize and remember this pain with your heart, you are ready to take care of it. You are ready to take into your arms that *newborn cosmic child* that is still crying out for your help. It is calling you through your negative emotions of fear, anger and despair.

One way of knowing how you are dealing with your cosmic birthing pain is to look at the area of relationships in your life. Often people try to find relief for their deepest emotions of loneliness and fear in intimate relationships. What they try to do is to fill their inner emptiness with the energy of someone else. The recognition, attention and care of the other person soothes their pain. In a sense, they are handing over their hurt child to their partner. This is a very dangerous game. Sooner or later, the partners will become emotionally dependent on one another. Their initial feelings of love and connectedness will change into a subtle or not-so-subtle power play. Whenever you are dependent on someone else for feeling loved and safe, you are claiming his or her energy for yourself and this will always lead to struggle and conflict in the end. You will end up feeling more lonely than ever. (See "Relationships in the New Era" for further discussion of this issue.)

You often think that *loneliness* is associated with a *lack of friends or a life partner* and that the solution lies in a new friendship or love relationship. But in this line of thought you assume that the cause of, and the solution to, your pain lies outside of yourself. If that is how you start a relationship, you are likely to eventually hold the other person responsible for your inner wounds and see yourself as the victim. To need someone else to fill up the emptiness inside you is to disempower yourself from the start.

The area of intimate relationships can make you very aware of the cosmic birthing pain you carry within. See how often you feel like you *need* the presence of another person in your life. This is in fact a signal from your inner being that you need to turn inwards and find the lost child within. The solution to your loneliness lies in this turning inward, in the careful embrace of that precious child within that has carried the emotional burden for you. When you take responsibility for that child, when you connect to it and guide it as a loving parent, you are setting your relationships free. You can now relate to other human beings in a free and independent way.

Pitfalls on the way to becoming a healer

Dear friends, it is with great pleasure and happiness that I bid you welcome in this place where you have gathered to hear me, an old friend of yours. I am Jeshua. I have been among you in my life on earth as Jesus. I have been human and I know of all that you go through as human beings in an earthly body and in an earthly life. And I have come here to help you understand who you are.

All of you who are present here and many among you who will read this text later on are lightworkers. You are angels of light who have forgotten who you really are. You all have gone through many trials on your journey on earth, throughout your many earthly lifetimes. And I know these trials from within.

You have now come to a point in your soul's history at which you are completing a cycle of lifetimes. At this point you are more and more connecting to the greater Self that you really are, the Self that is independent of time and space. You are in the process of allowing your greater, immaterial Self into your earthly being, into your everyday life.

You still find it hard to keep a steady connection to your greater or higher Self, because you have forgotten that you truly *are* this great source of light yourself. Nevertheless you have all started the journey within and along this journey you have felt the desire, even the calling, to help others on their way to inner growth and self-awareness. It is natural, especially for lightworkers, to want to share your insights and experiences with others. You are all born teachers and healers.

From the moment you take it upon yourself to guide others as a teacher or healer, you are likely to stumble upon a number of pitfalls. These pitfalls are the result of certain miscomprehensions about what it means to guide someone spiritually. They follow from misconceptions about the nature of healing and your part in it as a healer. It is about these pitfalls that I would like to speak today.

What is healing?

What is the essence of healing? What happens when someone "gets well," whether it is on the psychological, emotional or physical level? What happens is that this person is able to connect again to his or her own inner light, to his or her own greater Self. This connection has a healing effect upon all layers of the self - the emotional, physical and mental levels.

What every person is looking for in a healer or teacher is an energy space which enables them to reconnect to their inner light, the part of them that knows and understands. The teacher or healer is able to offer this space because they have already made this connection within. The healer has a frequency at their disposal, an energetic vibration which holds the solution to their client's problem. To be a healer or teacher means *to carry the energetic frequency of the solution in your energy field and to offer it to someone else.* That's what it is, nothing else.

Basically it is a process that can take place without words or actions. It is the energy itself that you have as a teacher or healer which has the healing effect. It is your enlightened energy that opens up the possibility for someone else to "remember" what they already know, to connect to his inner light, to her intuition. It is this remembrance, this connection that makes the healing happen. All healing is really self-healing.

To heal or teach, then, has in fact nothing to do with specific skills or specific knowledge that can be learned from books or by taking courses. Healing power cannot be acquired by something external. It is about the "frequency of the solution" that is present within your own energy field as a result of your own inner growth and clarity of consciousness. Often as a teacher and healer, you are all still involved in personal growth processes. Yet there are parts of your energy field that have become so clear and pure that they can have a healing effect upon others.

It is essential to understand that this effect is not something you have to work hard for. It is the client who decides whether or not to assimilate the energy you offer, whether to allow it in. It is the client's choice. You offer it by who you are, by "being there" for the other. It is not by the skills or knowledge you have learned from anyone else that you have a healing influence but purely by who you are, the inner road you have traveled. It is especially in the area of problems that you have gone through yourself at a deep emotional level that you can truly help others. Your light in these areas shines like a beacon to people who are still stuck in these issues, beckoning them gently to get out of them.

In the areas where you have healed yourself from deep-seated hurts and wounds you have become a true master, someone whose wisdom is based on inner knowing and genuine experience. Self-healing, taking responsibility for your inner wounds and enveloping them in the light of your consciousness, is the key to becoming a teacher and healer. It is the ability to heal yourself that makes you a lightworker. This creates the "energy of the solution" in your being, which offers to others a doorway to their own power of self-healing.

When you are treating clients or helping people in your environment, you often "read" their energy. You intuitively tune into them when you listen to them, give them advice or treat them with energetic healing methods. However the client or person you are working with is just as busy "reading" you. Just like you are tuning into their energy, they are, consciously or subconsciously, absorbing your energy. They intuitively feel whether or not what you say and do is in accordance with all of you, whether it is matched by what you radiate, your energy vibration. They feel who you are, apart from your words and actions.

It is in the reading of you by the client that the real breakthrough occurs. When the client feels free and safe in your presence, when they feel surrounded by a type of consciousness that empowers them to trust their inner knowing, then everything you say or do takes on a healing quality. When your words and actions are backed up by *who you are*, they become the carriers of light and love that can take the client into the core of their own light and love.

Whenever someone honestly asks you for help, this person is open to your energy in such a way that they can be touched by the purest and clearest part of you. This part of you does not stem from the books you read or the skills you have learned. It is the result of a personal alchemy, a personal transformation of consciousness that bears your unique hallmark. I would like to strongly emphasize this, as there seems to be a tendency among lightworkers (people who by their nature feel a strong urge to help others) to keep searching for a new book, a new method, a new ability that can help one be a better teacher or healer. *True healing is this simple.*

When I lived on earth, I conveyed a certain energy with my eyes. Something flowed out of my eyes that had an immediate healing effect on the people who were open to it. This was no magic trick or some unique skill I owned. I was in touch with my inner source of truth. I naturally radiated the divine light and love that were my heritage – just like they are your heritage – and I touched other living beings with it. It is the same with you. You are no different from me. You have walked the same inner road and gone through the same trials and sorrows to eventually get to the same point as I did when I lived on earth. You are all becoming conscious, Christed beings.

The Christ energy is your spiritual destiny and you are gradually integrating this energy into your day-to-day existence. It is the Christ within you who heals and teaches as a natural consequence of who the Christ energy is. Too often you still identify yourself with being the apprentice or the pupil who sits at the feet of a teacher and listens and asks and searches. But I am telling you that the time of being a pupil is over. It is time to claim your mastership. It is time to trust the Christ within and to bring this energy to manifestation in your everyday reality.

To become one with the Christ within and to teach and heal from that energy, you need to let go of a number of things. These things represent the pitfalls on the road to becoming a healer/teacher. I will differentiate among three areas in which these pitfalls occur.

The pitfall of the head

The first pitfall lies in the area of the head or the mind. You are very adept at analyzing things and categorizing them according to some general frame of reference. This might be handy in some circumstances but in general the mental, thinking part of you is very much a part of the world of duality. With the "world of duality," I mean a type of consciousness that divides things into good or bad, light or dark, healthy or sick, masculine or feminine, friend or foe, etc. It is a type of consciousness that loves to separate and label and that does not recognize the underlying unity of all phenomena. It is a type of consciousness that likes to work with general principles and a rational, objective application to individual cases. It does not really consider the possibility of another, much more direct approach to reality: the approach of intuitive knowing, or "knowing by feeling."

The Christ energy is outside of duality. The Christ energy constitutes the flow of Being that underlies all polarities. But the mind does not recognize the very existence of this mystical level of oneness. The mind would like to split up the ocean of Being into definable parts, categorizing it in such a way that it can get a rational grip on it. The mind likes to design structures, theories that can be placed over reality, over direct experience. Again this is sometimes useful and beneficial, especially in practical matters, but not so much when it comes to true healing and teaching, i.e. healing and teaching from the heart.

When you approach your client from a theoretical framework, you try to place their individual symptoms into a general category and you look to the theory to find out about this type of problem and the solutions to it. This is what you learn when you are trained to be a psychologist, social worker or any type of professional counselor. I am not saying that all this is wrong. But what I would like to ask of you is this: when you are working with someone, whether professionally or in your personal life, try to let go of all your thoughts and reasoning, all of your presumptions about what is the matter with the other, and simply *listen from your heart.* Tune into the other person's energy from a silent place within. Try to just feel with your heart and intuition where the other person is standing, what it feels like to be in their inner world. (See end of the channeling for a guided meditation to this effect.)

Often you foster a lot of ideas about what someone else needs to do to solve their problems. You analyze their problem and you think up the answer to it.

And you may even be largely right in your thinking. But the point is: your ideas are not necessarily attuned to the energy of the other person in the now moment. You might be completely out of touch with how they actually feel inside. Your help is only fruitful when it is attuned to the energetic reality of the one you are helping. It might be that he or she needs a wholly different approach than you can fathom with your rational mind.

I invite you to see and feel the other person purely from the still, intuitive place inside you. Allow yourself to transcend duality and to be filled with the compassion of the Christ within. I invite you to really be inspired by *the presence of the other*, when you offer them teaching and healing.

The solution is then often very simple. What is needed from you is not your knowledge but your wisdom. What is asked of you is not your judgment but your compassion and deep understanding. You are not there to provide the solution, to be the face of authority. You are there to be the face of love.

Let us turn to an example to illustrate this issue. Take parents who want to help their children with problems they encounter. Due to their experience, parents can often make better assessments of the consequences of certain actions than their children can. On the basis of this knowledge, parents often warn their children; they want to save them from harm and they advise them to do what they think is the right thing to do. This might seem to be a good way of helping, from the mind's point of view. And in some cases, it is very reasonable to do so.

However, very often, if a parent would tune into the child from a silent, intuitive place inside, the parent would find out that what the child truly needs from them is something else entirely. What the child often needs most is the trust and reassurance of the parent. "Trust me, let me be who I am. Let me make mistakes, let me stumble and keep your faith in me." When you connect to your child from a place of trust, you are in fact encouraging them to rely on their own intuition. This may help them make a decision that feels good to them and that is understandable from your point of view as well. If, however, you try to make your child do something from the notion that "you know better," your child will sense distrust in your attitude and this will cause them to resist you even more.

Children "read" you when you offer them assistance. It is in the nature of children to be keenly aware of the emotions behind your words. They can sense your underlying fear or judgment. They will often react to this emotion instead of to your words and when they react with aversion, they seem utterly unreasonable. However the parent may be acting "too reasonable," meaning that they do not recognize their own underlying emotions and are not trying to connect to the child in an open and honest way. To do so, the parent will have to let go of their preconceived notions and really open up to the emotional reality of the child. From genuinely listening to the cares and concerns of the child, a bridge of communication can be built.

I mention this example because it is so common and easy to relate to, and because we all know how difficult it is to support your children from an attitude of trust and openness. It is all about *letting go* – letting go of your ideas of "what should be," your wishes and desires, and truly letting the other person be. To envelop someone else with a space of openness and true, heartfelt understanding is to offer real healing power to someone. Often what really helps the other is your total acceptance of how things are. It is when you are not trying to change something from the level of the mind that you truly connect to someone and open up the doorway to love and compassion for them.

The pitfall of the heart

The second pitfall you come across when you endeavor to be a teacher and healer is in the area of the heart. The heart is a meeting point of many energies. The heart center (or chakra) forms the bridge between heaven and earth and between the higher and the lower energy centers or chakras. The heart "collects" energies of a different origin and is able to recognize the underlying unity. The heart enables you to transcend duality and reach out to someone else with love and compassion.

The heart is the seat of your ability to tune into someone else's energy and to feel what it is like to be that person. It is the center of empathy. Clearly then, the heart plays an important part in any form of spiritual teaching or healing. Many of you are natural *empaths* – you have a natural inclination to sense moods and energies from other people. This ability serves you greatly when you work with people.

However there is an important pitfall connected to this ability as well. Your sensitivity towards other people's energy may be so strong that you find it hard to distinguish between your own emotions and the emotions of someone else. Sometimes you absorb the other person's energy so strongly that you lose your sense of self. You may want to help someone else so much, especially since you know how they are feeling, that your energies get mixed up and you start to carry burdens that are not your own.

When this happens, an imbalance occurs. You are *giving too much*. You overstep your boundaries when you let yourself be carried away by the suffering of someone else and go out of your way to help them. The energy you give "too much" of will turn against you. This extra energy goes out to the other person but does not contribute to the solution of their problem. The client may be unable to integrate or receive this energy, or they may be frightened by it, or it may simply go unnoticed by them. You will end up feeling tired, annoyed and frustrated.

You can tell when you are giving too much by the signals your body and emotions are sending out to you. Whenever you feel empty, frustrated or heavy after you have seen a client or tried to help someone generally, this indicates that you have been trying too hard.

When you offer teaching and healing from a balanced, centered standpoint, you feel free, alive and inspired. After the meeting with someone has ended, you easily draw back your energy and touch base with yourself. You let go of the other person and no cords or strings keep lingering between your energy fields.

If an energy link remains with the other person because you so dearly want him or her to get well or be happy, that link has a destructive effect on your energy. By staying preoccupied with the client, you will absorb their emotional energies too strongly. You will give of yourself to alleviate their burden and this is where an emotional dependence which goes both ways comes into being between the two of you. The client starts to lean upon you, and your well-being will become dependent on their well-being. This entanglement of energies is not helpful to the client and it is depleting to you.

Why does this happen so easily when you start to help people? Why is this pitfall so difficult to avoid, especially for lightworkers? Where does this painfully strong need come from to heal and make whole, and to make the world a better place? In part, this natural desire in you is explained by your soul history as related in the Lightworker Series (Part I of this book). You have an inner mission to bring teaching and healing to this world. But the tendency to *give too much* stems from a pain in yourself that you are not totally aware of. This pain makes you "overeager" in giving.

There is a pain and sadness in your heart that makes you want to reach out for a new way of being, a level of consciousness more attuned to the natural divinity of all that lives. You are homesick for a more loving and peaceful reality on earth. In your present incarnation, you have not come to explore the ways of the ego. You are tired and weary of that. You have come to answer to an ancient song of your soul. You have come to help restore peace, joy, respect and connectedness on earth.

Your emotional body has been scarred by many lifetimes in which you endeavored to bring down the light of your soul and you encountered resistance and rejection. You have come here with great reservations and at the same time the old flower of passion has not withered within you. You are here again! But now, due to the pain that you carry within, you are like delicate and sensitive flowers who need a strong foundation in order to flourish and grow. The foundation you all need is a firm sense of being grounded to earth and centered in yourself.

By being grounded I mean that you need to have roots into the earth, to be aware of how earth reality works, to know what the elements are that you have to deal with while living in a physical body. Sometimes you are so enamored with the spiritual that you forget to take good care of yourself and your body. You get "spaced out" or too idealistic and unreal. You would often like to transcend earth reality but it is only *through the earth*, by feeling at home and at ease with the element of earth, that your soul energy can bloom here.

By centeredness I mean that you need to be true to your own feelings, to your own sense of what is right for you. As a human being, you have an ego or individual personality that separates you from others. The ego serves a valuable function. It enables you to focus your specific soul energy into

135

material reality. You do not want to give up your individuality to any kind of "greater good!" You are not here to eliminate your ego; you are here to let the light of your soul shine through your ego. You need your ego to manifest your energy outwardly.

Because of the pain you carry in your souls, because of your weariness of the old, because you want to reach out to the promised land of the New Earth, you can become ungrounded and lose your centeredness. You tend to push change where the situation is not yet ready, or you try to awaken people at a pace that is faster than they can handle. You become "overeager in giving." This eagerness may take the form of great involvement with a good cause or of caring intensely for the well-being of others. But there is an impatience and restlessness at the heart of it. You may feel inspired for a time, passionate and involved, but you will be disappointed at some point and then you will feel exhausted and angry because you have depleted your energy resources.

The pitfall of the heart, the pitfall of giving too much, stems from not accepting reality as it is. There is an impatience and a restlessness in you which makes it difficult for you to *let go*. It makes it difficult for you to keep the right emotional distance from the people you are trying to help or the causes you are involved in.

You *are* teachers and healers, you do have a mission on earth. But to truly fulfill it, you – paradoxically – need to let go of that dire need to change things, because your eagerness to do so has an edge of pain to it, the pain of not feeling at home on earth as it is now. True spiritual change always starts from a foundation of acceptance. To truly become the teacher and healer you want to be, you need to embrace your own pain and heal it. You need to find peace with your own deepest emotions of fear and anger. If you do, you will find out that the urgent need to give to others or to be involved in a "good cause" makes place for a very quiet feeling of peace and acceptance. This is when your radiance truly gets a healing quality to it.

Letting go of other people's pain and trials and completely allowing them the time and space to go through their own process may give you inner pain. This is because it brings you right back to your own loneliness and the sense of being lost in this earthly reality. The difference between this harsh and imperfect world and the reality you dream of, so much more pure and beautiful than this one, hurts you deep inside. It is your challenge to not run away from this hurt, to let it enter your awareness fully and to spread your angel wings around it.

Once you recognize your eagerness to help or fight for a good cause and become aware of the hidden pain in there, the part of not-accepting reality as it is, you can start to let go of it. As soon as you realize that your eagerness and impatience come from an inner pain and sadness, you can stop giving too much. You can focus on yourself and find ways to really be at peace with who you are. You can truly start to *give to yourself.*

This is when you become a fully grounded and centered lightworker, accepting of yourself and others. The only proper thing to do as a lightworker is to make your energy available to others. You teach and heal by radiating the "energy of the solution" that is present in your own energy field. Often you draw people to you with exactly the type of problems that you have gone through yourself. You have gone to the bottom of these issues yourself and therefore in these areas you have reached a knowingness and purity that have become part of your being. These are the enlightened parts of you. They are sacred and inviolable and cannot be lost. They are not built from learned knowledge that you can forget about. What you have to offer to others is not some tool or theory, it is *you* transformed by life, experience and the courage to face your inner wounds.

The "lightwork" that you have to do in this regard will come to you without effort. It will be something that feels very natural to you. To find your mission, the thing you are "meant to do" in life, you only need to be aware of what you truly long for and do the things you feel inspired to do. When you do so, you will put your energy out into the world and others will be touched and inspired by it, sometimes in ways you may not even be aware of. There's no more to be done, really. This is the lightwork you came to do.

Lightworkers who know the balance between giving and receiving will have more peace and enjoyment in their lives and therefore will radiate the "frequency of the solution" even more fluently from their energy fields. They are sensitive and empathic but they have a clear sense of their personal boundaries as well. They allow themselves to just as easily receive as to give and in that way both the flow of giving and the flow of receiving will become stronger in their lives.

The pitfall of the will

Now, I would like to discuss one more pitfall on the way to becoming a healer/teacher. I have mentioned one pitfall in the area of the head and one in the area of the heart and I would like to finish with the pitfall of the will.

The will can be localized in the solar plexus, a center of energy near the stomach. This center or chakra steers the ability to act, to manifest your inner energy outward on the physical, earthly plane. When the will is connected to your intuition, the quiet part of you that transcends duality, things will flow easily and effortlessly in your life. You will act from an inner sense of trust and knowing. When your solar plexus (which is also the center of the ego) is guided by the heart, you generally do the things you love to do and you feel joyful and inspired most of the time. The will (or ego) has then become the extension of the Christ within.

Often however when you try to help or guide others, you get out of touch with this flow. There is a part of you that wants to *do too much*. It seeks to achieve results by forcing or pushing things a little, even if your intuition tells you to let go or back off. Often it is your personal ego that craves visible results here. This has nothing to do with helping others! It has to do with a need for validation that you have, an insecurity which gets you out of touch with the natural flow of healing which is often slower and more unpredictable than you wish it to be.

You *do too much* when you feel like you are working very hard and your input is not really received or appreciated by others. Also when you have separated yourself from the natural flow of things, you often get distracted by outside judgments. You tend to rely on other people's ideas and expectations and you are afraid to fail in their eyes. The key to regaining your strength is to *not do anything* and to become really quiet within. It is only when you connect to your heart again that you can tune into the situation from a quiet and neutral space. Then your fear and insecurity disappear into the background and you can truly focus on what your client needs from you.

Often you do not need to do so much for him or her. You are first and foremost asked *to be* with them and to offer them "the energy of the solution" in a simple and direct way. You need to trust the *power of your presence,* even when you do or say nothing. Dare to be in that silent space when you are with someone. When you trust yourself, you will know in that moment what the appropriate thing to say or do is. Remember that often when it comes to offering guidance, less is more.

Letting go is love

Overcoming the pitfalls I described above always involves a type of *letting go*. It is about letting go of thinking too much, letting go of identifying too much emotionally and letting go of excessive use of the will. If you let all that go, however, and surrender to that most wise and compassionate part of you, you will find deep joy and fulfillment in your "work" as a teacher and healer. As the lightworkers that you are, you will experience a deep sense of self-realization and freedom. In being a teacher and healer in whatever way you express it, you feel connected to the Whole, to the oneness that underlies All That Is. Feeling part of this "fabric of Spirit", and playing your natural part in it make you feel like you are truly accomplishing your mission.

Meditation

This is an exercise that may help you get in touch with the issues mentioned in the channeling in a more direct, emotional way.

Sit or lie down in a comfortable position. Focus your attention on the muscles of your shoulders and neck and release any tightness or tension there. Do the same with the muscles of your abdomen, your arms and your legs. Then travel with your consciousness to your feet and feel your connection to earth. Feel how earth is carrying you and providing you with the security you need. Take a couple of easy breaths from your abdomen.

Now let your imagination take you back to a moment in time when you felt very down and unhappy. Take whatever situation comes up first. Go with it. Think again of that time in the past, of how you felt inside.

Then go to the "energy of the solution." Ask yourself: how did I get out of this? What helped me most of all? The energy that helped you the most may have come from yourself or from someone else; that doesn't matter. Just consider the kind of energy that lifted you from the lowest point.

Now let go of the past and think of someone in the present who is dear to you and who you have some concerns about. It might be your partner or child, or a colleague or friend. Let that person appear to you in your imagination and really take in their presence. Then ask: How can I help you? What would be the most valuable thing I could do for you? Listen with your heart. What is the other person showing you or saying to you? Feel the answer. Just allow it come to you.

Let go and focus your attention on your feet again, to your breathing, and return to the present.

The goal of this exercise is to become aware of what is truly helpful in a situation of emotional crisis or pain. This may be quite different from what you *think* is helpful.

Letting go of your birth family

Dear friends, it gives me great pleasure to be with you again. You are all brave warriors. Your very presence in a physical body on earth today speaks of your great courage and readiness to face up to darkness, within and without and to throw your light on it, the light of your consciousness. You are warriors in the spiritual sense and your weaponry consists of both compassion and discernment. One does not overcome the fears and illusions of your reality by love and compassion alone. These essential, predominantly feminine qualities need to be complemented by the masculine qualities of clarity and discernment. Compassion enables you to perceive the core of light in any expression of duality, for instance to recognize the light of someone's soul even if their personality is full of negativity. Discernment makes you aware of the presence of fear and power-related energies in any such expression and it enables you to distance yourself from it, to let it go from your energy field.

To know who you are you have to let go of what you are not. Discernment helps you let go of that which you are not. Discernment is the "energy of the sword," the energy that helps you set boundaries for yourself and find your own way. I call it the masculine energy and it is a necessary complement to the feminine qualities of understanding and forgiveness. I am stressing the importance of "the sword of discernment" in this channeling, for it is very relevant to the issue we will discuss today.

Today I would like to speak of your relationship with your parents and with your birth family in general. When you enter a path of spiritual growth, this issue will at some point be in the forefront of your attention.

One might look upon your birth in a physical body as a fall into darkness, if you dissociate it from any notions of sin or guilt. The birthing process is really a plunge into the deep that you have consciously decided upon from some part of your soul. At the core of your soul, you have decided to take upon you this present incarnation, and you felt the trust and perseverance needed to "accomplish the mission." However at the moment you plunge in, so to speak, you are soaked in a state of not-knowing, a state of temporary unawareness. As soon as you enter the material reality of earth, your consciousness becomes veiled or hypnotized by certain illusions which are nothing but the deeply ingrained habits of the majority of people on earth. This is the net that is cast around you.

When you enter the earth life, the memory of "the other side" is still fresh and alive. But you have no words to express it, no way of communicating the truth of it, the simple things like the unconditional love and safety that surround you everywhere you go. The energy of Home is still self-evident to you, like the feel of water to a fish. But then you enter the physical world and the psychological reality of your parents. You reach out to them, you want to keep that sense of Home alive but it seems that you are cut off, like a net cast around the "fishy part" of you. This is the birth trauma that has physical as well as deeply spiritual aspects to it.

The net that catches you as you fall is predominantly spun by your parents' way of being, their basic outlook on life, their ways of relating to themselves, their hopes and desires for you. When you were born, the collective consciousness on earth was still in the grip of ego based consciousness, as it is even now. Times are changing, but there is a kind of beginning stage in which things need time to gain momentum before real, fundamental change is actually brought about. At present you are still in these beginning stages, and the inner work you do is vital in this respect. So when you entered earth, you entered a reality dominated by ego based consciousness and you got acquainted with it through the energy of your parents.

When you enter the reality of ego based consciousness as represented by your parents, you get to deal with a number of pervasive illusions, of which I wish to name three important ones.

1. The loss of mastery

The first illusion is the illusion of the loss of mastery. This illusion makes you forget, while you grow up and become an adult, that you are the creator of everything that happens in your life. Most people do not recognize what happens in their life as their own creation. They often feel they are a victim of "greater powers" that make and shape their life. This is the loss of mastery.

2. The loss of unity

With the plunge into collective human consciousness as portrayed by your parents, you also lose your sense of unity with all that lives. The basic realization of the "oneness of all things" is slowly filtered out of your consciousness. You are encouraged to build your own ego. According to ego based consciousness, we are all essentially separate beings, struggling for our own existence, struggling for survival, nourishment and acknowledgement. We seem to be confined to our own body and locked into our own psychological reality with no true and open connection to "the other." This is the illusion of separation and the tragic sense of loneliness that accompanies it.

3. The loss of love

And then there is the loss of love, meaning the sense of unconditional joy and safety that belongs to the very heart of you like a natural birthright. As you enter the earth plane on which the energy of love is not self-evident at all, you gradually start to confuse love with all kinds of energies that are *not* love, such as admiration, wealth or emotional dependency. These confused notions of love affect your relationships and basically make you continually search for something outside of you to regain that sense of unconditional love that is actually deep inside you.

How these illusions or losses affect you depends on the specific energy of your parental house and your family environment. Generally the parental consciousness is a mixture of ego and heart, of fear and light. There are certain areas in which your parents are likely to be very attached to or hooked up with the illusions mentioned above. But at other points they may be quite enlightened, for instance by having experienced suffering and inner growth in some area which opened up their hearts. The specific way in which they are stuck in the illusions of ego based consciousness is different for each parent or family.

When you enter this specific configuration of energies that makes up your birth family, your consciousness is wide open with hardly a sense of personal boundaries yet. As a baby, you take in your parents' energies very thoroughly, like a basic imprint that has a deep effect on how you experience things later. There is no filter yet. It is only much later when you become aware of yourself *as yourself*, roughly during puberty, that you grow the consciousness needed to sift though these energies and find out what feels good and natural to you and what does not.

First you attach yourself very strongly to the paradigm of your parents, and then as you grow older and gain more self-awareness, you start to question your parents' outlook on things as you are looking for your own sense of identity. This psychological growth process is very much akin to the transition from ego based consciousness to heart based consciousness. The natural stages of earth life, the biological and psychological cycles and seasons, correlate with natural growth stages in the spiritual sense. The transition from ego to heart based consciousness often runs parallel with overcoming the limiting, fearful energies that controlled your birth family.

The cosmic birth trauma that you experience when you are born as an individual soul (see chapter *Cosmic birthing pain*, p.121) is to some extent repeated every time you begin a new earth life. At the time of your birth, your parents belong to the energy of the earth. They have already adapted to this dimension, to the laws that apply here. Often these are limiting laws which are not at all self-evident to the child. The parents thus represent the ego based consciousness for the child, the energy of the three illusions. The child meets these through the parental home, and the way in which they have taken shape in the parents will influence the child strongly for the rest of its life.

Especially in the first three months, the child takes in its surroundings very deeply. The energies of the parents sink into the child's consciousness unhampered by rational thought or defense. On the other hand there is still a "piece of heaven" in its memory, a part of the child's consciousness that is untainted by the illusions, that knows love, mastery and oneness as the natural state of being. This awareness collides with the ego based energies around it, and this is a deeply painful conflict. It can make the child want to turn around and go back "home;" it can cause grave resistance to life at the very start. It is actually the cosmic birth trauma repeated over again.

How does the child handle this collision or conflict of energies? Most often, it shuts down some parts of himself or herself. Some parts of the child's consciousness will go into hiding. The child will tend to comply with the energies of the parents, adapt itself to them, for it is wholly dependent upon them from the start. The child is in a very vulnerable physical state and it has a great desire to be nurtured and loved by the parents. Its memory of the natural state of oneness, love and mastery is actually *the child's gift* to the parents, but they are often unable to receive this gift, once they have been veiled by the energy of the illusions. They are thus unable to *truly receive the child.*

Parents have at some point been children as well, of course, and have gone through the same process. Parents do not consciously force their fears and illusions onto their children. However as adults they have unwittingly absorbed many energies of ego based consciousness.

At the moment of the birth of a child, parents often experience a temporary awakening. Watching this innocent little creature coming out of the womb, entrusting itself to the world, so open and vulnerable, stirs a deep sense of awe in almost anyone. This sacred moment opens the gates to Home wide open in the parents' consciousness and they – unknowingly – reach out to the divine core inside of them that knows unconditional love and oneness. They enter a sacred space for a while, and they feel *who they are beyond the illusions.* But often this is a temporary state of bliss, because afterwards things will settle down and "get back to normal." Their ways of thinking and feeling will tend to fall back into the patterns they were used to. And thus the opening to heart based consciousness closes down again.

And what happens to the child that grows up? Most children choose to adapt so strongly to the parental frame of reference that they lose touch with their original soul energy that they were still very much aware of in the beginning of their incarnation. In this first phase of life (until puberty) they are so involved in focusing themselves into this world and getting love and attention from their parents, that they themselves forget who they are.

How does this affect the child? The child has an unbridled longing for love and safety and when it stumbles upon fearful, blocked parts in the parents' energies, it will be confused by them. It will experience pain and a sense of abandonment. But it will hide these emotions from itself, because they are too painful to fully realise when you are in such a state of vulnerability and openness. What the child will do is put on blindfolds and create illusionary images of love. To survive emotionally, it will allow itself to be confused by the false images of the parents because if unconditional love is not available, conditional love seems better than none. The child will generally bend over backwards to get the love and safety it needs and remembers from Home. And therefore it will mistake the wrong energies for love. For example it will confuse love with a parent's pride in certain achievements or a parent's emotional need for the child.

Whenever the child achieves something that makes the parents proud and the child is complimented for it, they may feel their heart open up from gladness that they are liked and appreciated. But if the parental pride is not from a source of genuine understanding of the child, if it is not based upon what the child itself aspires to but more on what society expects from the child, then the pride is really a kind of poison. The child is rewarded for living up to external standards, whereas love means that one gets in touch with the child's inner standards – what they want to achieve in this lifetime for themselves. When attention is systematically focused on outer achievements, the child will be fooled into believing that achievement equals love and they will tend to grow a guilty conscience when they are not doing "what is right," what they are supposed to do according to external standards. As an adult, they may become someone who does not recognize when their boundaries are crossed or when they are working too hard. They will simply find that they feel the urge to achieve all the time, not understanding why working hard has become an addiction.

Another distortion of the true energy of love is when the child starts to confuse love with emotional dependency. Many children feel loved when they feel needed by their parents. They are actually filling a hole in their parents' heart, a hole that the parents have not taken care of themselves, and when the child steps into it, it offers itself as a *substitute parent*. It seeks to provide the love and support the parents are missing inside. In this way, it wants to please the parents and get the love it so sorely needs. But this kind of service is not love, of course. It is a dangerous entanglement of energies that will create a lot of difficulties later on in both the relationship between the parents and the child and in the intimate relationships that the child will enter as an adult.

Many parents have experienced a lack of unconditional love in their own childhood. They were not *truly received* by their parents either. This has left a deep seated pain and a sense of abandonment in their being. When they have a child themselves, they embrace it with mixed signals. On the one hand, there is genuine love in them but on the other hand, there is the subconscious need "to make up for the loss." Parents often try to heal their own emotional wounds through the relationship with their child. When they do so unconsciously, they use the child as a substitute parent – the child needs to give them the love they so sorely missed in their own childhood.

When that happens, the messages "I love you" and "I need you" get completely mixed up for the child. The child's energy will not be her own anymore, because it will feel sucked up by the parent's need, and this being sucked up will actually feel good to the child! It will provide a false sense of safety which by the time the child is an adult will make her feel like she is being loved deeply by someone when her energy is depleted and owned by that person. She will feel loved and appreciated when she is stretching her limits to give the most she can. She will interpret emotional dependency, even jealousy and possessiveness, as a form of love whereas these energies are diametrically opposed to it. This tragic loss of self is born from the association of love with need.

So far I have stressed that when you come to earth as a child, you are submerged into an "ocean of forgetfulness," a net of illusions that at first seems to tie you down very thoroughly. However from the soul level, you consciously *allow* yourself to be led astray. Deep down inside when you incarnate on earth, you trust that you will find the solution and the way out. It is your *mission* to find the way out of the illusions and to bring the "energy of the solution," the energy of love and clarity, out into the world, available to others.

At certain times in your life, there will be opportunities and possibilities that will help you fulfill this mission. As you grow up, you will meet certain people or situations that will invite or challenge you to find out who you are. You will be gently pushed or, if you are stubborn, violently provoked by life to "detangle the knot." You need to let go of the false images of love that were part of your upbringing, part of your parents' energy. This may trigger an identity crisis, similar to what has been described in the first part of this book as the *first stage in the transition from ego to heart*. It may seem that nothing is certain anymore and that everything you believed in is under scrutiny. Indeed, your soul will leave no stone unturned to bring you Home. Your soul will knock on your door incessantly until you open up and set yourself free.

Major events in your life are always geared to offer you opportunities to grow and return to who you are. But it takes courage and determination to get to the bottom of this quest and to regain the energies of the newborn child, untainted by the illusions of the loss of mastery, love and oneness. You will likely find yourself opposed to your own soul energy for a while, for it may lead you astray from what you regarded as normal and befitting for you. Your soul may seem a wayward guest to you, as you have been getting used to the ways of the world, the ways of your birth family.

It takes both the male energy of self-consciousness and discernment and the female energy of love and understanding to release yourself from ego based consciousness. Regarding your parents, discernment means that you distance yourself from the fear ridden and limiting energies they have fed you. Remember the importance of "the energy of the sword" that I mentioned in the beginning. To let go of your birth family in the spiritual sense, you need to be able to distinguish between their energy and your own and you need to be able to "cut the cords" that limit and suffocate you.

This is not primarily about expressing anger and frustration to your parents or telling them where they were wrong about you. It may be a good thing sometimes to try to make clear to them your position on things or your feelings about them. But in many cases, they may not understand what you are trying to tell them. They may not resonate with the part of you that is "different" and at odds with their outlook on life. Releasing the ties to the parental energy means first and foremost to release the energy *from your own mind and emotions*. It is about looking within and finding out to what extent you implicitly live by your parents' set of illusions, by their do's and don'ts which were based on fear and judgment.

Once you are clear about this and you allow yourself to let that go, you will be free to forgive them and really "leave the parental house." It is only after you sever the cords on the inner level and take responsibility for your own life that you can really let your parents be. You will have clearly said "no" to their fears and illusions (sword of discernment), but at the same time you will see that your parents are *not identical with* their fears and illusions. They also are children of God simply trying to fulfill their soul mission. Once you feel this, you can feel their innocence and you can forgive.

In a sense you have been the victim of your parents – your parents as they represented ego based consciousness in your childhood. You have temporarily and partly lived according to their illusions. In a way you had no choice, as their child. However to transcend your sense of being the victim here is one of the most powerful breakthroughs you can have in your life. It makes you a free person when you can recognize the deep energetic imprints from your childhood and consciously decide which ones benefit you and which ones you'd rather let go. This is mastery.

You then no longer subconsciously adapt to the wishes and longings of your parents when they are not your own. At the same time, you no longer rebel against them either. You can see the false images they offered you as simply not belonging to you, period. You do not need to judge your parents for burdening you with these aspects. You can be loving and discerning at the same time.

One might say that you are introduced to ego based consciousness through your parents and you transcend it through them as well, by letting them go in love and forgiveness and by recognizing yourself as the independent master that you are.

Lightworkers and their parents

At this point I would like to speak specifically about the lightworker soul in relation to his or her birth family. Lightworkers often carry within them an extra assignment in regard to their parents or birth family. When they come to earth, Lightworkers have the specific intention to awaken, to set themselves free from ego based consciousness and to plant the seeds of Christ consciousness on earth. More strongly than others, lightworkers want to teach and heal others, helping them grow towards a heart based consciousness.

For that reason, many lightworker souls are born with parents or in families which are heavily stuck in the reality of ego based consciousness. Because it is their intention to break open stuck and rigid energy patterns, lightworkers are drawn like a magnet to "problem situations" in which the energy is stagnant, like in a dead-end alley. The lightworker comes in with a certain awareness, a certain spiritual sense which makes him or her "different," not fitting into the family's expectations or ambitions. The lightworker child will somehow, by what she radiates or expresses as her truth, challenge the family's basic assumptions about life. She almost instinctively will do everything to get the energy moving and flowing again.

While the lightworker soul thus wants nothing more than to be of service to the parents and the family, they might look upon her as the odd one out, even as the black sheep. When the inner beauty and purity of the lightworker child is not recognized as such, she will often temporarily get lost in emotions of loneliness and even depression.

When they start their incarnation, lightworkers have the confidence deep down that they will find their way out, that they will overcome the limiting energy of their birth family. However when they are actually born on earth and grow up, they are exposed to the same dilemmas and confusions as any other child. In a certain sense they experience this confusion more deeply and more intensely. Because they are spiritually aware souls who are often older and wiser than their parents, they are very much aware that "something is not right" about the energy of their environment. On the inner level they clash head-on with the parents' energies, not understanding or resonating with their mind set or behavior. This clash causes great distress inside them, gentle and sensitive as they are. They have to find a way to survive emotionally, coping with the fact that they both love the parents dearly *and* are very different from them. This causes a lot of psychological problems in lightworkers ranging from loneliness, insecurity and fear to addiction, depression and self destruction.

Thus your journey to earth and to places of darkness where the energy is stuck and hostile is not without risk. It is a dangerous mission. Don't forget why I call you brave warriors! It is for this reason; you are like pioneers who venture out into strange and unknown territory. There are no signposts or markers. The environment in which you start your journey is inhospitable and does not feel like home. You will have to create the energy of home for

150

yourself, with only your own feelings and intuition as your compass. As a lightworker, you are a pioneer who wants to break the barriers of old and stifling thought patterns and release the energy stuck within. You are almost always the first one in your environment to do so. You do not meet your soul mates until later. It is the struggle by yourself that marks you as the true warrior that you are. You will have to find the way out by yourself and once you have done so you will attract likeminded spirits into your life, people who reflect your awakened state of being.

The solitary struggle you all have to go through to discover your light is the heaviest burden for you. On the soul level you have chosen this path consciously, but to live through it as a child of flesh and blood is a painful thing that wounds you deeply. I urge you to feel and recognize this pain in yourself, because only by connecting to it can you transform and release it. Once you know that wounded child inside that took the cross of alienation upon its fragile shoulders, you will get to the core of your burden. When you get to the core, the solution is nearby. You only need to embrace the pain of that child with a pure and deep awareness. From this awareness an energy of compassion and deep respect will reach out to the child. You will lift the cross just by being with yourself and truly loving and cherishing that part of you that is "different." This is how you bring the child home and fulfill your mission as the pioneer that you are.

Resolving family karma

The lightworker's assignment in regard to their birth family is *to become who they are*. In doing so, they accomplish their mission. It is not their task to change their family; it is not your job to change *anything outside of you*. You are not here to make the world a better place. You are here to awaken yourself. And yes, when you do so the world will become a better place, because your light will shine upon it and bring joy and enlightenment to others as well. But do not focus on the world, whether it is your family or any other relationship you enter.

The real work is to let go of all those bits of ego based fear and illusion that you yourself absorbed so deeply as a child. Getting to know these energetic imprints which partly created your personality, and releasing the parts of it that do not belong to you is a challenging and intense process. It is about peeling away all the layers of the onion; it is about being born a second time.

By stressing the profundity of this inner process, this *second birth*, I do not mean to discourage you. On the other hand I would like you to have deep respect for yourselves. You are the bravest warriors I know. You are pioneers who, by kindling your own light in places of darkness and hostility, pave the way for a new consciousness on earth.

It is not your job to kindle the light in someone else's heart. It is up to them if they do so. You may offer a spark, you may set an example, but in no way are you responsible for anyone else's awakening. This is important to stress especially with regard to your birth family. You often feel instinctively as a child and more consciously as a grown-up that you have to *save* your parents from their fears and illusions. Moreover you often think that you have failed in this assignment. You feel that you have not truly been able to help your parents in the way you had envisioned.

This line of thought rests on a mistaken perception of what helping really means and what your assignment is with regard to your parents. In reality, the situation is this. From your birth onward, you begin to absorb your parents' energies very strongly as if they were your own. You cannot easily distinguish any more where you begin and they end. Because you absorb their fears and illusions as well, you get intimately in touch with their emotional burdens. These burdens may have been passed over to them through several generations on either side of the family. There may be a karmic aspect to it, meaning that the same issue gets repeated over and over again until the "spell is broken." This you may call *family karma*. There may be issues relating to an unbalanced male or female energy, energies resulting from old slavery traditions, issues pertaining to certain illnesses, etc. This kind of karmic burden is solved when the energy stuck inside of it gets released and thus is not passed along to the next generation. Family karma is resolved when at least one member of the family breaks the link by *setting herself free* from the emotional burden that she absorbed from childhood and that may even be in her genes.

The family member who "breaks the spell" does so first and foremost by helping herself. It is about being focused on your own inner growth and expansion. This growth and expansion has an effect on the "energy of the family." It opens up the possibility for members of that family to find the way out as well. The lightworker who has freed himself of the emotional dead-end ally provides an *energetic trail* for others of his family. This he accomplishes by his inner work and what he radiates because of that, not by actually trying or even pushing others to change and move forward. What she offers her birth family energetically is the possibility of change. Her energy mirrors the possibility of change to them and that is all she needs to do.

Whether the family members pick up on the trail is entirely up to them. Never are you responsible for nor is your spiritual mission dependent upon someone else's decision to change or not. You may have freed yourself of the karmic burden that your family saddled you with and be ridiculed or rejected for it by your family, and yet your mission will have been entirely successful. You will have crushed the hypnotic hold that karmic patterns can have over a family line and if you have children, the emotional burden will not be passed along to them. This is what your soul mission is about.

Imagine you are living in a valley which is quite barren and dry. All of your community tells you that you cannot get out of this valley – it is all there is. You seem to be the only one to remember that there are much more lush and fertile lands than this. So after a lot of consideration, you decide to try your luck and climb out of that valley. The climb up takes a tremendous amount of strength and energy. Not only is the road very steep, there are no road signs or marks to hold onto either. While you are climbing up you leave a track behind you. At some point, you come up out of that valley and the landscape that lies before you overwhelms you with joy and a sense of recognition. You knew there was something out there that felt much more like home than your birth ground. Enthusiastically you peer down and look for your family. You would like them to join you and marvel at this great vista. You would like to share your victory. But you can see no one down there and when you notice some folks far off, they do not seem interested in your journey at all.

This is what happens frequently to lightworker souls. I ask you not to mourn the loss of your family in this respect. You will have offered them a great service by walking out of the valley, by clearing the way and leaving a track. This track will stay there and it will be used one day by anyone who wants to climb out of that particular valley. The track is an energy space that you have made available to them.

It is the building of this track that was your purpose when you were born with these parents and in this family. It is not your purpose to make your family go up as well or to carry them out of the valley on your shoulders! That is *not* your task. Whenever you try to figuratively drag your parents or family up that steep hill, you are hindering your own growth and you will be disillusioned and disappointed. It is not the way of spiritual growth and alchemy. Those others that you love and want to share your light with may choose to live in the valley for another century or more. It is up to them. But one day in their own time, they will uncover a little track that goes up and they will think: "Hey, this is interesting, let's go up and try this; I am not having a good time down here anymore." And off they go. They will start their own journey of inner growth, their own climb into the light. And isn't it wonderful, isn't it absolutely precious, that they will find marks along the way, a track for them to hold onto? They will have to go through their own struggles, but they will have a beacon set out for them which lightens their journey. As a pioneer you will have cleared the way though a wild and unknown territory and the road paved by you will be used with gratitude and honor.

To be really free and to regain your mastership as an independent spiritual being, you have to let go of your birth family. You have to let go of them, not only as their *child* but also as their *parent*. Let me explain this double bind. The child in you needs to let go of the hope that your parents will offer you unconditional love and safety. It has to turn to you for this and you have to help it let go of the angry, sad and disappointed part of the child that feels betrayed by your parents. This is the child part. However you also need to let go of the part of you that wants to be your parents' parent. It is typical of lightworker souls that at some point when they grow up, they start to feel like they are the parents of their parents. Because of their inborn desire to teach and heal and their developed spiritual awareness, they often see their parents' fears and illusions clearly and they want to heal them. This may get you into a lot of struggle with your parents because your desire to help them is often intertwined with an unconscious need to be recognized for who you really are. In other words, the wounded child speaks through you when you try to help your parents, and it is a recipe for disaster when you try to help others through the wounded parts of you. You will end up more wounded and your parents will likely end up upset or confused.

To let go of your parents means to let go of any desire to change them. You have to understand that it is not your task to lead them anywhere. Your mission is to deal with your own path – that is all. After you have truly parted with your parents, letting go of the double bind, you will find that a new space opens up between you and them, much more free and open. If they are still alive, the relationship with your parents may become less strained, as the energies of reproach and guilt will have left the scene. On the other hand, you may feel you do not want to visit them so often anymore. There may simply be a lack of common interests. In any case you will feel more free in this relationship, setting your own course through life without the need for approval by them or the tendency to get angry and upset if they do not agree with you.

In your life, you may now get in touch with people who belong to your "spiritual family." Your spiritual family has nothing to do with biology, genes or heredity. It is a family of kindred souls. Often you know them from past lives in which you bonded through friendship, love or a shared mission. It is very easy to get along with them, for you share an inner likeness; you belong to the same family. It is a kind of homecoming you experience. What made you feel different and lonely among other people first now becomes the foundation of your connection and mutual recognition. Bonding with your spiritual family is a true source of joy in earth life. The key to allowing it into your life is to find your own way "out of the valley" and to recognize the light within. When you are able to recognize your own light in an environment that does not mirror it back to you, you become independent and free. Unburdened by the karmic aspects of your history, the fears and illusions that held you down, you will attract relationships into your life which are based on love and respect and which reflect your awakened divinity.

Male and female energy

Dear friends, it gives me great pleasure to be with you again. I am so glad to be in your company. You have a tendency to look up to me, or to beings like me, as masters but we do not see it that way. We see you following your path on earth at a challenging time, a time when much is changing, and we see you growing towards your own mastery. We see you becoming the masters that you still look up to at times. And this is what it is all about – finding your own mastery! Do not follow any master that is brought before you by tradition or by books or by anything someone else is telling you. Find your own mastery – that's what it's all about.

Today I would like to speak about a theme that reaches back far into your history: the energies of the male and the female. These are old energies and a lot is going on with them right now.

First I would like to say something about the nature of the male and the female. These energies are two aspects of the One. They therefore are not really opposed or dualistic, they are one; they are two faces of one energy.

The male energy is the aspect that is outwardly focused. It is that part of God or Spirit that drives outward manifestation, that makes Spirit materialize and take form. The male energy therefore knows a strong creative force. It is natural to the male energy to be highly focused and goal-oriented. In this manner the male energy creates individuality. The male energy allows you to separate yourself from the One, from the Whole and to stand alone and be a specific individual.

The female energy is the energy of Home. It is the energy of the Primal Source, the flowing Light, pure Being. It is the energy that has not yet manifested, the inner aspect of things. The female energy is all encompassing and oceanic; it does not differentiate or individualize.

Now, imagine the energy of the female becoming aware of a certain movement inside of her, a slight restlessness, a desire for... reaching out, outside of her boundaries, moving outside of herself to attain experience. There is a longing for something new, for adventure! And then an energy comes to her that answers that longing. It is the male energy that wants to be of service and help her manifest in matter, in form. The male energy defines and shapes the female energy and by their cooperation the total sum of energies can take a completely new direction. A new reality can be created in which everything can be explored and experienced, in ever changing forms of manifestation.

The dance of the male and the female brings forth the fluctuating spectacle of created reality, of your creation. This is a spectacle of great beauty wherein the male and female energy worship each other and celebrate their cooperation and playful joining. And this is as it should be. The male and female energy belong together, they are two aspects of the One and together they celebrate the joyful manifestation that Creation is supposed to be.

It has been said that in the final realization of who you are, the only truth that matters is: I AM. And in this mystical mantra, precisely those two aspects merge. In the I is the male energy, in the AM is the female energy. The I is constricting, differentiating. It gives focus, it gives direction, it individuates: I, not the other, I. And then AM. AM is oceanic, all encompassing. It reflects the ocean of Home, the female energy, the inexhaustible source that knows no bounds, no differentiation. The flowing and joining aspect is the core of the female energy. In the I AM, the male and female come together and blissfully join their energies.

Now in the history of humanity and even before humanity existed, a conflict arose between the masculine and the feminine. I shall not go into the origin of this conflict now. But in your history there is a drifting apart of male and female energy so that they appear as opposite forces. The yin-yang symbol demonstrates the true situation very well. In the masculine there is always a core of the feminine, and in the feminine there is a core of the masculine, just as there is a white dot in the black and a black dot in the white. But in the course of history, this mystical unity of the masculine and feminine has been forgotten and these energies have become opposed to each other as black and white. The underlying unity was no longer recognized.

Right now, you are in the last phase of this history of conflict, in which the male energy has played the part of perpetrator for many centuries. The male energy has long been playing a part in which it oppresses, mutilates and destroys the female energy. It was not always like that. There have been times in which the female energy had the upper hand and wrongly manipulated and ruled the male energy. But that time is over. The conflict took a different turn at a certain point and the roles of perpetrator and victim were reversed. The male energy has been in power for a long time now and has misused this power in such a fashion that the female energy has been weakened and does not realize the integrity of her Being anymore. Whenever the masculine and feminine are in conflict, the disintegration of both is inevitable. Where the feminine gets victimized more and more and gets lost in self-denial, the masculine energy loses itself in ruthless violence and the kind of aggression you know from the many wars in your past.

The masculine and the feminine depend on one another. When they battle each other, the consequences are disastrous. But times are changing. Since the 19th and 20th centuries, the female energy is regaining its strength and rising above the role of victim. This resurrection comes from deep within the feminine energy. She has finally reached the outer limit of her self-denial. At this point she has looked herself in the face and has stated: this is as far as it goes.

By the way, this is how it always goes in the dynamic between victim and perpetrator. Change starts when the victim refuses to accept any more. The perpetrator could well hang onto his role for a longer while, for he has less of a reason to stop. Revolution starts where the victim refuses to accept any more and finally takes back her power. In all situations of repression, for example of women in their family or in society, the real moment of change is when the woman - or the feminine energy within a person - decides for herself: I will not take this any longer. This is when change truly starts to happen. External measures are useless until this moment presents itself.

159

The female energy has arisen and its star is rising. Actually the most urgent matter in this time and age is the transformation of the male energy!! It is now time for a new definition of male energy. I could have easily called this channeling "the rebirth of the male energy." For I want to stress that it is only in reunion with a matured and balanced male energy that the female energy can flourish again.

The female energy has in the past century and even before that regained power and strength. It has begun to flourish in a new and more balanced way. Despite the inequality of the sexes that is still present in your society, the rise of the female energy is unstoppable. However the female energy cannot gain full strength and vitality without cooperation with the male energy. This goes for the collective level as well as the individual. The female energy cannot make its final breakthrough without the support of and connection with the male energy. This is not because of an inherent weakness in the female energy. It is because of the essential nature of male and female energies: the fact that they are intertwined and can only fulfill their brightest potentials in cooperation. This is why it is imperative now that the male energy reshape itself and venture into the new!

When you look at the interplay between male and female on a collective level, the female energy is now in a position of waiting. She is waiting. At present there is a struggle going on *within* the collective male energy between the old and the new. A new wave of energy is dawning within the collective male energy that honors and respects the female energy. This new wave of male energy wants to join with the female and together enter the New Age. But at the same time an older wave of male energy is still active and trying to persist. This energy is clearly working in the series of terrorist attacks that has taken place all over your world. The male energy in its old role of heartless aggressor is thereby showing its nasty side. In the ones who commit these horrendous attacks there are very dark emotions: aggression, anger and at the same time utter powerlessness and helplessness. It is from this utter helplessness that they appeal to the most brute and destructive types of power display. This male energy we are speaking of is in its death agonies. It senses that there are important changes going on collectively and that humanity is on the threshold of a new era.

One of the problems you are now facing, while growing towards a more balanced cooperation between male and female, is how to deal with this kind of ruthless energy. What are we going to do about this old male energy that is trying to create as much havoc and destruction as possible in its downfall? Let me tell you this: its downfall is a fact. The struggle has been lost by the old male energy, but it will not surrender easily and it will resist to the very last with aggression and merciless attempts at domination.

Much will depend on how the inner collective attitude will be to these aggressors. Will you allow anger and powerlessness into your own energy field as a reaction to acts of violence? Then you open up to the energy field of the aggressors. At the very moment you feel overpowered by anger and resentment toward them they have reached their target. You are then sucked into their energetic vibration and you would be willing to kill as well: kill the murderers of the innocent. This is all very understandable, but is it vital to realize what's happening here. As soon as there are intense emotions rising up, it is wise to make a pause, in silence. Go back to the quiet, knowing part of you and ask: what is really going on here? It is all about your wisdom and discernment now, your ability to see through things and to feel what really is at stake. The world will not be taken over by terrorist powers; the old male energy has served its time and its dying hour is at hand.

The most important message I have about terrorism, this manifestation of old male aggression, is: stay conscious! Do not let yourself be taken off-center by emotions of powerlessness, i.e. by getting victimized. Know that no one will be touched by this aggressive energy if they do not allow it into their energy field. If you do not react with anger or hatred, you will not draw it to you. You will be safe and protected by your own light.

I now would like to pay attention to the more mundane individual level, the level at which you deal with the male and female energies within yourself. For on the individual level as well there has been a struggle between the male and the female energies. Everything that happens collectively mirrors processes at the individual level.

To illustrate the importance of balance between the feminine and the masculine on the individual level, I will speak of the energy centers in every human, which are also called the *chakras*. There are seven of them that you know of now and these are located along the spine, from the tail bone to the crown. I will go into all of these chakras briefly, to show you that they are all characterized by either a predominantly male or female type of energy.

161

The tail bone (root) chakra is the energy center that connects you to the earth. The energy in this chakra reaches out to the earth and allows you to manifest your soul energy in physical form on the dense, material level of reality. In view of the reaching out and manifesting type of energy in the tail bone chakra, you may call it a predominantly male chakra. A chakra is never completely male or female, but one may say that the male energy has the upper hand here.

The second chakra is called the navel (belly button) chakra and it is the center of emotions. This center allows you to experience emotions, mood swings, in short all the highs and lows of emotional life. It is a receptive center. That is why I call it a female center, a chakra in which the female flow of energy dominates.

The third chakra, also called the solar plexus, is a center of action and creation. This is a center which reaches out and allows energy to manifest in physical reality. You may compare it to the sun, the outpouring of rays and the power of the yellow sunlight (the natural color of the third chakra is yellow). In the solar plexus your thoughts, ideas and desires are transformed into outer manifestation. It is the chakra of action and outward expression. It is also the seat of the ego, meaning the earthly personality, without negative implications. The predominant energy is male.

The heart chakra is a receptive center like the navel chakra and it has the special ability to connect different flows of energy. It is the center in which the energies of the lower three chakras (earth reality) and the upper three chakras (cosmic reality) connect. The heart is the bridge between mind (head) and emotion (belly). From the heart you are also able to connect with others and transcend yourself. The heart transcends the boundaries of the ego and enables you to feel oneness with anything outside of you, even with All That Is. The heart chakra is the gateway to the energy of Home. It is clearly a center of connection and it is therefore predominantly feminine.

The throat chakra is male. From this center inner promptings, ideas and emotions are given physical shape through speaking, crying, laughing, singing, yelling etc. Here the inner life is expressed outwardly by communication through the voice and through language. This center enables you to make your inner life known to others by means of physical signals: words, sounds, concepts. It is a center of manifestation that enables you to focus your energy outwardly into the physical plane. It is also a center of creativity.

The sixth chakra, also called "the third eye" which is located in the middle of your head, is feminine again. It receives extra-sensory, intuitive impressions and transcends the boundaries of the physical (the five physical senses). It is the seat of clairvoyance, clairsentience, etc. Through this center you can feel the energy of someone else – the emotions, the pains, the joys – as your own. With this ability of empathy, you transcend the boundaries of the ego and you connect with "that which is not-you."

Finally there is the crown chakra, on top of the head. This chakra is neither male nor female. Or you might say: it is both. In this chakra, you rise above the duality of male and female. The crown chakra is an interesting combination of both energies. When this chakra is balanced, the consciousness therein is in a state of receiving as much as reaching out. There is a reaching "upwards" to other dimensions, where it seeks spiritual meaning or support, or to deeper layers of the Self. And at the same time there is a quiet and tranquil receptiveness, a knowingness that the answers will come in good time. It is a type of consciousness that is both highly focused and highly receptive. In this "state of mind" you come very close to the unity that underlies male and female energies, the energy of Spirit or God.

I have now sketched very roughly the movement of the male and female energy flows throughout the energetic body of the human being. Now I wish to speak of the lowest three chakras in particular. These are the chakras that are most connected to the earth, that are most involved with being in the earthly realm. This area of the lowest three chakras is of utmost importance in your inner road to healing, for in this area lie the deepest traumas and emotional scars.

You often feel you are earthly beings opening up to the spiritual. But we see it the other way around. You are spiritual beings opening up to the earth. The earth is a brilliant destination, a hidden diamond that has yet to reveal its true beauty. The earth is the Promised Land!

Heaven is your birth place. But you will not return to the state of consciousness that you remember as "Home" or "Heaven," to a state of purely spiritual being. The adventure of Creation brings you to new destinations; you are always expanding and progressing towards a wholly new type of consciousness. (We have spoken of this before in the last chapter of the Lightworker Series). Earth is an essential part of this journey.

However in your manifestations on earth and your attempts to express yourself there, you have suffered much pain. Almost all of you have severe emotional wounds in the lowest three chakras caused by experiences of rejection, violence and abandonment. This may have happened in past lives as well as in this lifetime. Almost all energy blocks in the upper chakras are related to emotional hurts in the lowest three chakras.

I will say a little about the tail bone chakra first. Your connection to the earth has become emotionally burdened, especially for lightworkers. Because you have met with grave resistance over many lifetimes, there is much fear and reserve in you when it comes to truly grounding yourself. Grounding yourself means being fully present in your earthly bodies and expressing your innermost inspiration in material reality. The resistance to grounding yourself fully has been discussed before (in the Lightworker series). It has mainly to do with you "being different" and having been rejected for it.

In the second chakra, the emotional center, you have also been affected deeply by experiences of being threatened or deserted (literally or emotionally) and by being severely restricted in your self-expression.

With these traumatic burdens in the lowest two chakras, the solar plexus (third chakra) is also heavily affected. The solar plexus has to do with life force, creative energy and power. You know few examples of what true power means. With this I mean power that is not aggressive and destructive. In the solar plexus chakra you often see that a person manifests himself or herself either in an aggressive, controlling way, or in a subdued, overly modest way. Both ways are the result of underlying feelings of helplessness, stemming from a wounded first and second chakra. In the third chakra it is all about finding a balanced way of dealing with power and control, it is about a balanced ego.

Ego is okay! The ego has a proper function; it lends focus to your consciousness which enables you to create and manifest as the separate individual that you are. Yes, you are part of a greater Whole but you are also "I," separate and different from anyone else. The ego is a necessary complement to the spiritual part of you that transcends the "I." The energy of the ego is fully honorable and justified in the energetic reality that you live. True power is in the joyful alignment of ego and Spirit.

The area of the lowest three chakras is the most important area in self-healing and inner growth. The greatest spiritual challenge to you now is to take care of this wounded area in yourself. Meditating to transcend physical reality or connect to elusive cosmic levels is not your main goal now. Your goal is to give your gentlest understanding and loving support to that hurt inner child within you and to restore its beauty and playfulness. This is your spiritual journey; herein lies the greatest treasure. Cherishing and respecting the human side of you, the child part of you, is your road to divine compassion and enlightenment.

I would like to draw your attention to the fact that within this energetic area, two out of the three chakras concerned are male. This shows that especially with regard to the male energies within each of you, much healing work is to be done. Therefore my message to you now is: heal the male energy within! The feminine energy is in many ways recovering and acquiring the strength needed to express itself fully and beautifully. The female qualities of intuition, sensitivity and connectedness are being appreciated more and more, individually as well as collectively. But it is not so clear what a balanced male energy truly looks like. The male energy somehow got lost in false images of what it means "to be a man," stereotypes that always boil down to power through aggression. It is vital to recognise and express the true nature of male energy. The female side now needs the balanced male energy to be able to truly fulfill her role. The female energy is waiting, not just at the collective level but also on the individual level. The female energy is getting out of its victim role, regaining its self-esteem and it is now wanting to manifest itself powerfully and joyfully through reunion with the male.

So, what then is the power of balanced male energy? This goes for the male energy in both men and women.

In the first chakra, a healed and balanced male energy leads to *self-consciousness*. The male energy does not have to fight and struggle anymore, it is present through self-consciousness. Presence, i.e. being fully present with all of your soul, is an essential quality of the first chakra. Being present self-consciously means to stay aware of yourself, remaining centered, not getting lost in someone else's opinions, expectations or needs. It is about finding the balance between connecting with others and being true to yourself. A balanced male energy in the tail bone chakra allows you to remain centered and aware of yourself while you interact with others and the outside world.

It is essential to develop this quality of self-consciousness, for it will protect and guide your female energy. The female energy is naturally inclined to connect with others (other living beings) and to be present with the other in a caring, nurturing way. The male energy makes for boundaries and helps find a balance between giving and receiving. With regard to the flowing, connecting female energies, the male energy in the lowest chakra fulfills the role of anchor and backbone. It is the point of coming home to yourself, the point of releasing ties to other energies you have connected with.

The solar plexus or third chakra fulfills the same role in a different way. This chakra is, as I said before, the energy center of the ego. You still have trouble with this concept of the ego. Especially among lightworker souls, there is a tendency to look upon the giving, self-transcending energies in the human being as "higher." But it is not so. You live in a world in which two energies play together and form the building blocks of Creation. One tends to connect and seek for unity, the other creates separation and individuality. And the latter energy is just as viable and valuable as the former one.

It is important to make peace with the male energy, to embrace your individuality, your uniqueness, your "I-ness." There is an essential "aloneness" in life which has nothing to do with loneliness, but which has everything to do with you being an "I," a unique individual. To embrace this aloneness does not stand in the way of experiencing deep connections to others. If you truly embrace your individuality, you become an empowered, independent and creative individual able to share your energy deeply with anyone or anything, because you are not afraid to lose yourself in it or give up your individuality.

The male energy of the solar plexus helps you become truly creative and empowered. That is what the female energy in you is waiting for. Your heartfelt inspiration wants to make itself known on the material level, it wants to come out in a very earthly manner and bring tidings of love and harmony to the earth. The female energy is the carrier of the New Age but it needs a balanced male energy to truly manifest itself and grow roots into material reality. That is why it is of such great importance that the energies of the first and third chakra are healed.

The energy of a healthy ego, the healed solar plexus, is *self-confidence*. In the first chakra it is self-consciousness, in the third chakra it is self-confidence. This is not the kind of arrogance you see in an inflated ego. It is about simply trusting yourself: "I feel that I can do it!" It is being aware of your own deepest inspiration, your own creative abilities and then acting accordingly. Let your energies flow out of you, trust your natural talents and gifts, trust who you are and show yourself to the world! Especially for you lightworkers who carry so much inner knowledge and wisdom, it is now time to show yourself and not hide anymore. It is time. This is your destination and in this you will find your greatest fulfillment.

Make peace with the male energy within. Do not hesitate to stand up for yourself, to receive abundance and to take good care of yourself. Be egotistical, in the pure and neutral sense of the word. You *are* an ego, you are an individual. You cannot and need not be forgiving and understanding all the time. It is not spiritual to tolerate everything and anything. Clearly there are moments at which you have to say "no" or even "farewell" and not compromise who you are. Do this without guilt or fear and feel how the male energies of self-consciousness and self-confidence empower you to let the delicate flower of your female energy flourish and shine.

It is all about the cooperation between the energies. Male and female energies have gone down together in a long and painful struggle. They will also rise together, for one cannot be balanced without the other. Now that the female energy is ready to rise from the ashes of humiliation and repression, there is an urgent need for a rebirth of the male energy. This rebirth of the male will become visible on a collective scale eventually, but it will first manifest in each of you separately, man and woman. You all are the keepers of these ancient energies within you, and it is your birthright to make their partnership equal and joyful.

Dealing with emotions

Dear friends, I am delighted to be among you again and to communicate with you in this way. I must say that this means a lot to me as well. I cherish these meetings for in this way I can come closer to you than from my own plane of reality.

Yet I always live inside your hearts and I wait for moments in your time when you are open and susceptible to my energy. My energy, the Christ energy that is being reborn in this time, is not solely *my* energy. It is not simply the energy of one man who lived on earth at one time; it is a collective energy field in which you take part in a way that is more profound than you realize.

You all made a vow once, you all set your intention to carry this energy forth into the reality of earth, to anchor it in earth. Many lifetimes, many centuries, you have worked on this mission. You are all in the process of birthing the Christ seed within and I am helping you. I was a forerunner, yet the sowing of the Christ seed was a collective effort. Even my coming to earth was possible only because of the field of energy that was present here, woven by you. We work together, we are a unity. Therefore I am accessible to all of you. I am not exclusively available to any one person. I am at the service of all of you.

Today I want to speak about an issue that touches you deeply and frequently in your day to day life. It is about *dealing with emotions.*

Last time I spoke about the energies of the male and the female which run through your energy field and chakras. I have emphasized the importance of healing the lowest three chakras as a part of becoming whole and complete unto yourself. I thought it was important to emphasize this as some of you who crave the spiritual tend to withdraw yourself, both in thought and feeling, to the higher chakras.

The heart, the third eye and the crown chakra are attractive to you, because these energy centers connect you with the higher realms that are so natural to you. But the real inner breakthroughs must now occur on a lower level, in the area of the lower chakras, closer to earth.

The area of the emotions is a vital area in your growth process towards freedom and wholeness. You are spiritual beings. You come from a plane of reality where the density and coarseness of earth reality was unknown to you. To cope with this has been difficult.

Throughout many lives you have tried to express your cosmic energy here on earth. And in this expression, in the channeling of your energy to earth, many deep traumas have been built up. The emotional body that you all have is rife with wounds and traumas. Of that I wish to speak today.

Anyone who walks the path of inner growth knows the importance of emotions: that you should not repress them, that you have to come to terms with them in some way, that you must ultimately release them. But how it all really works is not always so clear.

I first want to make a distinction between *emotions* and *feelings*. I am not concerned here with specific terms or labels and you may call it by different names, but I want to make a distinction between emotions in the sense of energies that are essentially *expressions of misunderstanding* and feelings or energies that are a form of *higher understanding.*

Feelings are your teachers, while emotions are your children.

Emotions are energies that have a clear manifestation in the physical body. Emotions are reactions to things that you do not really understand. Consider what happens when you are overcome by a fit of rage. For instance someone hurts your feelings unexpectedly and you feel yourself becoming angry. You can feel this very clearly in your body; in certain places you feel the energy go tense. This physical tension or tightening that follows the energetic shock shows there is something you do not understand. There is an energy coming toward you that you feel is unjustified. The feeling of being treated unjustly, in short the not-understanding, is vented through the emotion. The emotion is the expression of the not-understanding, it is an energetic explosion and a release.

When this happens, you are confronted with the following choice: what am I going to do with this emotion? Am I going to base my actual behavior on it? Am I going to use this as fuel for my reactions to other people or do I let the emotion be and base my actions on something else?

Before answering this question, I want to explain the nature of feelings.

Emotions are essentially explosions of misunderstanding that you can clearly perceive in the body. Feelings, on the other hand, are of a different nature and are perceived differently as well. Feelings are more quiet than emotions. They are the whispers of the soul that reach you through gentle nudges, an inner knowingness or a sudden intuitive action that later appears to have been very wise.

Emotions always have something very intense and dramatic to them. Consider anxiety attacks, fear, rage or deep sadness. Emotions take hold of you completely and pull you away from your spiritual center. In the moment you are highly emotional, you are full of a kind of energy that pulls you away from your center, your inner clarity. In that sense, emotions are like clouds hovering before the sun.

With this, I do not want to say anything against emotions. Emotions should not be repressed; they are very valuable as a means to get to know yourself more intimately. But I do want to state what the nature of emotional energy is: it is an explosion of misunderstanding. Emotions essentially take you out of your center.

Feelings, on the other hand, bring you *deeper* into yourself, into your center. Feelings are closely associated with what you call intuition. Feelings express a higher understanding, a kind of understanding that transcends both the emotions and the mind.

Feelings originate in a non-physical realm, outside of the body. That is why they are not so clearly located within one spot of the physical body. Consider

171

what happens when you sense something, an atmosphere or a mood, or when you have presentiments about a situation. There is a kind of knowingness within you then that seems to come from the outside and that is not a reaction from you to something external. It comes "out of nothing" ("out of the blue" as you so beautifully put it). In such a moment, you may feel something open up in your heart chakra.

There are many moments in which such an inner knowingness comes to you. For instance, you may "know" something about someone without having really talked with him or her. You can sense something about the two of you that later on will play an important role in your relationship. Such things are not easy to grasp in words – "simply a feeling" - and certainly not easily understood by the mind. (These are the moments in which your mind gets skeptical, telling you that you are making things up or are going crazy).

I would like to mention another energy that has more of a "feeling" nature than an emotional one. It is joy. Joy can be a phenomenon that transcends the emotional. Sometimes you can feel a kind of joy inside that lifts you up without a particular reason. You feel the divinity inside you and your intimate connection to all that exists. Such a feeling may come to you when you least expect it. It is as if Something Greater touches you or as if you touch a Greater Reality. Feelings are not so easily summoned and seem to come to you "out of the blue." Emotions almost always have a clear immediate cause: a trigger in the outside world that "pushes your buttons."

Feelings originate from the dimension of your Higher or Greater Self. You need to be quiet inside to catch those whispers in your heart. Emotions can disturb this inner silence and peace. Therefore it is vital to become emotionally calm and to heal and release repressed emotions. Only from your feeling which connects you to your soul can you make balanced decisions.

By being quiet and peaceful, you can feel with all of your being what is right for you at a certain moment. Making decisions based on emotions is making decisions from a non-centered position. You need to release the emotions first and get in touch with your inner core where there is clarity.

Now I want to go into the question of how you can best deal with your emotions.

I said that "feelings are your teachers and emotions are your children." The parallels between "being emotional" and "being like a child" are striking. Your "inner child" is the seat of your emotions. Also there is a striking resemblance between the way you deal with your own emotions and the way you deal with real children.

Children are honest and spontaneous in their emotions and they do not hide or repress them until adults encourage them to do so. The fact that children spontaneously express their emotions does not however mean that children experience their emotions in a balanced way. Everyone knows that children can be carried away by their emotions (rage, fear or sadness) and are often unable to put a stop to them. In such a situation, the child can almost drown in their emotions and that makes them unbalanced, i.e. out-of-center.

One of the reasons for this unbounded emotionality is that the child has only recently left a world in which there are hardly any boundaries. In the ethereal or astral dimensions, there were no such restrictions and limitations as there are in the physical realm, within the physical body. The child's emotions are often "reactions of misunderstanding" to this physical reality. Therefore when he or she grows up, the child needs help and support in dealing with their emotions. This is part of the process of "balanced incarnating" on earth.

So how do you deal with emotions, whether in yourself or in your children?

Emotions should not be judged or repressed. Emotions are a vital part of you as a human being and as such they need to be respected and accepted. You can look upon your emotions as your children who need your attention and respect *and* your guidance.

An emotion can best be viewed as an energy that comes to you for healing. Therefore it is important to not be completely swept away by the emotion, but to remain able to look at it from a neutral stance. It is important to *stay conscious.* One might put it like this; you should not repress an emotion, but you should not drown in it either. For when you drown in it, when you identify with it completely, the child in you becomes a tyrant that will lead you astray.

The most important thing you can do with an emotion is to allow it in, to feel all aspects of it while not losing your consciousness. Take for instance anger.

You can invite anger to be fully present, experiencing it in your body at several places, while you are at the same time neutrally observing it. Such a type of consciousness is healing. What happens in this instance is that you embrace the emotion, which is essentially a form of *misunderstanding*, with *understanding*. This is spiritual alchemy.

Let me explain with the help of an example. Your child has bumped her knee on the table and it really hurts. She is upset, screaming with pain and she kicks the table because she is angry with it. She considers the table to be the source of her pain.

Emotional guidance at this moment means that the parent first helps the child name her experience. "You are angry, aren't you – you are in pain, right?" Naming it is essential. You transfer the root of the problem from the table to the child herself. "It's not in the table, it is *you* who are hurt, it is *you* who is angry. And yes, I understand your emotion!"

The parent embraces the emotion of the child with understanding, with love. The moment the child feels understood and recognized, her anger will gradually fade away. The physical pain may still be present. But her *resistance* to the pain, the anger around it, can dissolve. The child reads compassion and understanding in your eyes, and this relaxes and soothes her emotions. The table, the cause of the emotions, is not relevant anymore.

In embracing an emotion with understanding and compassion, you shift the focus of the child's attention from outside to inside, and you teach the child to *take responsibility* for the emotion. You are showing her that her reaction to an outside trigger is not a given, but that it is a matter of choice. You can choose misunderstanding or understanding. You can choose to fight or to accept. You can choose.

This also applies to the relationship with your own emotions, your own inner child. Allowing your emotions in, naming them and making an effort to understand them, means that you truly respect and cherish your inner child. Making the shift from "outer" to "inner," taking responsibility for the emotion, helps to create an inner child that does not want to hurt anyone else, that does not feel victimized. Strong emotions – whether anger, grief or fear – always have the component of powerlessness, i.e. the sense that you are the victim of something outside of you. What you do when you focus not on the circumstances outside of you but instead on your reaction and your pain is that you "dismiss" the outside world as the cause of your emotions. You do not care that much about what gave rise to the emotion. You completely turn inward and you say to yourself: okay, this has been my reaction and I understand why. I understand why I feel the way that I do and I am going to support myself in this.

Turning toward your emotions in such a loving manner is liberating. It does require a kind of self-discipline. Releasing outside reality as the "source of the evil" and taking full responsibility yourself means that you acknowledge that "you choose to react a certain way." You stop arguing about who is right and who is wrong, who is to blame for what and you simply release the whole chain of events that happened outside of your control. "I now experience this emotion in the full awareness that I choose to do so." That is taking responsibility. That is courage!

The self-discipline in this is that you give up on being righteous and on being the helpless victim. You give up on feeling angry, misunderstood and all the other expressions of victimhood that can feel quite good at some times. (Truly, you often cherish the emotions that bug you the most). Taking responsibility is an act of humbleness. It means being honest with yourself, even at your weakest moment.

This is the self-discipline that is asked of you. At the same time, this kind of turning inward requires the highest compassion. The emotion you are honestly prepared to face as your own creation is also looked upon with gentle understanding. "You chose anger this time, didn't you?" Compassion tells you: "Okay, I can see why and I forgive you. Perhaps when you feel my love and support more clearly you will not feel inclined to take that response next time."

This is the true role of consciousness in self-healing. This is what spiritual alchemy means. Consciousness does not fight or reject anything; it encircles darkness with awareness. It encircles the energies of misunderstanding with understanding and thus transforms ordinary metal into gold. Consciousness and love are essentially the same. Being conscious means letting something be and surrounding it with your love and compassion.

Often you think that "consciousness alone" is not enough to overcome your emotional problems. You say: I know I have repressed emotions, I know the cause of it, I am aware but it does not go away.

In that case, there is a subtle resistance within you to that emotion. You keep the emotion at a distance, from fear of being overwhelmed by it. But you are never overwhelmed by an emotion when you consciously choose to allow it.

As long as you keep the emotion at a distance, you are at war with it. You are fighting the emotion and it will turn against you in several ways. You cannot keep it outside in the end. It will manifest itself in your body as an ache or tension or as a feeling of depression. Feeling down or weary frequently is a clear sign that you are repressing certain emotions.

The thing is that you need to allow the emotions to fully enter your consciousness. If you do not know exactly what emotions are there, you can very well start by feeling the tensions in your body. This is a gateway to the emotions. In your body it is all stored. For instance, if you feel pain or tension in the area of your stomach, you can go there with your awareness and ask what is the matter. Let the cells of your body speak to you. Or imagine that right there, a child is present. Ask the child to show you what emotion is predominant in him or her.

There are several ways to connect with your emotions. It is vital to realize that the energy that got stuck in the emotion *wants* to move. This energy wants to be released and therefore it knocks at your door as a physical complaint or as a feeling of stress or depression. For you it is a matter of really opening up and being prepared to feel the emotion.

Emotions are part of your earthly reality – but they should not get a hold over you. Emotions are like clouds for the sun. Therefore it is so important to be aware of your emotions and to deal with them consciously. From a clear and balanced emotional body, it is much easier to contact your soul or inner core through your intuition.

In your society, there is much confusion about emotions. This is evident, among other things, from the amount of debate and confusion there is about how to raise your children. Children clearly are much more emotionally spontaneous than you are as adults. This creates difficulties. What if some of your moral boundaries are crossed? What if the situation gets out of hand and chaos arises? Does one have to discipline children or let them express themselves freely? Do their emotions have to be controlled or not?

What is important in a child's upbringing is that they learn to understand their emotions, to understand where they come from and to take responsibility for them. With your help, the child can learn to see their emotions as "explosions of misunderstanding." This understanding prevents your child from "drowning" in their emotions and going out of control. Understanding liberates and brings you back to your own center without repressing the emotions. The parent teaches their child to deal with emotions in this way by being the living example of it.

All the questions you have about dealing with your children also apply to yourself. How do you cope with your own emotions? Are you hard on yourself? When you feel angry or sad for some time, do you discipline yourself by saying: "Come on, get yourself together and move on"? Do you suppress the emotion? Do you feel that disciplining yourself is good and necessary? Who taught you this? Was it a parent?

Or do you go to the other side? Do you wallow in your emotion, not wanting to let go of it. This also is frequently the case. You may have felt for a long time that you were a victim of some situation outside of you, for example your upbringing, your partner or your work environment. At a certain moment, it may have been very liberating to get in touch with the anger inside you about the negative things that influenced you. Anger can enable you to break free from these influences and go your own way. However you may get so enamored with your anger that you do not want to give it up anymore. Instead of becoming a doorway, it becomes a way of living. A form of victimhood then arises which is anything but healing. It holds you back from truly standing in your own power.

It is very important to take responsibility for your own emotions and not to make absolute truths of them. When you give them the status of truths, instead of looking upon them as "explosions of misunderstanding," you will base your actions on them and that will lead to uncentered decisions.

The same happens with children who are allowed too much emotional freedom. They run wild and become uncontrollable; they become little tyrants and that is not right. Emotional chaos is just as unpleasant for the child as it is for the parent.

In short you can either be too strict or too lenient in dealing with your emotions (and, by analogy, with your children). I want to go a little more into the "lenient" way, for that seems to be more of an issue nowadays. Since the sixties there has been a collective realization that it will not do to suppress your emotions, for then you are stifling your spontaneity and creativity, indeed your very soul. Society will produce disciplined and obedient children who care more for rules than the whispers of the heart and that is a tragedy – for society as well as the individual.

But what about that other extreme: what about justifying emotions in such a way that they take over and rule your life?

You can very well observe inside you whether there are emotions that you cherish in such a way that you regard them as truth instead of what they really are: explosions of misunderstanding. These are emotions you have identified with. The paradox is that often enough, these are emotions that cause you much suffering. For instance: powerlessness ("I cannot help it"), control ("I'll handle it"), anger ("it's their fault") or grief ("life is miserable"). These are all emotions that are painful but yet, on another level, they give you something special to hold on to.

Take powerlessness or the "victim feeling." There can be advantages to this emotional pattern. It may give you a sense of safety. It releases you from certain obligations or responsibilities. "I can't help it, can I?" It is a dark corner you're sitting in but it seems a safe one. The danger of identifying or "merging" with such an emotional pattern for a long time is that you lose touch with your own true freedom, your innermost divine core.

Things may have entered your life path that have justifiably provoked emotions of anger and resentment within you. This may have happened in your youth, later on or even in past lives. It is very important that you get in touch with these emotions consciously and that you become aware of the anger, sadness or any other intensely charged energy within you. But at a certain point, you need to take responsibility for your emotions, for they constitute *your* reactions to an outside event.

Being centered, being in a state of clarity and spiritual balance, means that you take full responsibility for all the emotions that are in you. You can then recognize the emotion of, for instance, anger within you and say at the same time: this was my reaction to certain events. I surround this reaction with understanding, but at the same time I intend to release it.

Life is ultimately not about being right; it is about being free and whole. It is *very* liberating to release old emotional responses that have grown into a lifestyle.

One might say that it is all about the subtle middle road between suppressing emotions and drowning in them. On both sides, you have been raised with opinions and ideals that are not in accordance with the nature of spiritual alchemy. The essence of spiritual growth is that you do not suppress anything, but at the same time you take full responsibility for it. *I* feel this, *I* choose this reaction, so *I* can heal it. *Claiming your mastership* – that is what my message is about truly.

Perhaps it is not really a middle road, but a different road. It is all about spiritual mastership. In accepting all there is within you, you rise above it and become its master. Mastership is both strong and gentle. It is very allowing and yet it takes great discipline: the discipline of courage and honesty.

Claim your mastership, become the master of the emotional bits and pieces that torment you, often behind your back. Get in touch with them, take responsibility. Don't let yourself be driven by unconscious emotional hurts that sidetrack you and block your road to inner freedom. It is *your* consciousness that heals. No one else can restore the power over your own emotions for you. There are no external instruments or means to take away those emotions. It is in becoming aware of them with strength, determination and compassion that they are released into the Light.

Becoming whole and free on the emotional level is one of the most important aspects of growing spiritually. I want to finish by saying: do not make it more difficult than it is. The spiritual path is a simple path. It is about love for yourself and inner clarity. It does not require any specific knowledge or any specific rituals, rules or methods. All things you need for your spiritual growth are *within you.*

At a quiet moment, go to the feeling side of you. Let this feeling side of you tell you what needs to be clarified and cleansed within you. Trust your intuition. Work on it. Believe in yourself. You are the master of your life, the master of your unique path to love and freedom.

Sexuality and spirituality

Dear friends, I rejoice at being with you again. When I see you, I do not so much see you as the physical bodies that you look at in the mirror. It is your inside that I feel and see, the inner movements of your thoughts, feelings and emotions. I am here to support you on your journey.

There is a theme that I would like to discuss today that has had a great impact on you throughout your history on earth. It is about sexuality and how it is experienced by men and women.

This is not an easy subject. Sexuality has become burdened with many judgments, fears and emotions. Hardly any aspect of it is spontaneous and self-evident anymore. This is the same as saying that the childlike aspect of sexuality, the aspect of the freely exploring innocent child, has become lost. You are full of fear and tension when it comes to sexually expressing yourself.

I want to address this burden in this channeling, but first I'd like to say a little about what sexuality means from a spiritual perspective.

Sexuality is the dancing together of male and female energies. Originally sexuality was more than a physical act. It was meant to be a dance in which all levels or aspects of you and your partner participate.

I will distinguish among four levels or aspects that can play a role in this dance of energies.

Four aspects of the sexual experience

First, there is the *physical level*, the aspect of the physical body. The body is innocent. The body knows sexual desire and lust and this is something that is spontaneously present within the body. The body seeks gratification of its desires and it is the human, or the soul consciousness in the human, that determines the way in which the sexual desire is applied and manifested. Again, the body is innocent. It knows lust and desire. There is nothing wrong with that. It can be a source of fun, play and enjoyment. But the body cannot itself choose in what way it is going to express its sexual energy. It is you the human being who is in charge and the body needs your leadership.

When you would like to experience sexuality in the most loving way, the seat of leadership will be in the heart. When you let your heart take charge of your sexual energy, it will find its most joyful expression. The alternative is to let either your thoughts (judgments) or your emotions rule the sexual flow and you will see that this will cause several blockages in your energy, but I will speak of this below.

The second aspect of the sexual dance I wish to distinguish is *the emotional level*. Sexual union is a deeply emotional act. If you ignore this aspect, you are not fully present in the act and you cut yourself off from the real meaning of sexuality.

In a previous channeling called "Dealing with emotions," we have gone into the issue of emotions extensively. We highlighted the powerful emotions of fear, anger and sadness and discussed how they can take you out of your center. When any of these powerful emotions is working in a relationship between two people and they are not consciously recognized and addressed, it will come up when they are intimate together. These emotions may cause psychological reactions of resistance or closing down when you are physically intimate, or the body may be unable to feel lust or excitement.

Whenever there are these psychological or physical blockages, it is important to deal with them at the level at which they have arisen: the emotional level. When you try to take away physical symptoms without looking at the underlying emotional dynamic, you are disrespectful of yourself and your body. When the body resists intimacy it gives you a message, pure and clear, that there is an emotional blockage. This may be due to a problem between you and your partner, or it may be an emotional hurt you carry with you from the past. Whatever it is, it needs to be addressed and taken care of in a gentle and loving way before the sexual energy can flow freely.

Next to the emotional level is *the level of the heart,* which is the seat of feeling. In the same channeling I just mentioned ("Dealing with emotions"), we distinguished between emotions and feelings. Feelings belong to the domain of intuition and inner knowing. Your feeling side speaks to you through quiet whispers, filled with wisdom and compassion. Emotions are more dramatic in nature and we called them "reactions of misunderstanding," for that is what they essentially are: explosions of not understanding what is happening to you. (See the channeling for clarification.)

When the heart opens up between sexual partners there is trust, love and safety between them. When the heart is present in a sexual meeting, you allow your intuition to take note of what is happening between you when you get physically intimate. You do not hide your emotions, you speak openly of them. Old pain may surface and it is accepted as such. You are accepted as you are and this kind of acceptance is the greatest healing power there is. When you connect your heart energy with your sexual energy, great healing can take place in an area that is much in need of it.

However, the heart can also play a subtle role in preventing you from experiencing sexuality in a joyful, loving way. The heart may have closed itself off from the joy of sexuality for different reasons. First there may be a desire in the heart to rise above the physical reality of earth. Second there may be religious dogmas at work that keep the heart from opening up to what sexuality really is. I will address both of these issues now.

The heart can have a strong inclination to rise above the dense plane of material reality. It is a kind of homesickness. There may be a longing there for unity that is not at all aimed at sexual union, but in fact carries within it a subtle rejection of the earth realm (and of sexuality as well). Many of you

183

know the desire to transcend this reality. Many of you remember the energy of love and harmony that you have experienced in non-material realms before you incarnated on earth. Your heart cries out for the ease and the lightness of this vibration. You try to drink in this energy when you meditate. Often the higher chakras are activated in this way, meaning the heart, the throat, the third eye and the crown chakra. They open up, while the lower three chakras (solar plexus, belly and tail bone) which are vital to your earthly self are more or less abandoned.

In a more unnatural way, this also happens when you take drugs. When you take mind-expanding substances, the upper chakras are artificially ripped open and you can temporarily experience ecstasy and bliss that make you forget the dense and heavy aspect of earth reality.

Although the desire and the longing for transcendence are understandable, it is important to make peace with earth reality. Otherwise you will create an artificial separation between the upper part and the lower part of your energy field. You will give preference to being in the upper part of your aura with your consciousness and you will grow a subtle or overt resistance to the reality of the body, the emotions and sexuality. This creates an imbalance in your energy field

When you are homesick in this way, try to feel the reason and purpose for your being on earth right now. Your reason to be here is not to transcend earth but to bring Home down to earth. This is a sacred journey.

The second reason for the heart to shy away from sexuality is religious dogmas, often from past lives. There may have been lives in which you took vows of chastity or in which you were taught to feel shame or guilt about bodily pleasure and sexuality. These energies may still linger in your heart. Because of them you may have negative judgments about or subtle resistance to physical intimacy. These judgments and sentiments do not rest on truth. Again I wish to say that the body itself is innocent. Lust, desire and all the physical processes that make you long for sexual union are natural, healthy processes. The imbalances that occur in the area of sexuality are almost always due to the non-physical levels, of which I have now discussed two.

The fourth and last level is *the aspect of the mind.* On the mental level there can be moral or spiritual beliefs that keep you from enjoying sexuality. Most of these beliefs are religious in nature.

On the spiritual level you may feel that the physical body is a kind of prison. The non-physical reality of the "higher realms" (as you call them, not I) is so glorified that the physical reality gets undervalued. This occurs frequently among lightworkers. Especially among them there often is resistance to the pleasure and enjoyment that sexuality can provide. This stems partly from religious and moral beliefs and partly from sheer inexperience with this aspect of life. Most lightworker souls have spent many lifetimes as priests, nuns or similar roles, withdrawn from the community, without a partner or family. They focused so much on the spiritual that the area of sexuality was neglected.

In spiritual or religious people there is often a lack of respect for the body in its natural expression. This is truly regrettable for it is the expression into matter that is regarded on our side to be the most sacred journey for a soul to go on. To sow and reap the seeds of your divinity so far away from Home in the reality of matter and form is a sacred undertaking. It is a divine, creative act of the highest order.

Perhaps you have at some time been present at someone's deathbed or you have witnessed a childbirth. In those moments, the souls enters or lets go of the dance with matter. Both points in time are surrounded by an atmosphere of sacredness. You can sense this as a deep, enveloping silence filled with honor which announces the coming or leaving of the soul. There is but the deepest respect on our side of the veil for what you do at those moments. The dance with matter is sacred. And you detest it so often!

Sexuality in its true meaning is a dance in matter which at the same time rises above matter. In balanced sexual self-expression you transcend material reality without ignoring or repressing it, without abandoning the lower three chakras and without seeking ecstasy only through the upper chakras. Complete sexuality integrates all levels of your being. Sexuality bridges the gap between matter and spirit.

When two people are physically intimate in a loving way, all the cells in their body vibrate a little faster – they start to dance a little. A gateway is opened to an energetic reality with a slightly higher vibration and a lighter feeling. After a sexual joining in which all of you participates – your body, soul and mind – you feel peaceful and joyful at the same time. There is a quiet ecstasy. The cells of your body have tasted the energy of love and in that moment you brought the reality of Love a little closer to you. You channeled the divine energy of Love that so dearly wishes to flow through you and that has only the greatest respect for your sexual nature.

If the energy on all four levels flows together in a sexual joining, it is an act of divine creation. That children are being born from such an act is only natural. When the dance of male and female is performed in such a joyous way, only goodness and sweetness can come of it. If a child is conceived in such a way, it enters the earth realm on a slide of love and light. It is the most loving welcome that a soul can have on earth.

Because the sexual energies are so precious, we ask you: please deal respectfully with your sexuality. When there are problems, fears or tensions around it, do not judge sexuality in itself or give up on it, for it is a natural part of you and a sacred one.

Sexual problems and the battle of the sexes

I would now like to go into the history of sexuality and then say something about the specific problems that women and men experience nowadays in their sexual self-expression.

Much has happened in the area of the sexual. At its core sexuality carries a great potential of light, but because of that there is also the potential for great misuse. The history I wish to speak of is one of the power struggle between men and women. This history is ancient and actually began at the time when the extra-terrestrial galactic empires started to interfere with life on earth. (See Part I, the "Lightworker series", for a detailed account of this process). Before that earth was a kind of paradise, a Garden of Eden in which beauty and innocence prevailed. We will not discuss this era here but will simply note that you are in the end phase of a power struggle that is much older than the 5,000 years of written history.

In the last stage of this history, men clearly played the role of perpetrator and oppressor. But it was not always so. There have been times in which the woman was much more powerful in the public as well as the private domain of life. She oppressed the male energy as well in cruel and sadistic ways. Woman is not naturally the oppressed or subdued sex, you know, nor is she by definition the most loving sex. Your stereotypes of women as sweet but powerless and of men as tough but insensitive say more about the last phase of the above mentioned history than about men and women as such.

There have been times predating written history in which matriarchal societies were regarded as standard. In those times women also used their energies in a destructive way, being disrespectful of the individual life force and creativity in each human being. There was a time when women had power over men. Women controlled and manipulated men by using the powers of emotion and intuition that they have a natural affinity with. They also used their psychic abilities to control men. For example there were sacrifices and rituals where men were tortured and killed.

I want to stress for your official history that this aspect draws a one sided picture of the relation between men and women. The oppression of woman by man has been evident for the whole period covered by your written history. But the grudge and hatred that men have displayed (and may still display) against women has not come from nothing. In addition to the cultural traditions and habits that influence them, there are also deep emotional wounds in the male collective soul that stem from a much older era.

Without going into detail about this era, I would like to invite you to *feel* for yourself whether it is possible that you experienced this. For women the question is: can you imagine that you exerted power over men once and that you successfully tried to control their energy? And for men the question is: can you imagine that this took place on a large scale and that you were "the weaker sex?" Maybe you will receive certain images or fantasies by asking this question inside. Let your intuition show you and watch the emotions that surface. This may be surprising.

Within the collective male, soul hatred and resentment had arisen because of this ancient history. This has come out in oppression of the female energy in the area of politics but also in the area of religion, particularly through the church. The idea that sexuality is sinful or at best a necessary evil is a male line of thinking that was influenced by hatred and grudges resulting from the repression of male sexuality in another era. Male sexuality was at that time considered to be an instrument for procreation without respect for the feeling side of men and the emotional ties between a father and his children. Often children were raised by the mother in separation from the father and hardly any attention was paid to what the father thought and wanted. Important values were passed on through the mother figure and the inferiority of men was one such value. Man was a workhorse rather than an equal partner.

In addition to the church being a bulwark of frustrated male energy, the world of science also displays hostility to the female energy. Although science and religion are in many respect natural enemies, they are united in their resistance to the intuitive, flowing aspect of the female energy. The church dogmas are rigid and stifling but the scientific method is limiting too in another manner. While the impetus behind modern science was enlightening and innovative (in the desire to dethrone false authority), it has gotten stuck in a narrow kind of rational thinking that doesn't allow the female energy to participate. Scientific thinking is analytical and logical but it does not open up enough to the imagination and to extrasensory (intuitive) sources of observation. The aversion that many scientists have to "the paranormal" and to anything that cannot be explained by rational reasoning is however partly due to a soul memory of pain and humiliation dating back to a time when psychic powers were abused by women and were used against them as an instrument of manipulation.

I speak of this ancient history because I would like to make clear that in the "battle of the sexes" there are ultimately no offenders and victims, no "good guys and bad guys," because you all have been both. It has been a struggle between the male and the female energies in which these energies became opposites, whereas they originally were complementary to each other. In this day and age both men and women are invited to join forces again and to rediscover the joy and honor of the original dance of female and male.

Essentially the female energy is leading and inspiring while the male energy is serving and protecting. The female energy is the inspiration behind any creation; the male aspect takes care of the manifestation in form and action. Both energies work through every human, through every individual, whether male or female. Whether you are a man or a woman is not really relevant; it is the balance and relationship between both energies within you that counts.

Blockages in female sexuality

I will now speak of energy blockages in the area of sexuality which specifically apply to women or men. In women, it is the area of the first and second chakra (tail bone and umbilicus) that is most battered and hurt as a result of sexual oppression and violence over the centuries. For quite some millennia women have been framed into a subservient role in almost all areas of society and this still goes for many places on earth. With regard to sexuality, this inequality manifested as rape, assault and humiliation on a large scale. As a result of this many women, indeed the collective female soul, have suffered incredibly. There are deep emotional wounds which need time, love and utmost care to heal.

Often the drive for sexual union is felt by women as a longing of the heart or as a spiritual feeling. But when they get physically intimate they may find that they cannot express their sexual energy freely because of energy blockages in the first and second chakra. In those energy centers there are (soul) memories of sexuality that was forced upon them and humiliated them. These experiences were so painful that the woman withdrew her energy, her consciousness from the area of the belly. When this part of the body is now approached again in a sexual way, the muscles instinctively tighten or the emotional body automatically signals resistance. The physical cells are aware of the trauma and do not go along so easily with the invitation to dance. They want to shut off and create a barrier to protect you from more aggression. This reaction is utterly understandable and should always be dealt with in a most respectful way. Using any kind of force to take away the resistance is in a way violating the hurt centers again.

When you have these emotions as a woman, it is very important to become fully aware of them; there may be anger there, resistance or fear with regard to physical intimacy. And all of these emotions are often older than the relationship you are in, older even than this lifetime. There may be very old traumas in those lowest chakras that have caused deep emotional scars.

Specifically I would advise women who recognize this pain to get acquainted with lifetimes in which they were the offender/perpetrator (as opposed to victim). Or if you find it difficult to access previous lifetimes, get in touch with the "energy of the offender or powerful woman" inside you. This may sound very strange but the reason is this. When you have been the victim of sexual violence this has caused a lot of anger in your energy field. There may be anger there from several lifetimes. This anger blocks you and keeps you imprisoned in a feeling of powerlessness and victimhood. To release anger you need understanding. You need to understand why and what for; you need to see the larger picture. When you can imagine yourself as a powerful woman who could be merciless and cruel towards men and feel inside that this is also a part of you, then the anger can dissolve. A more thoroughgoing understanding can arise, an inside knowing that you are part of a larger karmic story in which you played both the role of offender and of victim. It is nearly impossible to release your emotions of pain, powerlessness and victimhood without also looking at the other side of you, the "dark side."

You need not necessarily go back to past lifetimes to recognize this dark part inside you. You can also become more aware of it by watching yourself in your day-to-day life. When you feel this energy (e.g. the will to exert power or hurt others), you can sense that you have not only been the helpless victim of outside circumstances. There is a karmic tie between offender and victim; both roles reflect aspects of yourself.

As soon as you know and accept your dark side, you can look at your own inner wounds in a different way and start to forgive. When there is understanding, anger can dissolve and you can get in touch with the layers of emotions beneath: the sadness, the grief, the pain that is there on many levels, also in the body itself.

It is very important for women to acknowledge the offender aspect in themselves and to work with it. When there is hatred and grudges in you with regard to sexuality, realize that the more hatred and anger you feel, the more you identify with the role of victim and the more you rob yourself of your freedom. Try to feel inside you that in the arena of sexuality a karmic game is being played out in which you have fulfilled both roles, the good guy as well as the bad guy. From there you can get to a place of forgiveness – forgiving yourself as well as someone else. Things happen for a reason. Acts of violence and repression may seem meaningless, but there is always a story behind them. And whenever there is sexual violence involved it leaves deep impressions on all four levels of the human being.

Blockages in male sexuality

With regard to the male experience of sexuality, the blockages that occur are mostly on the level of the heart or the head. At these levels there may be a fear of surrendering, a fear of deep emotional intimacy. Most of the time this fear reaches farther back than you can remember. It relates to the era in which women dominated men. This made the game of sexual attraction, that initially was innocent and spontaneous, threatening. Men learned that it was dangerous to openly show their emotions and open their heart to their partner.

Within men there are deep seated fears about surrendering to their feeling side, and these fears need not necessarily manifest on the physical level. They may participate in the physical act of sex while keeping their feelings separate. So the man may be sexually present at the physical level while his feeling nature is (partially) absent. His emotions are locked away because of his fear to open up and become vulnerable to rejection once again. There are old soul remembrances there of being abandoned and emotionally scarred.

Patience and love

In general the energy blockages are somewhat different in men and women. Therefore it is very important to communicate openly with each other about what you feel and sense when you are together. When you truly trust your partner, you can investigate without shame where your sexual energy gets stuck when you are intimate. This you can do by simply becoming aware, when there is a flow of excitement and intimacy arising between you, to what extent you are allowing yourself to feel and express it. See if you feel stuck or blocked in any part of your body or in any part of your emotions and feelings. Do you feel a warm glow in your heart when you are together? Do you feel a spiritual openness towards the other? Are you prepared to meet the other in his or her totality?

It sounds strange but you are afraid of real intimacy. You all strongly desire a fulfilling relationship. On the streets almost every billboard refers to the ideal of an emotionally and sexually gratifying relationship. But true intimacy frightens you. When someone else comes very close and you are asked to take off all your masks, all kinds of inhibitions arise that you were not aware of. In the moments that they surface try not to judge yourself for it. Instead see it is an opportunity to investigate those inhibitions and blockages within you. No one is free of them. Nearly all people have blockages that prevent them from experiencing sexuality in the full sense that I described in the beginning. That is why I want to ask you all to look at the flow of sexual energy inside you with loving awareness – whether you are alone or in a relationship – and to treat those blockages you find with care and respect. Force is the worst counselor in these matters. Patience and love are vital.

Keep the longing for a true and complete experience of sexuality alive! You need not throw away the baby with the bath water. The desire is sound. The road to a full and joyful experience of sexuality may be long and winding. But along the road you will grow love and compassion for yourself as well as for others, and this is so immensely valuable in your human world.

You are healing an ancient history of struggle between men and women. The male and female energies want to come together again and join in a dance of joy and creativity. Anything that you contribute to this at an individual level has a positive influence on the collective soul of men and women. Your self-love makes the energies of patience and love available for others.

Work, money and creativity
The flow of ease and the flow of enough

Dear friends, it is with joy and affection that I am among you today. I know you so well and it seems to me as if we met each other yesterday. In the realms where I dwell, time is not so important. I recognize you very well although your manifestation, your physical appearance, is different from the times I knew you.

I am Jeshua. I have lived on earth in a human body, as Jesus. I have been a human being among people just like you. Nothing human is foreign to me. It is from this experience with human existence that I come to support you with your own development, with your birth into the New Era. A New Era is on the way. A transformation is going on these days with which all of you feel a strong connection.

I want to tell you something else about myself. On earth I was a human being of flesh and blood and I had formed a channel with the energy of Christ. The Christ energy was flowing outward through me and that was my essential contribution to the earth at that time. But the Christ energy is not mine alone; it belongs to all of you. All of you are planting a seed, bringing a part of that energy here to earth today and in that lies your biggest fulfillment.

However this transformation from the old to the New Era uproots and shakes up many things. The area of work and money is very much involved in this "uprooting," for this is precisely an area in which the old energies are particularly active. You could characterize these as the energies of power and ego.

The old energies have been so strongly active within this field that you may find it quite difficult to have a well-balanced attitude towards work and money issues. In your job, in the organization or company you work for or in the people who are your colleagues, you are confronted with society. Many times you ask yourself: how do I cope with energies that I have no affinity with and yet are surrounding me every day? In this encounter of the old and the new you would like to know how to deal with this friction.

On the basis of the energy centers in your body I would like to elucidate this issue a little more. The aura that belongs to each human being contains seven chakras or energy centers. In the solar plexus which is the third chakra (near the diaphragm or the stomach), the will is located. It is in this center of personal will that power and ambition are seated. In the era of the old energy, the old time human being, people have been living to excess from this center. This has to do with an attitude of being keen on winning, of putting one's own interests first and of fighting at the expense of others. An attitude like this is often born out of fear and a feeling of being lost. It is not my point to pass judgment on these energies. I just want to mention that they are often active from the solar plexus, the third chakra.

One chakra higher we find the center of the heart. The heart connects you with your higher origin, with energy spheres you once dwelt in and from where you bring along ideals that contrast sharply with the energies of power and ego.

Now what happens in the present transformation of consciousness is a passing along of the wheel from the solar plexus to the heart. That doesn't mean that the solar plexus should be abandoned or pushed aside altogether. It is not true that you should "get rid of the ego." It is more a matter of passing along the steering wheel to another level of being and in so doing, founding your life on the energy of the heart. All of you are seeking to achieve this in one way or another, either in your personal life or specifically in the field of work and creativity. All of you feel a kinship with the shift toward the energy of the heart. You all sense that you can live your life with much more joy and tranquility that way.

With regard to the question of how do I deal with ego based energies (inside you and around you), the essential step that is asked of you is to connect from the heart with the energies of the solar plexus (the will and the ego) and to

194

guide them in a loving and affectionate way. It is the connection between the heart and the solar plexus (more generally between the higher and lower seated chakras) that provides you with abundance in the field of work, creativity and money.

Now how do you know whether you are acting from your heart or from fear or ego? I would like to point out two important characteristics of the heart energy which may help you recognize it in your own daily life. The first characteristic is the absence of struggle and the presence of ease and simplicity. I will simply call it *the flow of ease.*

The flow of ease

You are used to struggling and fighting for the things you want. Especially in the area of work there is a lot of competition and ego battle. Often you have to act like someone you are not to get recognition and validation. This opposes the longing of your heart. The heart longs for a much more natural kind of presence. The heart energy does not exert pressure and is very smooth and gentle by nature. The heart energy speaks to you through the intuition. The heart gives gentle pushes and suggestions and will never tell you something that is emotionally charged with fear or pressure.

In your daily life you can clearly notice whether things are going smoothly and finding their natural way or whether you repeatedly encounter resistance to something you are trying to achieve. If the latter is the case it means you are not – or not completely – in alignment with your heart energy. The secret of the heart energy is that it performs miracles not with force, but with ease and tenderness.

Daring to trust your intuition is the most important way to get aligned with the energy flow of the heart which I call "the flow of ease." Acting on your intuition in the context of work and creativity, even if this goes against the culture of your work environment, will create unexpected possibilities and opportunities for you. It will bring you closer to your own divine Self and empower you on the heart level, and it will by itself attract to you places and people who fulfill your heartfelt desires.

When you experience problems at work, when you feel that you are not at the right place in your particular work environment, spend some quiet time alone. Find a moment of stillness in which you let go of all the thoughts and ideas that you have absorbed from your social environment and all the fears and worries that go with it. Try to look at these thoughts and emotions from a deep and quiet spot at the center of your heart. See them for what they are; they are clouds hovering in front of the sun but they are *not* you. Go to that core of sunshine in the your heart and ask your Self what is wise for you to do right now. Connect to your ancient and wise heart, the source of your highest creativity, and ask your intuition to tell you what is the right thing to do at this moment. Do not try to base your actions on outside opinions, on social standards of behavior that especially in the field of work can be overwhelming. The social or collective consciousness in this area is strongly based on fear: fear of losing your job, fear of social failure and fear of poverty. All these fears may overshadow your intuition and yet there is an inner voice that tells you what to do right now. The key is to dare to listen to this voice and you will see it will come up with genuine answers.

When you try to go to that inner core, self doubt may block you and make you dismiss your heartfelt intuitions and inclinations as unrealistic and wrong. Self doubt may prevent you from trusting the spiritual path that is laid out for you. By your spiritual path, I mean the path of experiences that brings you in touch with your highest creative source, the creative energies that want to flow outward through you. These energies are already present. But you can only recognize and manifest them in the outer world by listening to and trusting your own feelings. Your soul speaks to you through your feelings. There are no external warrants or securities. Trust is essential. To accept the direction where your feelings are taking you and to act upon your intuition is to open yourself up to the guidance of your heart and to truly make the shift from ego based consciousness to heart based consciousness.

You have reached the end stage of the domination by the solar plexus. Your soul has entered this incarnation with the intention of releasing this way of being, and you are all highly motivated to express your creativity from the heart. I ask you to trust yourself at this stage and to continue on this path, for you are already bringing into this world a new energy which is of great value. This energy often effects changes without you knowing it; you do more good than you realize. You help birth the New Era by trusting the flow of your heart and daring to follow the flow of ease. Therefore have no doubts and continue on your path.

The energy of the heart is much more quiet and gentle than the competitive and harsh energies that often rule the arena of work. For that reason it takes courage and strength to stay centered in the heart, when you are surrounded by these ego based energies. But I tell you this: following the flow of your heart will ultimately bring you to creative possibilities that are quite real and practical, and it will bring you abundance on the material level. It is an act of faith and courage to entrust yourself to this flow.

I said that I would mention two important characteristics of the energy of the heart. I started with the flow of ease. I would now like to speak about the flow of abundance which I will call *the flow of enough*.

The flow of enough

The energy of the heart is the source of true abundance in your life. Abundance has to do with all areas of your life reaching from the physical, material level to the emotional, social and spiritual level. You are meant to enjoy yourself and to be nurtured on all these levels. At this point I want to address the issue of material abundance in particular, as it is of extra relevance to lightworker souls.

Lightworker souls and spiritually oriented, idealistic people in general tend to condemn money. Money is considered to be sinful by them, to be a lower energy. The reason for this condemnation is that they have come to associate money with power and wealth at the expense of others. Money has practically become synonymous with power. This association is one of the main reasons why the flow of material abundance has become blocked in many of you who read this.

Also lightworker souls who have a great spiritual zest associate money with the base and trivial things of life which need to be transcended. Here many convictions are active which date back to past lives of austerity and abstinence from the material world. These lifetimes were often spent in solitude, aimed solely at spiritual liberation. The energy of these lifetimes still resonates throughout your energy field. It results in a kind of "strictness" that is narrowing you down.

However money is innocent. Money is a flow of energy that actually represents pure potentiality. Money offers opportunities, money is potentiality and there is nothing wrong with that. Nor is it the case that by receiving money you act at the expense of others. With money you are able to create beautiful and good things for others. By receiving it joyfully, you expand the flow of abundance for both yourself and for others. The creative spiral always generates a receiving flow also, so that receiving and giving are balanced out. This is the way of the heart. Therefore do not be afraid to receive money.

It is sad to watch how you, when you truly share your highest gifts and talents with the world, still have reservations about asking and receiving from the world what you want and need for yourself. Many old judgments prevent you from truly standing up for yourself and enjoying the receiving part. But the secret of the universe is balance. The universe knows that you need to be sustained on all levels to express your highest potential in this lifetime. There is nothing sinful about that. When you are truly creative from the heart, you will attract a receiving flow as well and only by allowing it in will you keep the outward flow of creativity alive and vibrant.

You may not be consciously aware of the fact that you are blocking the flow of money in your life or that you have a tacit aversion to money. Take some time to examine your innermost thoughts and emotions about money and you can easily see how they are blocking the flow of abundance in your life. Please realize that you are meant to enjoy life on earth! It is a natural thing to take joy in beautiful things that caress the senses or fill the heart with inspiration. This is your home, your dwelling place for quite some time so please allow yourself to create your material surroundings as you wish them to be. Simply loving the earth and material reality alone will create a flow of abundance. The earth will listen to you for she wants to provide you with everything you need, not just to grow and evolve as a spiritual being but also to simply enjoy life as a human being.

So please consider your attitude toward material abundance at the deepest level and feel how the flow of abundance indeed offers you the possibility to help build a new earth, to realize your dreams on the densest plane of reality. This is not the time to withdraw yourself from society, to meditate by yourself on top of a mountain. It is time for participation. It is time to let your energy flow into this world and freely receive all that comes back to you in return. Do not be afraid to receive abundance. Honoring your own input, receiving enough in exchange for your efforts, is part of being a well-balanced spiritual human being.

I would like to say a little more about the word "enough." I told you that the energy of the heart is characterized first by the *flow of ease*. When things succeed easily and all you need appears spontaneously on your path, it is a sign that you are going with the flow of your heart. The second energy flow I distinguished is the *flow of enough*. *Enough* means everything that I need right now to be a fulfilled human angel is available to me. To live in the flow of enough means that you feel satisfied with and thankful for what you have. You feel nurtured by what surrounds you on the material, emotional, mental and spiritual level. That is abundance. That is *having enough.*

Experiencing the flow of enough means that you enjoy what you have in the Now. All of you know that to experience abundance is a subjective state of mind. It depends on the circumstances. The amount of material abundance that you have does not necessarily relate to the amount of pleasure you experience. Experiencing abundance is not about being rich; it is about experiencing riches in all that surrounds you. You have to discover for yourself the kind of material abundance that satisfies and fulfills you. For some people this could mean living on their own in a secluded hut where they can enjoy nature to the full. For others it implies a luxurious place in town where they enjoy the hustle and bustle of the city. There is no judgment on this from our side, from God or from Spirit.

You need to find out what enough means for you. The key is to find the flow that makes *you* happy, that gives *you* the feeling that you are living life to the fullest. That is the flow of enough. You can recognise it not by the amount of material goods you possess but by the sense of joy and fulfillment you have in your everyday life. *Enough is a feeling*, not a thing.

You can be out of tune with this flow in two ways. You can want "more than enough" or you can want "less than enough." If you want "more than enough" you crave material wealth that you do not really need or are capable of truly enjoying. Too many possessions make life complicated and actually take away some of your joy. Joy thrives on a good and simple life. When you seek to have more than enough you often do it to feel a safeguard for the future. You can get addicted to the feeling of having money just for the security of it. But that is not to experience abundance in the Now. It is to experience lack in the midst of material wealth! To really be in the flow of enough, you need to let go of fear and dare to enjoy yourself with what there is. This very enjoyment will attract more of the same into your life; it will maintain the flow of enough. If you start thinking that you need more material security, however, you go into fear whereas what you need is more trust and less fear.

If you settle for "less than enough" you are also stuck in fear but here it is the fear of truly opening yourself up to the world, expressing yourself and receiving back from it as well. You are afraid to live life to the fullest. You might think you are not worthy of it, not capable of it or that it is sinful to be all that you are and to receive full recognition for that. What you need is to feel your natural beauty and innocence. You are meant to express yourself and to be loved for who you are. The world becomes a more beautiful and radiant place if you share the gift of your soul with it, and it wants to bless you with enough in return. The universe is geared to abundance and you can be a part of that flow if you open up to your real nature which is pure and unconditional love.

"Enough" is the natural state of being. You are all here to experience enough; the flow of enough is available to all of you. It is quite meaningless to settle for less. It is not true that you will improve yourself spiritually by abstinence or self-imposed poverty. More likely you will develop feelings of bitterness or hostility because of it. Please do not try to seek some kind of spiritual justification for your lack of abundance. You are all here to enjoy life to the fullest, to let your creative energy flow into the world and to receive joy, satisfaction and material abundance in return.

Creating the flow of enough

When you feel yourself to be out of the flow of enough, take a look at your present living circumstances and interpret this as an energy message to yourself. "This is how I create reality now." Do not judge yourself or anyone else for it. Just take note of it.

Then feel the energy of your present environment – whether it is your house, your social life or your work – and compare this with what you truly long for in your heart. Take some time to really feel what you want. Do not merely content yourself with a vague sense of dissatisfaction or unrest but clearly define to yourself what you want in your life.

In doing this you become aware of "lack" of that which is not there. Take note of the pain in you because of this, but do not dwell on the sense of lack or dissatisfaction. This is not an exercise to make you feel bad. Rather focus on the longings you have and realize deeply that this is what your soul wants for you. Be convinced that these longings point in the direction of what your soul has planned to do in this lifetime. You will be supported by the universe to make it come true.

Your focused, silent and open awareness of these heartfelt desires is enough to make the changes happen. Realizing who you are is the biggest magnet to change in your everyday life. It is not necessary or even useful to push for change on the material level. The key is to feel deeply (but not emotionally) what you are longing for and to then leave it in the hands of your heart. Just release and trust.

Things will start to change in your life. Perhaps you will first start to look more closely at some of your deeply ingrained habits in the area of thinking, feeling and reacting to people. Then relationships or jobs that do not serve your true goals may break apart and fall away. You can trust that you will get into a flow that will slowly but certainly bring you to your goal. Pay attention to the things that happen in your life. The things people say or do to you often contain an underlying message that tells you where you stand in relation to your goal.

All that you need on the physical level to realize your heartfelt desires will appear in your life in an effortless way, out of the blue. It will enter your life with ease and elegance. It may seem miraculous and at the same time feel perfectly appropriate. It is not your grasping, trying, pushing and forcing that will get it to you but your silent awareness of your truest needs, your honesty to face up to them and your courage to trust and let go. Honoring the longings of your heart with such focus and surrender will bring the reality of enough to you.

Illness and health

Dear friends, I welcome you warm-heartedly and send you all my love. I love you all so dearly. My love for you is not only universal in nature but it also has a personal touch, for I have known many of you when I was here on earth among you.

I am Jeshua. I have lived on earth as Jesus and I have been among people to testify to the love which is available to all of us from the Source that lies within ourselves. Now the time has come for you to take over the torch. You are the seeds that blossom today. This is the meaning of the rebirth of Christ. I, the one man who once lived on earth, am not the one who is bound to return; instead the universal power of the Christ energy is now being birthed within you. I am so pleased to support you in this process by being with you in this way.

At the beginning of this session, Pamela and Gerrit asked me which subjects I would like to address and I told them: "It does not matter, I just want to be with them." I simply want to touch you with my energy and to remind you of your own greatness. In extending my energy to you, my sole purpose is that you feel the flame of clarity within, the flame of your truth. That is the essence of the Christ energy. I have been an early carrier of this flame but now it is time for you to carry on the torch. It is important to acknowledge who you are on the inside. You carry this torch with you and you must realize that the time has come to show it to the world, for the world is waiting for it. This is a time of transformation, a time of great changes which show many faces, both dark and light. The time is ready for people who have a wider view, who can watch all manifestations of dark and light from a calm and peaceful state of mind and who are able to be present in love, without judgment.

Today I will talk about illness and health. But remember: basically it is my concern to let you feel that I am here, to let you feel that you are equal to me and that I am equal to you. We are one, we are carriers of a particular Light energy and we have been working for a long time, during many lifetimes, to ground this energy and anchor it to the earth. That is your job. That is your mission.

The time has come to let go of me as someone you look up to. I am a brother and a friend to you, not a master you should follow. I want to surround you with the energies of love and truth. That is all I can do. Now it is your turn to stand up for yourself and to let the Light of your torches shine.

Illness and health – this is a subject that comes up in the lives of all people sooner or later. First I would like to say something about what illness actually is. *All diseases have a spiritual origin.* I will explain this by drawing a distinction among the different bodies you have. In addition to the physical body visible to all of you, you also possess an emotional body, a mental body and something you may call a spiritual body.

Illness mainly starts in the emotional body. It is from here that certain blockages settle themselves in the physical body on the material level. Often beliefs from the mental body contribute to the development of emotional blockages and thus to the manifestation of illness. I am talking of deeply ingrained beliefs or habits of thinking. Often these are beliefs about what is right and wrong about yourself.

Judgments may literally create a blockage in your emotional energy system. At those places where the blockages arise where the emotional energy is not allowed to flow freely, something of a dark energy becomes visible in the aura. This energy may settle down in the body. It need not necessarily be so, for this process takes quite some time and there is enough opportunity to turn things into balance emotionally, before a disease displays itself.

Generally your emotions tell you when your energy is not flowing, and when you turn your attention to their message and honor it, the blockage gets released. For instance you may feel upset or angry every time you have to do a particular thing and if you look more closely at those emotions, they will tell you that you are forcing yourself to do things that do not truly affirm who you are and who you want to be. However if you systematically ignore your anger and force yourself to do things you truly don't feel good about, then the emotion goes underground, so to speak. It removes itself from your awareness and it expresses itself in your physical body. The repressed emotion is an energy that wants to be heard by you. When it expresses itself through the body it will manifest as a physical complaint.

Generally a physical complaint or illness points at an emotion inside you that you are largely unaware of. The physical symptom makes it visible to you on another level and in this way actually helps you get in touch with the blockage. In this way physical symptoms or pain are the language of the soul. The soul longs for full communication among all of its parts. The soul feels happy when there is a free flow of energy and a continuous renewal of all aspects of itself. Blockages prevent the energy from flowing freely and that depresses the soul.

Illness thus has the function of an indicator: it shows you where you are in need of healing. Although illness seems to be negative in the sense that you are bothered by all kinds of symptoms and pains, the key is to interpret illness as a message or a signpost. In doing so it becomes easier to cooperate with the disease instead of resisting it.

The soul has many ways to communicate to you. The soul's favorite way is to speak to you through your intuition: quiet feeling tones, hunches, soft whispers of the heart. If it cannot reach you in that way, you will be alerted by your emotions. The emotions speak a louder language. They clearly show you that you have to look within and find out what is igniting that emotional response. Whenever you are strongly affected emotionally you need to find out why and what it means to you. If you become silent and listen carefully, the soul will tell you. If you resist or deny your emotions the soul will speak to you through your body. The body is an intelligent being, highly responsive to not just the material things (like food and liquids) you take in but to the emotions, feelings and thoughts you have. *The body is meant to be a communicator.* It is not a mere vessel to dwell in. It has an intelligent function to play in helping the soul express and know itself in matter.

How can you learn to understand the language of your soul if it is expressed through the body as an illness? At the moment the disease manifests itself it may not be clear what message is conveyed by it to you. In fact you have denied the emotion it represents consistently for a long time, so it is by definition not obvious what your illness has to tell you. Understanding the spiritual meaning of the illness is *a process.* It is a quest, an inner journey on which you gradually restore the communication process.

To embark upon this journey, you first have to *accept your illness.* The initial reaction to illness is often one of denial or resistance. You would prefer the disease to disappear as soon as possible because it frightens you. You are scared of failure, decline, imperfection and ultimately death. The panic that seizes you when you are confronted with physical failure or illness prevents you from opening up to a broader perspective on illness. You could consider illness in another light. You might experience it as a messenger of change, as an invitation to return to something precious that you have lost.

To comprehend and cooperate with the "signpost function" of illness, it is very important to say *yes* to the symptoms and pains which display themselves in your body. In saying *yes,* in accepting the state of your physical body and in being willing to listen to the language of your soul through it, you have actually solved half the problem. The real problem is not the disease itself but that which it represents, the underlying blockage(s). The disease buttonholes you so to speak and forces you to look at the underlying blockage. In turning to the disease and saying *yes* with your heart and soul, you will already have solved part of the blockage without even knowing precisely what the disease wants to tell you. Part of the communication is being restored just by your willingness, your patience and determination to take this inner journey upon you.

However, to say yes and embrace the illness is not easy for you. You may find yourself resisting it, being angry or desperate about it and therefore not listening to what the malfunction is already telling you. Frequently you get specific clues. For instance the body's inabilities indicate that you must let go of certain obligations, spend more quiet time by yourself, be less active and more attentive to your needs. Although you may not yet know how to interpret your physical situation from a spiritual level, quite often the behavior that the ailment forces upon you is a big clue. By limiting yourself in certain areas, it is putting a spotlight on things that were in the dark before. How is it with your ability to be patient and gentle with yourself? Can you really take good care of your physical *and emotional* needs? Illness always brings up these questions, and to confront and accept the emotions they arouse is part of the healing process.

To really start the healing process you have to say yes to it all: the pain, the discomfort, the anxiety, the insecurity and the anger. You have to look it in the eye, be friendly with it and reach out your hands to it. It is coming to you for healing. It is not something you have to get out of the way as fast as possible. It is not a coincidence that it has entered your life now.

If you ignore your body's language and you keep resisting the disease, it is very difficult to get through to the spiritual essence and meaning of the disease. There is too much anger and fear surrounding it. You only achieve true inner freedom in coming face to face with your disease, with your pain and discomfort and also with your feelings of fear and disgust. Embrace them and then ask them quietly and with an open consciousness: what do you want to tell me?

In your society it is not self evident to be intimate with your own body. Talking to your body like a being that deserves love and respect is not considered to be natural. You are dished up many idealized images in your society about what your body should look like, what fitness and health imply and what you should or should not eat and drink. There are all kinds of rules and standards about what a long and healthy life is like.

But all these idealized pictures bear no relationship to the path of the soul. The path of the soul is highly individual. Therefore to find the truth about any illness, ailment or distress that you suffer in your body, you need to tune into yourself in a very intimate way, leaving behind all these general, often artificial standards and rules. You are asked to release all these outside standards and to search for your own truth deep within.

This is a great challenge to you, for the fear and panic that seize you in the case of an illness make you look too quickly to authorities outside yourself. You reach out to external authorities for advice and comfort. This may be a medical doctor or an expert in alternative treatment; basically it makes no difference. The key is that out of fear, you tend to give up your own responsibility and partially hand it over to somebody else.

Of course there is nothing wrong with listening to an expert's advice and quite often this is a very sensible thing to do. But always you need to take this knowledge inside you and weigh it in your own heart. Feel whether the advice resonates with you or not. Only you are the true creator of your life, the master of your own body. Only you yourself know what is best for your own body. In the deepest sense of the word, you are the creator of your own body.

Since illness represents a stuck emotion that is partly beyond the scope of your consciousness, it is not always easy to understand what the disease or the symptom represents. Sometimes it seems very hard to find out what the soul is trying to tell you by a specific disease. At this point you need to go inside and examine yourself thoroughly, in the sense of gradually becoming aware of the kind of energy that manifests itself in the disease and what it is trying to tell you.

Regaining intimacy with your own body requires practice; it is not self evident. Do not give up on it too easily. When you are dealing with persistent complaints, try to examine them once again. Take a moment to relax yourself and then travel with a neutral awareness to the places in your body where the illness is expressing itself. Ask the pain or the disease to take the shape of a living being so that you can talk to it. Ask it to appear as an animal, a child or a human being. Or ask it to appear as a guide, in whatever shape. Use your imagination! The imagination is a precious instrument to discover the deepest stirrings of your soul.

If you do so and when you notice that your body answers – with images or feelings – you will experience joy. You will feel happiness about the regained intimacy. The body speaks to you and its role as a communicator is restored! This is a breakthrough. As soon as you realize that you are able to know your body from the inside and that you are the only one who can do this for yourself, you will feel more confident. This self confidence makes it easier for you to feel what the disease is trying to tell you. It prevents you from brushing aside the answers that you receive from your inner self because they do not fit in with general ideas from the outside world. Intimacy with the body is very precious in all circumstances but particularly when the body is ill or in distress.

The way to let your body talk is love. You will not encourage communication with your body if you try to remove the disease by ardently repeating healing affirmations or visualizations to yourself. That still is form of struggle or resistance. The key is that you come to understand the meaning of the sick part of your body. If you understand this, things will be transformed and emotional blocks can be removed. This is how the healing process works – not fighting the disease, one way or another, but accepting it like a friend who wants to show you the right direction. This is difficult to understand, for illness frightens and distresses you. However accepting and understanding your illness is the only way to true healing. Illness wants to take you back home.

Chronic and terminal illness

The purpose of illness is to obtain a better and deeper understanding of yourself. Once you do this and go along with the inner healing process, physical recovery is often the result. However it does not always work this way. Some diseases do not disappear even when it seems you have gone down to the root of the underlying emotional blockage. This is the case with chronic diseases.

In the case of a chronic disease there are persistent physical problems that keep recurring. Especially during vulnerable periods in which you more or less lose touch with your inner self, the symptoms recur sometimes even in an increasing degree. This can be quite demoralizing. Therefore it is important to consider the disease from a broader perspective.

People with a chronic disease undertake quite an arduous task. On the soul level, they have agreed to confront the fears that come up in the context of their illness and to confront idealized pictures of how someone should perform in life. To take up this challenge shows great courage.

It often happens that a soul chooses a chronic disease to work out a specific issue in a highly focused way. The disease throws you back on particular emotions each time. There is an emotional pattern that accompanies the illness. To deal with these emotions time and again is quite a heavy task but it bears many fruits for the soul.

Quite often these lives have a great profundity and an inner richness that is not always noticeable to others. Therefore it is not supportive to constantly strive or hope for an improvement of the medical condition. The fact is that the disease often proceeds in a spiral movement, helping you grow on the inner level in circular movements upwards, although apparently you relapse into the same physical symptoms each time. On the spiritual level, you do not fall back but you reach ever greater depths in dealing with emotions that possibly have been overlooked by you in the past, even in past lives.

This also applies to hereditary or congenital physical defects. In this respect you sometimes speak of karma but I am careful with this concept, as you have a tendency to associate karma with crime and punishment. This is not how it works. The soul has the sincere desire to know itself to the fullest and to be free. This is its deepest desire. Starting from this ardent wish the soul sometimes undertakes ailments, diseases and physical defects which help it reach its aim. It is certainly not a question of paying off your debts. It is a deep intent to be set free and sometimes the best way to get there is to experience extremely difficult circumstances within your own body. For this intention we can only have the greatest respect, especially in your society where inhuman ideal images are cherished as to how to be functional, useful, beautiful and successful. These idealistic ideas make it even more difficult to live your life with a handicap and to nevertheless experience it as meaningful and joyful.

Finally I want to say something about incurable terminal diseases. Sometimes it will be obvious that someone will not survive a disease anymore. The body gradually succumbs to the disease. The "earthly frame" does not persist. At that moment what does the soul that finds itself within the body do? As long as you keep resisting the disease, you cannot get in touch with your soul and your inner knowing that tells you that it is time to say goodbye. Sometimes you sense in advance that you have to leave, but the idea strikes you with such horror and sorrow that you keep on fighting. You are eager to try another treatment or wait for that new medicine to be launched.

This is quite understandable and I certainly do not want to condemn this attitude, but you are hurting yourself in a terrible way. If you let go and allow death to come closer, you will notice that death is not an opponent but instead is a friend. Death releases you from the struggle.

If you go along with what death wants to tell you, you will pass through several stages before the actual process of dying takes place. These stages have to do with a gradual release of all earthly things – of your beloved, of your earthly surroundings, of your senses with which you observe everything around you. This is a beautiful, natural process.

It would be a pity to overshadow this process by an attitude of battle in which you try to hold on to life at any expense. Often by then the body has already become so fragile that life is not worth living anymore. Let it go. Death is a liberator who is there to serve you. Death is not your enemy. Death brings you new life.

When you are with someone who is incurably ill and when you feel that person knows that they are going to die, try to talk about it softly and carefully. It is a relief to the person who is passing over. The dearest and most precious thing you can do for a dying person is to sit next to them and hold their hand. There is nothing else you need to know or to be able to do in accompanying a dying person.

Terminal care is very important in your society. One day all of you will face this within your own family or your circle of friends. Simply be present with a dying person and feel the journey that is arriving. Feel the mighty, powerful moment in which the soul leaves the body and returns to the other realms, to its home.

Do not consider a disease that leads to death as an enemy who you will lose to in the end. It is not a battle. Quite frequently death comes to release you from even more pain and misery. You are certainly not a loser. You will simply continue your path in another way.

Sometimes there are particular issues you would have liked to live through or overcome during this life and these issues cannot be finished. This may distress you and not just you but those who stay behind as well. Nevertheless I ask you to leave this in peace, for there is a deeper wisdom at work that is guiding you and will bring you and your loved ones together in new and better circumstances. One day you will be together again and will celebrate life.

Today my biggest plea with regard to illness is to really embrace your illness. Surround the illness with love and awareness and let it lead you into a deeper understanding of yourself. Entrust yourself to the illness and allow yourself to enter into a more profound communication with yourself. Surrender does not mean to be passive or bitter about your illness but to cooperate with it in an active way, like a friend.

I embrace you all with my love and I ask you to feel my presence today, the presence of the Christ energy. Feel the love available to all of you in sickness and in health. There is so much love everywhere around you and you can feel it as soon as you let go of your judgments. You have so many judgments about what you do and don't deserve, about what you are doing right and what you are doing wrong, about all the things you still have to do and achieve. Let it go. Love is present here and now for all of you.

The Gatekeepers

Dear friends, today I am here with joy and pleasure and I extend a warm welcome to every one of you. Our meeting makes a difference. It is not only a lecture in which you listen to words but my presence here which merges with yours creates an energy space which helps anchor light in the earth.

You are the gatekeepers to the light. You are the ones on earth who open the gate to more light, the light of the New Era. The old world is gradually passing away. Old structures of power and ego based consciousness have lost their strength and will gradually sink to the bottom of the ocean. A new society, a new state of *being* arises which is based on love and on the values of the heart.

You are all so much a part of this transformation. Sometimes you do not realize enough how closely you are associated with this transformation process. Also your contribution is different from what you often think it is. During this transition from the old to the new it is you yourself, your own energy body, that is changing. In addition to the physical body you dwell in, you are also a compilation of energy, partly perceptible and partly imperceptible. You are all walking sources of energy. Each of you individually radiates a certain vibration, an energy field which has its effect on the environment, often without you being aware of it. It is this radiation or energy field which is the determining factor in everything that happens around you, in all the things you attract into your life. You may also call it "a state of being." It is this very state of being which enables the earth changes to take place. For if many groups or individuals change and refine their energy field, this will attract another energetic reality to earth. This is the global transition which is taking place now and which starts in the individual.

Of course there are many realms around the earth – astral and spiritual realms – which are willing to help you realize this transformation, this enlightenment. But *you* are the gatekeepers. You are the ones on earth who open the gate to the light. If this gate does not open, the light cannot be embedded in the earth. Therefore it is so important to believe in yourself, to know and to feel inside that you are doing exactly the job for which you came to earth.

All of you are working on the inner level to bring about a spiritual transformation in your being. And this is the very thing you came for: the inner work of raising your vibration in a world that does not always comply with and sometimes resists your purest intentions. You are the lightworkers, you are the pioneers of a New Era. From love and harmony you will give birth to the New Era in your own heart. In this way, by doing the inner work you will attract a material reality that is far more beautiful and caring than it has been for many ages.

The point is not so much what you do in your daily life or which profession you have. Whether you are a carpenter or a therapist, a homemaker or a professor, it makes no difference. What really matters is your "state of being," the energy that you send forth, the energy that you *are*. It is not what you *do* but who you *are* that is the source of transformation.

Now I would like to ask you to feel the energy here in this room for a moment, to feel the collective energy of all of us together. I can only be here *through you*. It is when you accept me in your hearts that my energy can flow into you and out through you here on earth. Whenever you open up your heart to me, I come in and let my light shine. But *you* are the ones who open the gate and I thank you for that. You are doing the job you came to do here. The earth is changing. From the ashes of the old times a new world will arise.

I would like to say something about how this New Era feels inside. I do not so much want to consider the external symptoms but the inner signs. There is a big transformation going on in your emotional body. The emotional body is very sensitive to fear, to anger and aggression and to all strong sentiments which easily pull you out of your center. You are all working on the refinement of your emotional body. You are doing this by a process of internalization: taking responsibility for the emotions you feel, examining them and following them back to their source(s). In this process of internalization you do not search for the cause(s) of your problems in the outside world anymore but you look for them within yourself. Thus you take responsibility for your own energy and that is a big step forward. As soon as you take responsibility for everything that exists inside you, you can become aware of blocked emotions and transform them. This is the very thing you are working on at this time.

In the New Era the emotional body will settle down. You will live in a much more intuitive way than you are used to. Your environment will also comply with this intuitive way of living. There will be peace and quiet in your heart. Do you feel how much you are longing for this? I feel and see how you are yearning for a state of awareness in which the energy between you and others can run freely, in which you can openly show your love, in which you can rely on the safety of the world and the people around you. You long for that state of awareness in which you know that all is well and you can be just who you are.

It is a sense of freedom and safety that you long for. And I tell you once again that this energy is completely available to you. But *you* are the ones who must open the gate to accept that divine energy into your soul. I and many others in the beyond are right next to you to help and support you. I ask you here and now to feel my energy, to feel that my energy is available to all of you. You are really working on a new birth. Feel the silence in your heart, feel the inner space that allows you to release the old energies and make way for the new. The freedom which you are all craving is near.

Just before the new arrives there is always a difficult stage: the death struggle of the old. Right before dawn is the darkest hour when all the old fears come to the surface, all the grief and anger which you have accumulated during your life and the many lives before when there was darkness on earth. All this comes to the surface in order to be integrated. Do not let yourself be deceived by appearances. It is a good sign, a sign of progress, when all this negative energy enters your consciousness. It means that you are strong enough to pass the test.

You are all working on the completion of a cycle of lives that has been dominated by an inner struggle between light and dark, between self-awareness and the illusions of power, fear and ignorance. An appeal is made to all of you to look into the depths of your soul and to rediscover the light, the flame of divine light in there.

Now I would like to point out three pitfalls which you may encounter in releasing the old. They all have to do with the emotional body and they also are deeply connected to the fact that you are a lightworker.

1. Spiritual anger

The first obstacle is anger. Here I am talking about a type of anger that is actually motivated by a longing for harmony and justice. It is what you might call spiritual anger. I will explain the origin of it.

When you started your cycle of lives on earth you all had an inspiration. This inspiration is strongly connected to the Christ energy. My coming to the earth, the coming of Jeshua (or Jesus) was a beacon to you, a source of inspiration. In me you recognized an energy which you all have inside. In former times you all had made the decision to anchor this energy on earth. But in the cycle of lives in which you tried to do so you experienced a lot of resistance. And this has caused harm to the emotional body. The emotional body is nothing else than the child within you. Your inner child is the lively, free part of yourself which spontaneously acts and reacts from its emotions. This child has suffered a lot during the lifetimes in which you sought to accomplish your inner mission of seeding the Christ energy on earth.

A part of you is always cosmically inspired and from the level of your higher self or soul, you know and feel the meaning of all that happens to you. You can see things from a perspective of light and knowledge. But there is another part to you which is your earthly personality. This is *the inner child* or your ego; it is your humanness, however you may call it. On this level of you, there can be a lot of fear and lack of understanding about what is happening to you, even if your soul knows that "it is all right" and that it serves a higher purpose.

During your lifetimes on earth you were often inspired to plant seeds of light in the form of new ideas or attitudes, but you were frequently misunderstood

216

by your environment. You were rejected, neglected or even annihilated. From these experiences of being unwelcome, much emotional trauma resulted. The child within you did not understand why it had deserved disapproval. Your soul did understand but your earthly self, your emotional body, had to deal with deeply traumatic experiences that arose out of persecution, violence and disapproval. All of you carry these traumas within you as scars on your soul.

You have all come to earth to bring light into this reality, starting from a past history which is quite complicated. (For the whole story see the Lightworker Series, in the first part of this book). I just need to mention that there was a type of personal karma involved when you decided to start your cycle of lives on earth. There have been times in which you yourselves were immersed in darkness, living to gain power and control over the earth souls, among others. Your mission on earth was to make up for these former lives, to bring back love and justice to humanity.

While this inspiration, this torch of light, was burning strongly in your hearts there was at the same time a lack of understanding in the inner child part of yourself. And therefore such a thing as spiritual anger arose. The child part inside you had no understanding of your own karmic contribution to the darkness and projected the evil outside of itself. The child part within you wanted to fight for the good and the just out of emotional motives. The child part inside you had little tolerance for the resistance and slowness of earth reality and it was impatient. Starting from this child part, spiritual anger was born.

Spiritual anger means that you can be immensely affected by the evil of the world, by the suffering of innocent people, by the destruction of the earth, by the wrecking of the plants, the trees and the animal world. All these things – political and social inequality, the apparently unnecessary dying of so many children, the wars, the violence – anger you. These are matters which affect you deeply and which can stir up anger inside you and so you feel powerless.

It is characteristic of lightworkers that they let themselves be carried away by this anger and that they go beyond their limits in this regard. They lose themselves in their desire to change and improve the world. This can be a passion to change things on the political or social level or it may emerge as a desire to help people on a personal level, as a profession or in your private life.

The desire to help and change things often contains a form of spiritual anger although this may not be noticeable. After all you seem to simply "want the best" for someone else or for society. But surely there is anger inside you when you feel inclined to force somebody – no matter how subtly – to change their behavior or their emotions. Often you do not notice that the time is not yet ripe for it.

Each time when you feel an intense indignation or an enormous passion to change things or when you have feelings of powerlessness and anger towards things as they are, you are in the pitfall of spiritual anger. You want too much at once. You are heedless of reality as it is for you are seized by an emotion, the emotion of anger. I ask you to be aware of this and to let it go, for this kind of inspiration that is charged with anger takes you away from your center. It will not offer you the true inspiration, the peace and quiet in your emotional body that help you embody your light on earth.

You achieve the state of truly embodying your light on earth by being entirely centered in your own being, in a pure and calm state of mind. In this state you can feel that you are *in* the world but not *of* it. Being of the world means that you attach value to everything you observe with your senses: violence, war, illness, destruction. If you regard these with your physical senses only you can easily get angry. Therefore we ask you to take a step backwards and to feel inwardly what spiritual dynamics are taking place in the things that upset you.

There is a secret meaning in suffering. Each soul, each living being on earth is here to unfold itself, to express itself and to learn more about what it is to be human and spirit at the same time. Each soul proceeds according to its own path of development. And you are asked to respect this, to take a step backwards and to concentrate entirely on yourself, on your own light. The energy, the truth, the vibration that you radiate as a result invites people or animals or plants to come into your energy field and experience a healing vibration. This is the work you came for. There is no need for you to stand on the barricades. There is no need for you to fight for this.

Your real spiritual work is not a *doing* but a *being*. When your spiritual energy is in balance, the healing energy you send forth to others flows easily and effortlessly, without physical or mental exertion. It feels light and smooth, not exhausting to you. Things and people show up spontaneously on your path and turn to you for healing.

Each time you lock yourself in indignation and anger, even if it concerns injustice or suffering that you find unbearable to watch, I ask you to step backwards and move into the center of yourself. Enter the silence and accept that things are as they are. Accept that everything completes its own cycle and has its own development, including the people who are dearest to you. Set them free too. It is enough *to be* there for them, nothing more and nothing less.

2. Spiritual depression

A second pitfall I would like to address is depression or melancholy. I have just described in broad outline a history in which you all as lightworkers have fallen prey to resistance, persecution and violence. This has left scars on your soul. It may have hurt you so deeply that you have lost the courage to let your light shine once more into this world. You may frequently feel depressed and life may seem meaningless to you. You may feel that you are unwelcome in this world, that you do not fit in with your kind of energy. You feel that you are different.

Feelings of depression or gloominess result from a lack of self confidence. On the one hand you may know very well that you carry a spiritual light within, that you are a sensitive, compassionate and wise person. But on the other hand there is a wounded child inside you who wants recognition and appreciation from the outside world. There is a part of you that craves external attention and safety. But you never seem to get enough of this or you cannot find the sort of recognition you really seek because you are different. Often your environment does not recognize the real you and therefore cannot acknowledge and nourish you.

Your wounded, inner child will never be healed by something from the outside but only by yourself, your own power and wisdom. It is in taking care of your own pain and sorrow and in having faith in yourself at times when no one else has it that you really achieve self confidence. Once you have opened up this source of power you will attract a physical and social environment which supports you and your deepest aspirations.

Everyone who suffers from spiritual melancholy or depression experiences a strong desire to transcend earthly reality and return to a realm of harmony and light, in which peace and safety prevail. To all of you I ask, I pray to your souls to trust and stand firm in your inner light again. The light that provides love and security is available to you here and now. It is burning in your own heart and it is only asking you to focus your attention upon it again. We in the beyond are eager to lighten your burden but no one can help you as long as you do not believe in your own light and kindle it yourself.

It is extremely important not to let yourself be bogged down by feelings of despondency or depression. This is a dangerous pitfall in which you could lose your way completely because you lose touch with who you really are: the angel, the creature of light who dwells within you. During moments of depression or nostalgia, it can be helpful to be quiet and merely breathe. Be aware of the movement of breathing throughout your body and with each inhalation and exhalation you can say out loud or softly within: "I am who I am. I am good as I am."

I surround you with my light. Once you have slightly opened the gate to more self confidence, to a feeling of self respect that really stems entirely from your inner self, the light will shine inside: the light of our own Greater Self, the light of the Christ energy and the light of all the helpers, guides and angels who support and love you from the realms around the earth.

The time of transformation has arrived. Right now when the time is difficult I ask you to continue with heads held high and to focus on the horizon of the New Era. A reality of harmony and love is waiting for you; it is your inheritance and many of you will taste this even in this lifetime. The key is to have faith in yourself and to trust that you will be given all that you need. Do not fear the dark, for the light inside you is stronger. Your light will never be defeated. The reality of light is waiting in love and patience until you extend your hand and open the gate.

3. Fear of your own strength

Finally I want to mention another obstacle that causes a lot of commotion in your emotional body. I am still talking here about energies which restrain you from achieving inner peace and clarity. It may be anger, it may be depression but it may also be fear and this is the third obstacle.

Fear has mainly to do with a lack of trust in your own inspirations, feelings and intuitions. If you doubt your own feelings, you worry a lot and you invoke a whole series of emotions which take you further and further away from your center. When you are full of fear your intuition is blocked. The intellect and the emotions gain the upper hand and subsequently create a panic-stricken and chaotic situation. The intellect and the emotions need the intuition, the heart as a foundation. Only then can they serve you in a useful way.

If you leave out the heart, the intellect will work overtime and the emotions will not have a moment's peace. Then fear may get a grip on you and manifest itself in all kinds of situations. You may doubt your ability to do the things you are normally capable of doing. You may start to question the self-evident and make a problem out of everything. There is a kind of nervousness inside you which makes it impossible to be with yourself in a quiet and peaceful way.

The key here is to set yourself free from all the worrying and to go back to your heart, to your feelings. What do you really feel underneath all those restless thoughts and confused emotions? In breathing calmly in your belly you are able to go back to your foundation. Then you may feel a relief inside, a point of silence which is beyond your thoughts and emotions. You may then experience the thoughts and emotions that you have as a cloud surrounding you, a cloud that you can focus your attention on or not. You will then have recovered your sense of freedom, your *ability to choose* a certain thought or emotion.

If you believe that your thoughts are *true* or your emotions are *true*, you will be entirely absorbed by them and you will keep on following the track of these thoughts and emotions. But it is possible to step backwards and say: "Stop, I leave these thoughts and emotions for what they are and I am going back. I am going more deeply into myself and I will feel what is really going on, why I am harboring these thoughts and emotions now." As soon as you take that step backwards you will rediscover your own strength. Your self confidence will again flow freely. The dark clouds will dissolve and peace and clarity will return. This step must be repeated frequently since the intuitive nature, the living from the heart has not yet become self-evident to you. Therefore you experience a lot of fear.

You are releasing old certainties. No more do you rely unconditionally on what your father and mother told you, on what your teachers taught or on the rules your superiors prescribe to you. You do not blindly trust the results of the intellect or of science anymore. And you also know how unstable your emotions can be and that they are not a measure of truth either. Because you have released all these certainties – and that is a sign of strength – fears may turn up and you may feel like you're drifting around by yourself on a rough ocean. However it is exactly this situation that really forces you to go inside and to feel from deep within, from your own unique foundation: "Who am I? What is my position in this world? I do not let myself be guided by the external world but only by my own inner compass." It is this very compass through which you will enter the New Earth.

Every time you make contact with this inner center and take a step backwards you will find a renewed clarity within your soul. From there you can watch your emotions without being absorbed by them. You can watch your anger and send it love. You can observe your depression and lend yourself a helping hand. You can look at your fear and send it the energy of deliverance.

You are your own Messiah.

There is no Messiah outside of you. There are thousands of Messiahs willing to reach out to you, but only *you* can open the gate of your heart and accept the light. This is basically what the coming of the New Era is about: you opening up your hearts. You are the ones who actually live on earth, we are the helpers. You are the ones who take the action and for that we can only show the deepest respect. We are always available to you to let you share in our love and our light.

You are brave, you are courageous. You are the warriors of the New Era. I ask you to believe in yourself and your mission. And every time when you feel overwhelmed by heavy emotions or by dark thoughts, take a moment's rest and connect to your inner self, the center of silence within. That is the anchor of the New Era. The anchor has been dropped already. Peace already exists in your heart. The only thing you need to do now is to return to it, time after time, to keep anchoring yourself once more to that focus of peace and clarity.

Do not get stuck in drama and commotion. Emotional turmoil is not a friend of truth. But do rely on the quiet, peaceful and clear voice of your heart and be aware that you are not alone. We stay next to you with every single step you take on this path. I love you and I ask you to accept my energies of love among you. It is my ardent wish to serve you at this historical moment and to support you on your sometimes laborious way to the light.

Accept my love.

Relationships in the new era

Dear friends, with much joy and happiness I am with you today. My energy flows among you and as you can feel, this is not a lecture in the traditional sense. I am passing on a certain energy (in addition to information) and you are as much a part of this as I and Pamela and Gerrit. In our being together here, we create a field or vortex of energy in this room, in this opening to the earth. Therefore this place is sacred. At any place where people – angels in human bodies – come together and join with the intention of seeding their light into the earth, the ground becomes sacred.

I would like to briefly say something about the phenomenon of channeling which has become so popular recently. You all know the concept of prana, which is employed in yoga and eastern philosophy. Prana is a spiritual energy that you take in with every breath. The idea is that you do not merely inhale oxygen when breathing in but also a life force energy, a cosmic energy which exceeds the physical and enables you to live. Now what I'd like to point out is this: just as everyone inhales prana along with oxygen in breathing, everyone channels continuously in his or her own way. Channeling is not reserved to a few people with a special gift. Channeling is the most natural thing in the world. You see, you cannot live without cosmic energy. You cannot exist, live and thrive without taking in cosmic energy. Just as you cannot live from oxygen alone, you cannot function even in a basic manner without some connection to the cosmic energy that is your home. Earth and cosmos, oxygen and prana, both are necessary to manifest yourself completely as a human being in earth reality.

In the previous channeling I have called you the gatekeepers, the ones who open the gate to more light on earth. But you are also the bridge builders, the ones who mediate between the cosmic and the earth realm, the ones who channel cosmic energy to the earth. This is something you actually do and it is something you *need* to do in order to feel joyful, purposeful and healthy. You are channeling whenever you use your intuition, whenever you go deep within and sense how things are for you and how you would like to change them. At these moments you form a channel with your higher self and you connect to the wisdom of non-earthly, cosmic realms which can support you in reaching your goals here on earth. Every one of you channels in some way to realign yourself with your greater being that is outside of space and time.

Today we share our energies and join to channel a cosmic energy which is trying to find its way to earth in this New Era. The New Era is no longer a vision of the future. It is already manifesting itself in the daily life of innumerable individuals. If you read the paper or watch the news it may seem that the time is not ripe yet. But the awakening brought forward by the New Era starts at the level of the individual, not at the level of governments, institutions and organizations. It is in your own everyday existence that a new flow of energy presents itself. It is the flow of your heart that invites you and beckons you to live and to act according to its lightness and wisdom. This is how the birthing of the New Era takes place, by ordinary individuals being attentive to the whispers of their heart. Spiritually the foundation of any real change or transformation is always laid on the individual level. The energy which is awakened in your hearts will gradually find its way through institutions and organizations which still hold on to the old paradigm of ego based consciousness. Old bulwarks of power will break down, not by violence but by the tender energy of the heart. If the heart takes over the lead the old will collapse, not under the pressure of power and violence but under the pressure of love.

In this New Era relationships undergo a major transformation. Relationships are the source of the deepest emotions within you, reaching from great joy to deep agony. In relationships you may become aware of an inner pain that is essentially much older than the relationship itself, even older than your human existence.

In this age you are invited and often challenged to achieve a deep self-healing in the field of relationships. Because of the new energy now presenting itself it is possible to transform the destructive elements of a relationship into a positive, equal flow of energy between you and the other person. However healing and personal transformation may also mean that you let go of relationships in which you cannot properly express yourself. It frequently means that even if you love someone dearly, you may have to say goodbye, because your own inner path takes you to a different place. Whether it leads to renewal or to parting in a relationship, you are all challenged to face the deepest issues in this area of personal bonding. The call of the heart, the heart based energy which marks the New Era, has entered your daily lives and you cannot ignore it anymore.

To explain why relationships can hurt you so much and turn your life completely upside down, I would like to say something about an ancient pain you carry within your soul. It is a pain which is very old, much older than this lifetime, older even than all your former lives on earth. I want to take you back to your original birthing pain as a soul.

"Once upon a time" all was whole and undivided. Can you imagine this? Allow your imagination to travel freely for a moment. Just imagine: you are not in a body, you are pure consciousness and you are part of a huge energy field that surrounds you in a comfortable way. You feel that you are part of this unity and are being cherished without conditions. Feel how this energy field encloses you as an immensely comfortable blanket, as an abundantly loving energy which allows you to explore and develop freely, without ever doubting yourself or your intrinsic right to be who you are. No anxiety, no fear. This sense of comfort and security constituted the pre-birthing conditions from which you emerged as an individual soul. It was a cosmic womb. Even if it is far removed from your present state, your heart still aches for this sense of completeness and wholeness, the feeling of absolute safety you experienced in that blanket of love and benevolence. The sense of oneness you remember was God. Together in this blanket of love you *constituted* God.

Within this divine consciousness or blanket of love, it was decided at some point to create a new situation. It is very difficult to put into human words but perhaps you can imagine that in God, this unity awareness, there was a longing for something different, something other than unity. There was, so to speak, a longing for *experience*. When you are completely assimilated into a wholeness of pure being, you do not experience things – you simply *are*. In spite of the ecstasy and the total safety in this state of being, there was a part of God, a part of this cosmic awareness, that wanted to explore and to evolve. This part "departed from itself."

You *are* this part of God. At a certain point your consciousness agreed to this experiment of departing from unity and becoming an "I," an entity in itself, a defined individual awareness. This was a huge step. From the bottom of your being you felt that this was a good thing. You felt that the longing for creativity and renewal was a positive and valuable aspiration. However the moment that you actually departed from the field of oneness, there was pain. For the first time in your recollection, for the first time in your life there was deep pain. You were torn loose from a realm of love and safety which had been completely self-evident to you. This is the birthing pain I referred to. Even during this first intense experience of desolation, something in your innermost being told you that it was all right, that this was your own choice. But the pain was so deep that at the outer layers of your being you got confused and disoriented. It became quite difficult to keep in touch with the deeper knowledge inside, the inner level at which you *are* God and where you know that all is well.

The tormented part that arose at that time I call the *inner child.* Your soul, your unique individuality, carries within itself the extremes of a pure divine knowledge on the one hand and a traumatized cosmic child on the other hand. This unity of God and Child, of knowledge and experience started off on a long journey. You started off as an individual soul. *You* started to investigate and experience what it is like to be an I, a defined individual.

God had transformed a part of Godself into Soul. The soul needs experience to find again its divine origins. The soul needs to be alive, to experience, to discover, to self-destruct and to recreate in order to feel who the soul truly is, namely God. The self evidence of being one and whole had been shattered and had to be regained by experience. This in itself was a great feat of creativity. The birthing of I-consciousness was a miracle! It had never existed before.

Often you try to transcend the boundaries of your I-ness in order to experience oneness and deep unity again. You might say that is the very aim of your spiritual quest. But consider for a moment: from God's point of view it is the I-ness, the separateness, that constitutes the miracle! The state of being ONE was the normal situation, "how it had always been." Within the miracle of being an individual soul lies an immense beauty, joy and creative power. The reason that you do not experience it like that is that you are still struggling with your birthing pain as a soul. Somewhere deep inside you the primal scream of anguish and betrayal still resounds: it is the recollection of being torn apart from your Mother/Father, from the omnipresent blanket of love and safety.

On your journey through time and experience you have gone through so many things. You have tried all different kinds of forms. There were quite a lot of incarnations in which you did not have the form of the human body, but that is not so relevant now. What matters to me in this context is that throughout this very long history, you were guided by two different motives. On the one hand there was the zest for exploration, creation and renewal and on the other hand there was the homesickness, the sense of being cast out of paradise and an overpowering loneliness.

By the adventurous, progressive part in yourself, the energy which pushed you out of the cosmic womb, you have experienced and created a lot. But due to the birthing pain and homesickness you carried within, you also had to deal with a lot of trauma and disillusion. Your creations were therefore not always benevolent. During your journeys through time and space you have done things you have regretted later on – things you might call "bad" (in quotation marks). These actions were, from our perspective, merely the result of the determination to plunge into experience and venture into the unknown. You see, as soon as you decide to become an individual, to break away from the self evident oneness, you cannot experience light only. You have to find out everything anew. So you will also experience the dark. You will experience all there is, up to all the extremes.

At your present point of evolution, you come to realize that everything stands or falls with the power to truly embrace your "I-ness." It is about truly embracing your own divinity and from that *self-awareness*, experiencing joy and abundance. In the moment of your cosmic birth, the moment that desolation and pain enveloped you, you started to feel tiny and insignificant. From that moment on, you started to look for something that could *save* you – a power or force outside of you, a god, a leader, a partner, a child, etc. In the awakening process that you are now experiencing, you realize that the essential safety you are longing for is not to be found in anything outside of you, whether it is a parent, a lover or a god. However strongly this longing or homesickness may be triggered in a particular relationship, you will not find this essential safety there, *not even* in a relationship with God.

For the God you believe in, the God who has been handed down to you by tradition and who still heavily influences your perception, is a God outside of you. It is a God who outlines things for you, who lays out the way for you. But that God does not exist. *You* are God, you are that creative part of God who decided to go its own way and to experience things in a wholly different way. You had the confidence that you would be able to heal yourself from the primal wound of birth. You could say that the expansive energy of exploration and renewal is a male energy, whereas the energy of unification, joining together, the energy of Home, is a female energy. Both these energies belong to the essence of who you are. As a soul you are neither male nor female. Essentially you are both male and female. You started your journey with both these ingredients. And now the time has come to let them work together in harmony which means to truly experience wholeness in yourself. After having denied your own greatness for such a long time, you will start to realize finally that there is no alternative but *to be the God you are longing for.*

This is the ultimate breakthrough to enlightenment: to realize that you yourself are the God you are craving. There is nothing outside you that can bring you into the heart of your own power, your own wholeness. You are it, you are the one and you have always been the one! *You have always been waiting for you.*

To light this flame of self awareness within brings such joy, such a deep sense of homecoming that it puts all of your relationships into a new perspective. For example you feel less concerned about the things that other people tell you. If someone criticises or distrusts you, you do not automatically take it personally. You feel less affected or eager to react. You let it go more easily and the need to defend yourself, both to yourself and to the other person, drops away. When you are easily affected emotionally by what another person thinks of you, this indicates that inwardly there is a self contempt that makes you give credit to the negative opinions of others. You do not solve this self contempt by seeking out a conflict with the other but only by going inward and getting in touch with the emotional wounds within yourself. These are much older than this specific moment of rejection.

In fact all pain of rejection, all relationship pain, goes back to the original, unhealed birthing pain. It may seem as if I'm taking a huge step here for there are all kinds of complex situations in relationships which seem to indicate that the cause lies closer. It may seem as if your pain is caused by something your partner has done or not done. It may seem as if something *outside* of you causes the pain. And therefore you think that the solution to your problem lies in the behavior of the other. But let me tell you: fundamentally you are working on healing an ancient pain *within yourself.* If you are not aware of this, you may easily get entangled in relationship issues that can be extremely painful.

Especially in male/female relationships (love relationships), you frequently try to forge a kind of unity and safety between you that resembles the primeval state of oneness that you vaguely remember. Subconsciously you are trying to recreate the feeling of being comfortably wrapped in a blanket of unconditional love and acceptance. There is a child within you who is crying out for that unconditional acceptance. However if this child in you puts his or her arms around the child part in your partner, too often it results in a suffocating grasp that blocks both partners from genuine self expression.

What happens is that you become emotionally dependent, and then you are going to need the love or approval of the other person for your well-being. Dependence always calls into being power and control issues, for to need someone is equal to wanting to control his or her behavior. This is the beginning of a destructive relationship. To give up your individuality in a relationship, guided by a subconscious longing for absolute unity, is destructive towards yourself as well as towards the other person.

True love between two people shows two energy fields that can function in complete independence from each other. Each energy field is a unity unto itself and connects to the other on the basis of that unity. In relationships in which partners are dependent upon each other, you will find an uncoordinated striving for "organic wholeness," not wanting or being able to function without the other. This leads to an entanglement of energies which can be observed in the auric fields as energy cords by which the partners feed each other. They feed themselves with the addictive energies of dependence and control. This kind of energy entanglement indicates that you do not take responsibility for yourself, that you do not face up to the old soul wound that only you can heal. If only you would address this deepest pain and take

231

responsibility, you would see that you do not ever need someone else to be whole and you will liberate yourself from the destructive aspect of the relationship.

Karmic relations

In this context I would like to say something about karmic relationships. By this I mean relationships between people who have known each other in other lifetimes and who have experienced intense emotions with regard to each other. The hallmark of a karmic relationship is that the partners carry unresolved emotions within such as guilt, fear, dependence, jealousy, anger or something of the kind. Because of this unresolved emotional charge, they feel drawn to each other in another incarnation. The aim of the renewed encounter is to provide an opportunity to resolve the issue at hand. This happens by recreating the same issue in a short period of time. When they first meet, the karmic "players" feel a compelling urge to get nearer to each other and after some time they start to repeat their old emotional role patterns. The stage has now been set to face the old issue anew and perhaps handle it in a more enlightened way. The spiritual purpose of the renewed encounter is for both partners to make other choices than they made during that former lifetime.

I am going to give an example here. Imagine a woman who, in a previous lifetime, had a husband who was quite possessive and bossy. For a while she accepted this but at a certain point she decided it was enough and she broke off the relationship. Afterwards the husband committed suicide. The woman felt remorse. She believed that she was guilty. Shouldn't she have given him another chance? She carried this sense of guilt with her for the rest of her life.

In another lifetime they meet again. There is an odd attraction between them. At first, the man is exceptionally charming and she is the center of his attention. He adores her. They enter into a relationship. But from now on he becomes increasingly jealous and possessive. He suspects her of adultery. She finds herself in an inner struggle. She is angry and upset that he wrongly accuses her but she also feels a strange obligation to be forgiving and to give him another chance. He is a wounded man, she thinks; he cannot help it that he has this fear of being abandoned. Maybe I can help him get over this. She justifies her behavior in this way but in fact she allows her personal boundaries to be violated. The relationship negatively affects her self esteem.

The most liberating choice for the woman would now be to break off the relationship and go her own way without feelings of guilt. The pain and fear of the husband are not her responsibility. His pain and her sense of guilt have led to a destructive relationship. Their relationship was already emotionally charged because of another lifetime. The meaning of the renewed encounter is that the woman must learn to let things go without feelings of guilt and that the man must learn to stand on his own feet emotionally. So the only real solution is to break off the relationship. The solution for the woman's karma is to let go of her sense of guilt once and for all. The mistake she made in her former lifetime was not that she abandoned her husband but that she felt responsible for his suicide. The departure of his wife in this lifetime would confront the husband again with his own pain and fear and it would offer him a new opportunity to face these emotions instead of escaping them.

You may recognize a karmic encounter by the fact that the other person immediately feels strangely familiar to you. Quite often there also is a mutual attraction, something compelling in the air which urges you to be together and to discover each other. If the opportunity is available, this strong attraction may grow into a love relationship or a heavy infatuation. The emotions you experience may be so overwhelming that you think you have met your twin soul. However things are not as they seem. In such a relationship there will always be problems which sooner or later will surface. Often the partners become involved in a psychological conflict that has power, control and dependence as the main ingredients. By this they repeat a tragedy which they subconsciously recognize from a former lifetime. In a past life they could have been lovers, parent and child, boss and subordinate, or some another type of relationship. But always they touched a deep inner pain in each other by acts of unfaithfulness, abuse of power or, by contrast, too strong an affection. There was a profound encounter between them which caused deep scars and emotional trauma. That is why the forces of attraction as well as repulsion can be so violent when they meet again in a new incarnation.

The spiritual invitation to all souls who are energetically entangled in such a way is let each other go and become "entities-unto-themselves," free and independent. Karmic relationships as mentioned here are almost never long-term, stable, loving relationships. They are destructive rather than healing relationships. Quite often the basic purpose of the encounter is to succeed in letting each other go. This is something that could not be done in one or more past lifetimes but now there is another opportunity to release each other in love.

If you find yourself in a relationship that is characterized by intense emotions, that evokes a lot of pain and grief but from which you cannot break free, please realize that nothing obligates you to stay with the other person. Also do realize that intense emotions more often refer to deep pain rather than to mutual love. The energy of love is essentially calm and peaceful, light-hearted and inspiring. It is not heavy, exhausting and tragic. If a relationship gets these traits, it is time to let it go rather than "work on it" once again.

Sometimes you convince yourselves that you have to stay together because you "share karma" and you have "to work things out together." You call upon the nature of karma as an argument for prolonging the relationship, while you are both suffering immensely. In fact you are distorting the concept of karma here. You do not work out karma together; karma is an individual thing. The karma at stake in such relationships as mentioned before often requires that you let go completely, that you withdraw from such a relationship in order to experience that you are whole unto yourself. Again, resolving karma is something you do on your own. Another person may touch or trigger something inside you that creates a lot of drama between you. But it remains your sole task and challenge to deal with your own inner hurt, not with the other person's issues. You only have responsibility for yourself.

This is important to realize because it is one of the main pitfalls in relationships. You are not responsible for your mate and your mate is not responsible for you. The solution to your problems does not lie in the behavior of the other person. Sometimes you are so connected to the inner child of your partner, the emotionally hurt part inside, that you feel you are the one to "rescue" it. Or your partner may be trying the same with you. But this is not going to work. You will be reinforcing emotions of powerlessness and victimhood in the other person, whereas it would be more helpful ultimately if you drew the line and stood up for yourself. It is your destination to be able to feel whole and complete, entirely on your own. That is the most important condition for a truly fulfilling relationship.

Healing relationships

There are healing and there are destructive relationships. A characteristic of healing relationships is that the partners respect each other as *they are*, without trying to change each other. They take much pleasure in each other's company but they do not feel uneasy, desperate or lonely if the other person is not around. In this kind of relationship you offer understanding, support and encouragement to your loved one without trying to solve their problems. There is freedom and peace in the relationship. Of course there may be misunderstandings now and then, but the emotions they bring up are short-lived. Both partners are prepared to forgive. There is a heart connection between them as a result of which they will not take the other person's emotions or mistakes personally. Because it does not trigger a deeper layer of pain, they do not attach so much importance to it. Emotionally both partners are independent. They draw their strength and well-being not from the approval or the presence of their mate. He or she does not fill a gap in their lives but adds something new and vital.

In a healing relationship partners may also know each other from one or more past lifetimes. But in these cases there is hardly ever an emotional karmic burden as described above. The two souls may have known each other in a past life in a way that was essentially encouraging and supporting. As friends, partners or as parent and child, they have recognized each other as soul mates. This creates an indissoluble bond throughout several lives.

I will give another example. A young man grows up in a poor family somewhere in the Middle Ages. He is gentle and sensitive by nature and he does not fit in very well with his surroundings. His family consists of hard working, rather rough people who think little of his dreamy, unpractical nature. When he is grown up, he enters a monastery. He is not really happy here either, for life is tightly regulated and there is little human warmth or companionship among the people living there. There is however one man who is a bit different. It is a priest who has a higher rank but who has no air of authority and who is truly interested in him. Now and then he inquires how things are going and he allots him a few pleasant jobs like gardening. Each time they look at each other there is a sense of recognition, something like-minded between them. There is a silent connection from the heart. Although

235

they do not meet very often or speak much, the priest is a source of hope and encouragement for the young man.

In a following lifetime this man is a woman. Once again she has a gentle and dreamy nature. She has difficulties standing up for herself. When she is an adult she gets bogged down in a marriage with a man who is authoritarian and bossy. At first she fell for his distinct, powerful charisma but later on she realizes how his dominance restricts and oppresses her. Nevertheless she finds it very difficult to set herself free from him. At her work she sometimes mentions the subject to a colleague, a somewhat older man. He encourages her to stand up for herself and to stay true to her own needs. Each time she speaks with him she intuitively knows that he is right. Then after a great deal of inner conflict she divorces her husband. The contact with her colleague changes now. She feels affection for him. He turns out to be single. She feels so much at ease with him that it seems as if they have known each other for ages. They start a relationship which is affectionate, relaxed and encouraging for both of them. The sympathy which was flowing between them in a former lifetime now takes shape as a fulfilling relationship as husband and wife.

This is a healing relationship. The woman has taken an essential decision in leaving her husband and choosing for herself. With this she has affirmed her emotional independence. This has created the basis for a loving, well-balanced relationship with a congenial soul.

Twin souls

At this point I would like to say something about the concept of twin souls, probably familiar to all of you. The idea of twin souls exerts a deep attraction for you. However it is potentially quite dangerous, because it can be interpreted in such a way that it *reinforces* the birthing pain and emotional dependence in each of you, rather than resolving it. This happens when you conceive of the concept of twin souls in such a way that there is another person who perfectly suits you and makes you whole. This is the concept of the twin soul as your other half. You then assume that the oneness and safety you are missing so deeply will be found in someone else who is the perfect match for you.

According to this immature notion of twin souls, the souls are considered to be two halves who together make up a unity. Usually the two halves are

236

respectively male and female. So this notion not only suggests that you are incomplete unto yourself but also that you are essentially male or female. You can probably see that this notion of twin souls is not healthy or healing from a spiritual point of view. It makes you dependent on something outside of you. It denies the divine origin which implies that you are *everything*, male and female, and that you are whole and complete unto yourself. It creates all kinds of illusions which bring you far away from home. And by "home" I mean your own self, the divinity of your "I-ness." No soul is meant to be someone else's other half.

Twin souls do exist and they literally are what the word implies: they are twins. They are souls with the same "feeling tone" or vibration, or you could say with the same birthing time, as is the case with biological twins. The particular time of birth, this unique moment in time and place, makes for a uniquely charged feeling tone inside the souls that come to life. They are not dependent upon each other in any way. They are neither male nor female. But they are certainly tuned into each other as kindred spirits.

What is the reason for the creation of twin souls? Why do they exist? You often think that the raison d'être for something is the learning process it effects. But this is not the case with twin souls. The reason for the existence of twin souls is not to learn something. The aim is simply joy and creativity. Twin souls have no function within duality. You will meet your twin soul when you are transcending duality, when you identify yourself again with the God inside yourself who is whole and undivided and who is able to take any form or appearance. Twin souls meet again on their journey back home.

Let us go back for a moment to the beginning of the journey. The moment you leave the state of oneness and become an individual, you enter duality. Suddenly there is dark and light, great and small, sick and healthy, etc. Reality is split. You have no frame of reference anymore for who you really are. At first you took your identity from "being-part-of-a-whole." Now you are a single part torn loose from the whole. But without your conscious knowing, someone accompanies you who is equal to you, who resembles you as closely as anything could. You took up "the same space" in the blanket of oneness, so near to each other that you didn't know you were two until you were born. What connects the two of you is something beyond duality, something that antedates the history of duality. This is hard to put into words properly, because it defies your usual definitions of identity in which you are either one or two and cannot be both at the same time.

Now you were both setting out on a journey, a long journey throughout many experiences. Both of you have experienced the extremes of duality, to discover gradually that your essence does not lie in duality but outside of it, in something which underlies it. As soon as you become deeply aware of this underlying oneness, your journey back begins. Little by little you feel less attached to external things such as power, fame, money or prestige. You understand more and more that the key is not *what* you experience but *how* you experience it. You create your own happiness or misery by your state of awareness. You are discovering the power of your own consciousness.

Once you have gone through all the highs and lows of duality there will be a moment when you meet your twin soul. In the energy and appearance of your twin soul, you will recognize a very deep part of yourself, your essence beyond duality, and by this very recognition you will start to understand yourself better and become aware of who you really are. Your twin is a frame of reference for you that carries you outside of the limited beliefs about yourself that you took in during your life and lifetimes before. You liberate yourself by seeing this reflection of you in your twin; it is like a reminder and it has nothing to do with emotional dependence. Meeting each other helps each of you to be stronger and more self-aware individuals, expressing your creativity and love on earth. It accelerates your return journey as it helps you step up to a higher level of oneness while fully retaining and expressing your I-ness, your unique individuality.

Ultimately we are all one. We are supported by an energy which is universal in all of us. But at the same time there is individuality in all of us. The twin soul is to some extent the link between individuality and oneness. It is like a stepping stone to oneness. If you connect with your twin soul consciously and materially, you will bring about the creation of something new: a third energy that is born out of their combined action. That energy always helps to enhance unity awareness on a larger scale than just the two of them. Because they are on their way Home, twin souls feel inspired to anchor the energies of love and oneness on earth and they do so in a way that accords with their own unique talents and skills. In this manner the twin soul love builds a stepping stone between "being one" and "being One."

There is a deep inner bond between twin souls but that does not alter the fact that they are complete unities unto themselves. Their joining together brings about love and joy and their meeting enhances creativity and self-realization. They support each other without falling into the pitfalls of emotional dependence or addiction. The love between twin souls is not meant to make each other whole, but to create something new: *instead of the two becoming one, the two shall become three.*

Healing the cosmic birthing pain

You will meet your twin soul at some point. Please let this knowledge be enough to you. Try not to dwell upon hopes and expectations that take you out of the here-and-now. What matters in this very moment is that you fully realize that the love and safety you deeply desire are present within yourself. The key is to realize that this absolute self-acceptance can never be given to you by anyone else, not even by your twin soul.

Not only in love relationships but also in parent-child relationships, there is the temptation to find absolute oneness or safety in the other. Think of a parent who secretly wants his child to realize all the dreams he did not fulfill, or a child who as a grown up still clings to her parents and considers them to be her absolute safe haven.

It is important to become aware of the underlying dynamics and motives in your relationships and to heal them in the light of your consciousness. Your cosmic homesickness is not going to be healed by or in a relationship. This will be done by you alone, by the full realization of who you are, by realizing your light, beauty and divinity. This is the destination of your journey.

Also you will not return to the state of oneness from whence you came. The "blanket of love" from which you were born constituted your *embryo* stage. Now you are becoming mature gods. You will create a field of absolute safety and love from your own heart and allow others to share in this without any conditions. That is the essence of God: unconditional love that radiates, creates and cherishes without any agenda, without any calculation.

I would like to ask you now to be silent for a few moments and to truly feel your I-ness, your unique being unto yourself. If you are surrounded by people, then for a moment feel your "I" very strongly. Unconditionally, you are this part of God. It is not something that can be taken from you, it is an undeniable presence that IS.

And now feel how this undeniable fact of your I-presence can be a source of joy and strength to you. Say yes to the miracle of your own being and embrace it. Yes, I am I. I am separate and unique, my own being. I may connect deeply with others but also ever remain an "I." You may think that behind this fact lies solitude and desolation but please go beyond these *thoughts* and feel the power and vitality within you. If you really say yes to your individuality, you experience self-confidence and trust. On that basis you will create loving relationships and the solitude and desolation will dissolve.

When feelings of loneliness and desolation overwhelm you, take the child within you on your lap. Notice the hurt in this child. It is longing for the total safety it once knew as an embryo. It wants to see that safety reflected in the face of your partner, in the face of your child, in the face of your mother or father, in the face of a therapist. Then show the child *your* face. *You* have the face of an angel for this child. *You* are meant to heal this child in the most absolute way you can dream of. Neither I nor any "master" is able to do it for you. We can only show the direction. You yourselves are the saviors of yourself.

Finally I would like to invite you to feel our joining together for a moment. Even if you are not present and you are reading this material, feel our connectedness. Do not focus on the I-ness now but on our togetherness in a very free and easy way. Feel the energy, feel what brings us together. It is a longing for a state of wholeness. Now imagine that we are surrounded by the most powerful energy there is, the energy of your awakened selves, the energy of the angel within you. Let us breathe in this energy and take a minute to deeply feel its power.

Thank you for your presence.

The Children of the New Era

Dear friends, I bid you a cordial welcome. My energy flows among you and is discernable to you as the energy of home, a Home that you are moving towards and a Source that you are coming from. My energy is not merely the energy of one man who lived on earth two thousand years ago. I represent a Source energy in which you all take part and in which your higher selves are present as one, as a group energy.

On this level of oneness there is an oversoul which you may call the Christ energy and which covers us all like an umbrella, including me, Jeshua. It is from this energy that we bring messages to you on earth and hold up a mirror to you when you have temporarily lost yourself and cannot find the way. It is the energy of your own higher self, your soul family, your oversoul, that we wish to show you. We remind you of the Source that you descend from and from which your deepest inspiration stems.

The inspiration that joins you together has to do with bringing Light on earth. It has to do with the arrival of the New Era. Your incarnation here and now on earth is deeply connected with the transitional times you live in. Now what I wish to speak of today is the arrival of a new generation of children on earth. These children show other qualities than you are accustomed to from the past. How has this come about? Where does this phenomenon come from? For that I have to take you back in time and show you how you have been the pioneers of the new wave of energy that these children are bringing in.

There have been times on earth when the energy was heavy and tight. Everything was prescribed by rules and regulations with little room for the imagination and the intuitive powers which bring along a loving and playful energy. For ages this heavy energy took possession of the earth. I was a pioneer in breaking the hold of this suffocating energy, in bringing Light to a dark reality in which power and oppression were prevailing. There was oppression of the imagination, the freedom to express oneself, the energy of the heart.

In the course of this history, the Second World War became a turning point. In the wake of this wartime, a new era and time spirit was born which is familiar to you as the revolution of the sixties. It also meant a spiritual revolution. The energy of the heart was reborn at that time and although the energy of the sixties was to some extent free-floating and naive, it nevertheless constituted a breakthrough. It heralded in a new and vibrant energy.

All of you who were born during the period around and after the Second World War have been pioneers of the new era. It is from a spiritual foundation created by you that a new generation of children has now appeared, who recognize the song of your heart and carry it further. I would like to speak about these children now.

These children come in with an energy that is purer and higher than ever. By "higher" I mean that they are able to keep more of their soul energy intact as they arrive on earth. Another way of putting this is to say that the veil between your material reality and the spiritual realm has become thinner because of the pioneering work that you and many others have done during the decades after the Second World War.

In those days a lot was laid open; traditional authorities were called into question, new concepts came to the surface and influenced the collective consciousness of humanity worldwide. At first sight this led to confusion and chaos, but the energy of the heart always leads to confusion and chaos in the eyes of those who love rules and structures and who look up to an unfaltering authority to hear the truth. Those days are gone. You are all aspiring to feel and found the energy of truth and clarity within yourself. This inner work paves the way for a new era on earth. You all have one foot in the old era and one foot in the new. The transition to the new is a long, gradual transformation. The children who are being born now are already standing within the new era more than you have ever done. Nevertheless there is an important connection and recognition between you and them.

To clarify this let me say some more about the various groups of children that are now entering the earth. All of you who are present here and all who feel particularly drawn to this message are lightworker souls. I have talked about the characteristics of lightworker souls and their history throughout the ages in channelings past (see the Lightworker Series). You are old and bring in the wisdom and experience of many, many lifetimes. Because of all that you went through, you have developed a sensitivity in your soul which makes you wise and compassionate, but vulnerable as well. Many times you felt you were "different" and did not fit in so well with your social environment. Especially in times when order, discipline and repression of the feelings were the normal way, this caused you deep suffering and it injured your feeling centers. But the sensitivity that is characteristic of you, you can now clearly see reflected in the eyes of the lightworker children that are being born on earth.

This is the first group of "new age children" I would like to distinguish. They are lightworker souls who are basically the same as you but they enter through a different gate or veil on earth. They are less burdened with the energy of the old era, like you were. You had to deal with old educational methods, well-meaning but often stifling methods of raising children, which often repressed the child's original sense of wonder, imagination and self-esteem. All that has been changing over the past decades. There is more freedom, more room for feeling, more understanding of the importance of the emotions, more respect for the individual nature of each person.

The lightworker souls that are now entering are thus differently received, in a different energy, and this enables them to bring more of their soul energy and their cosmic light through the veil. Their sensitivity is therefore clearly visible and it can also cause imbalances, but I will go into that further below.

I would like to distinguish a second group of "new age children." They are the earth souls. They do not historically belong to the family of lightworker souls that we have been speaking of before (see the Lightworker series for the distinction between lightworker souls and earth souls). Their development is deeply intertwined with the evolvement of life on earth. They are now as a group going through the early stages of letting go of ego based consciousness and moving towards a heart based consciousness. The earth souls who have entered in recent times display a greater sensitivity. This is because of their own inner development but also because the veil is thinning and there is more room for emotional self expression. They are also part of the new wave of energy that is now coming in through the children.

Then there is a third group I wish to distinguish. They are currently called the crystal children by your spiritual literature. These children are relatively new on earth; they have not spent many lifetimes here, although they have a rich experience with other dimensions or planes of existence. They have incarnated there in other forms than the human body. You might also call them the star children. Their energy is often dreamy and they are also characterized by a great sensitivity. In their case there may also be physical symptoms like food allergies or skin problems which have to do with difficulties in getting accustomed to the energy of earth, the density and crudeness of material realty. These newcomers on earth bring along a very refined, ethereal energy and they need ample protection and safety to be able to ground themselves fully.

We have now named three groups of children who are *all* children of the new age. Thus we might say that all children incarnating presently are part of the New Era, according to their own nature.

You who are hearing and reading this are especially acquainted with the lightworker souls, because you are one yourself. All of you are deeply inspired to bring Light onto earth and at the same time, you carry within old wounds of rejection and loneliness. Because of this, it is not always easy for you to feel a loving and safe connection with the earth. But it is this very point that is of utmost importance in helping the new children ground their energy and lead fulfilling lives. Experiencing a loving connection to earth reality yourself is a precondition for being able to coach and support them and to offer them the emotional safety they need.

I will now mention some of the problems these children might meet and what you can do about it whenever you are in touch with them as parent, teacher or therapist. Some of you feel called to work with them and this is very appropriate, since you are especially adept at recognizing their underlying motives and inspirations. You recognize aspects of them that were repressed and smothered in you during your childhood or later on. This is why encountering these children can affect you at a deep emotional level for you see in them a reflection of yourself, your own love, your originality and also your pain. Indeed these children may just as well experience the pain of not feeling welcome on earth. Even if times have changed, it is not self evident that they will find forms of manifestation that match their vibration and level of consciousness. This has several reasons.

The first is that their energy or vibration does not yet match the energy of earth and of the collective human consciousness. They are ahead of their time. This lack of understanding between the old and the new is familiar to you from your own experience. There is a knowingness and a heartfelt wisdom in *you*, the older generation, that has not been fitting very well into your societal reality. It goes against some deep-seated traditional values and notions and has met with scepticism and distrust. The children have to deal with this resistance too, for it is not yet gone. Moreover (this is the second reason), material reality on earth has a slowness to it because of its density. Dreams and desires do not manifest quickly or easily. To truly realise your deepest inspiration, you have to be able to connect yourself to the earth at all levels: emotional, physical, mental and spiritual. Only then can your energy find fertile ground and only then can the seeds of your soul sprout and flourish.

For the children of the new era it will be of great importance that they are able to ground themselves, meaning that they will know how to connect their cosmic energy, which can be sweeping, passionate and inspired, to earth reality. It is important that they grow the patience to channel their soul energy to the energetic reality of this planet. Also it is vital that they have patience with those parts of humanity and society that are walking behind and that are not yet able to grasp the wisdom they offer, or that even interpret their behavior as obstinacy and rebelliousness.

A collision is taking place here between the old and the new that may cause problems. The energy of the new children will often be misinterpreted by people who are part of the old mentality which says that discipline, order and obedience are the prerequisites for the full development of the child's abilities and personality. Now *you* are actually the ones who stand in between the old and the new here and who are able to build a bridge. You have suffered because you had to control and keep inside much of your true spiritual energy. You know what it is like to feel blocked in your self expression. You therefore understand the new children quite well, you understand their need to break free from rules based on authority and oppression of the feelings.

These children need to have room for self exploration and individuality and at the same time they need to understand the value of *loving discipline*, as opposed to authoritarian discipline. They have to learn how to channel and manage their energy without repressing themselves. This is precisely the issue that you are dealing with yourselves on your own inner road. For all of you it is vitally important that you are able to channel your cosmic energy, your inner spark of light through your body into earth reality. In particular it means that you have to deal with the emotions that block you from truly being present in the here-and-now and from expressing yourself in material reality.

It is one of the biggest issues for lightworker souls, their "complex" so to speak, that they carry a lot of spiritual energy on the upper side of their energy field (shoulders and head) which stagnates and cannot find its way down. The energy cannot properly connect to the earth, which is another way of saying that you keep your energy inside and that you feel unable to express yourself satisfactorily. This can be the case either in your private relationships or in your working environment, where you might feel less fulfilled and creative than you could be. All of this has to do with not being completely grounded. And the reason why the energy cannot go down and incarnate fully is that there are emotional traumas located in the area of the belly which block or interrupt the flow. Therefore it is of great importance to focus your attention and awareness on these parts of you that are in need of emotional healing.

It is vital that you acquire a fully embodied, grounded spirituality and that you do not keep this energy locked into the upper part of your auric field. In such a fashion this energy can cause a naive and imbalanced form of spirituality which may give you ecstatic feelings and great enthusiasm every now and then, but which lacks the "body" to really connect to earth and manifest itself outwardly as a satisfying job, a stable, loving relationship and/or material abundance. The spiritual energy must connect to the emotional body and from there on to physical reality. What blocks the flow are old wounds: emotions such as fear and anger, feelings of inferiority, disappointment and bitterness about life. These are the emotional hurdles you bump up against and I tell you that dealing with these basic emotional issues is the key to finding ways of supporting the new children. Your emotional healing will provide you with the means to help the children ground themselves in a loving yet disciplined way. For by steadily addressing these issues, you will set out an *energetic trail* for them.

What does emotional healing mean? I would like to speak of this again, although it has been dealt with more thoroughly in earlier channelings (see "Dealing with emotions" especially). You have all known times in which the emotions were repressed and considered more or less taboo. Especially the older ones among you grew up in a generation where this was standard. In the sixties a counter reaction followed and the emotions were set free, sometimes to the other extreme of exaltation. Emotions were put above reason. Rationality had to be set aside temporarily, to freely investigate and transgress the boundaries of tradition. And it was fruitful to do so for a while, but the free exploration of suppressed emotional energies also has some pitfalls to it. One does not transform and heal the emotions by giving free reign to them and letting them control you.

The essence of spiritual freedom is that one *acknowledges* all emotions and allows them to be there, while at the same time remaining *fully conscious,* i.e. embracing them with your own angelic consciousness. The unsolved emotional energies within you are like small children: confused, sad or frightened, coming to you for comfort. By you I mean: to the angel in you, your higher self. In this manner your higher, angelic self *descends* into your own emotional body to do the healing work that is your mission. And when you do so, your Light flows downward, through the lower energy centers (chakras), through your arms and legs and out into the world. This is what it means to ground your angelic or soul energy.

It is a process that requires self discipline. I use the word discipline to point out that this does not happen automatically. The process of self healing requires a steady and honest focus on your inner life and a willingness to face up to all the emotions inside. It is about acknowledging them as yours, taking responsibility for them and not feeling a victim of the past, of other people or society. No, you are the angel who has absorbed these emotions and who has the power to transform them. That is the reason you came to earth: to transform your fear, anger and sadness into love, forgiveness and understanding. By doing so, you will create for yourself a life of joy and fulfillment and you will be at peace with the reality of earth. And thus you set out an *energetic trail* for the new children who are and have been arriving.

They come in with a higher energy, thanks to your pioneering work, but without the assurance that this energy will find firm ground to stand on.

To prepare such ground all of us, society at large, will have to open up to the new and different aspects of these children. We need to welcome them and allow them to express their energy freely and at the same time teach them to develop the focus and patience to channel their energy to the reality of earth. They need to express their soul energy, their cosmic inspiration, in material forms that belong to earth. So they must feel able to express themselves emotionally, mentally, creatively and spiritually in language, communication and organization. It is important that they feel invited to bring their energy into this reality, even if it means they have to go through internal or external resistance and difficulties.

The message of the new children, their clear, crystal energy, can only land on fertile ground when we help them establish a loving connection to earth. With regard to this aspect, you yourselves are going through a fundamental transformation process in which the emotional body is the key. You are all in the process of taking responsibility for your deepest emotions and gradually releasing them in the light of your own angelic consciousness. Your angel self has compassion for the deep fear and gloominess you can experience in this earthly realm. It belongs to the essence of the Christ energy that it descends to the lowest point, where darkness seems all around, and makes Light's presence known. It is no great feat to spread light in a cosmic realm of love and safety.

The true power of the Christ energy is that it pierces through the darkest cells, that it brings love where hopelessness abounds. On earth, a planet so lovely and rich and yet so removed from oneness and love, the Christ energy prepares a seed bed and opens up new vistas. You all are sprouts of this seed and pioneers of a new era. Even if your road seems difficult and heavy, you all have accomplished a great deal and by your own inner changes have helped open the gates for the new wave of light energy now pouring down on earth.

Even now, it will not be easy. Even now, a lot of darkness is coming to the surface: abuse of power, fear, old energy. Therefore I ask you to keep faith in your mission: to bring the light of your sprouted Christ energy to your own inner darkness. The children of the new era will be grateful to you. They need you but they also will give you something in return. They carry happiness in their hearts, a delightful freshness and a living remembrance of Home. They shine with joy and love like a budding flower, full of promise. This energy can open up your heart and stir a sense of playfulness and light-heartedness in you. All of you who feel old and worn out, who have gone through a lot: reach out your hands to the newcomers! They need your support and experience and they will bring love and merriment into your lives. This is a process that touches you all, whether you are dealing with children directly or not. It touches you all.

I would like to conclude with a moment of silence in which I ask you to connect to the earth. The earth itself is an intelligence, a being with a soul who is looking forward to the arrival of the new children. She is smiling to herself when she looks at you, for when you arrived here, in another time, you were such beautiful children too. You were the pioneers and the mediators. Feel the gratefulness of the earth to you. You are so tied in with this huge process. Then feel the arrival of the new children, full of anticipation and inspiration. They are also here to *help you*. Their liveliness and wisdom will cheer you up and remind you that the new age is dawning, that the longest mile is indeed the last mile home and that the flowers of love and peace will truly blossom.

Biography and some notes on channeling

In this biography, I explain a little more about my personal background and spiritual development. Many people have asked me how I got acquainted with channeling and how the connection with Jeshua came about. This biography does not so much offer an explanation of the phenomenon of channeling as a personal story about what it means for me.

Prelude

I was born on September 6, 1968 in a small village in The Netherlands. In my childhood, I had a strong interest in the children's Bible and in stories about the life of Jesus, which was strange because my parents were not religious in any active way. At age 12, my grandmother died. I had loved her dearly and she was like a parent to me, since she lived in our house as part of our family. After her death, we – my mother, aunts, cousins and I – got very interested in literature about the afterlife, psychic phenomena, etc. This interest remained until I went off to the university at 19 years of age.

I started my studies in philosophy at the University of Leiden and after a year I had turned into a sceptic, thinking all this religious stuff was highly superstitious and irrational. I fell in love with the rationalist approach in philosophy and I worked and studied hard. I graduated *cum laude* and was then offered a position as a Ph.D. student at a different university in The Netherlands. My field of research was the contemporary philosophy of science. Meanwhile, at age 23, I had started a relationship with a somewhat older man who was successfully pursuing an academic career as well. We lived together in a nice house and I thought I was quite happy.

This was not really the case, as I found out through meeting a young man who I fell deeply in love with. He was a philosopher and Ph.D. student as well and, in contrast to my partner, he believed in "spiritual things" while at the same time being sensitive, intelligent and rational. This stirred something deep within me. I had this old interest in the spiritual, but it had become forbidden in my academic environment and now there was someone, who I would now term as a soul mate, reminding me about a part of me that had been kept hidden too long. We could talk endlessly about philosophy and spirituality. We fell in love, I left my partner, the house and the city I lived in, but we did not live happily ever after. Our relationship was short-lived and ended in what I experienced as great emotional trauma. Our heavy crush completely uprooted both our lives, but due to character differences and emotional turmoil, we could not build a life together and we broke up after less than six months.

Crisis

I was renting a small room on my own at that time, living like a poor student again. I didn't mind about the material backslide though. I was torn apart with grief and sadness because this soul mate and lover had left me. It felt like nothing mattered to me anymore and I couldn't care less about the completion of my Ph.D. thesis. Then, seemingly out of nowhere, I was offered a scholarship which enabled me to stay one semester at the University of Harvard in the United States. I could simply attend classes that I liked, without much pressure on me to do anything in particular.

So I undertook this journey, all on my own, and it was an incredibly deepening experience for me. I felt totally alone for the first time in my life, and I could only endure it, *bear it* so to speak, with no solutions at hand. Intellectually I had become empty. The interest I took in academic philosophy had completely withered and I had to try really hard to stay awake during the courses I took at one of the world's most famous universities. My mind could not take in anything intellectual anymore. I was very tired and after classes I just slept or spent time with my kind roommate, who was lonely too and had just come out of an unhappy marriage.

In a bookstore near the university, I discovered a book by Seth, channeled through Jane Roberts. I had never read channeled material before, and at first I did not understand anything about it. But I felt drawn to it again and again and after a while, reading this material became the highlight of my days. It was not merely the content that struck me as quite original and profound; it was the energy that touched and uplifted me. It was to me the first thing that called me back to life again.

252

Stuck again

After my stay in the U.S., I decided to finish my Ph.D. thesis, although I knew I would not pursue an academic career anymore. In 1997 when I was 29 years old, I graduated with a doctorate in philosophy, and by then I had found a nice apartment for myself again, and I valued and enjoyed my independence. I had grown, I had overcome the worst crisis in my life and I had to some extent recovered. I had had to learn one of the most difficult lessons for me: that one cannot completely lose oneself in a relationship, that one has to accept one's own "individualness."

I had always experienced falling in love as almost a religious thing, like I was waiting for someone or something to lift me up from the incomplete state of aloneness, enabling me to feel ecstatic oneness and complete recognition. This desire for transcendence or oneness, rising above the boundaries of me, had eventually driven me to utter loneliness and despair. I was now recovering from this with a new sense of awareness, but still I felt quite lonely. I then met a former fellow student, and he was the only one at that point in my life who I could talk with, really talk with, about the things that mattered to me. We got involved and lived together for almost four years. It was more like a brother-sister relationship though. I told myself this was for the best, since too much passion had gotten the better of me and I still felt disillusioned about that former relationship.

Meanwhile I had to prepare myself to find work, now that I had said goodbye to university life. This was not as easy as I thought. My boyfriend and I planned to teach philosophy courses and do counseling work, and take part-time jobs just for the money. I started working as a secretary in various jobs, but I was appalled at how office life works: the power struggles, the gossips, the humiliation of not being able to express one's true abilities as a secretary. I was utterly naive, since I had spent ten years at the university, working at home most of the time and having lots of freedom to organize my work as I pleased. After a couple of years, I moved into a more prestigious job, but I ended up being very stressed.

Then came a turning point. I had an aura reading from a woman who later became my teacher. The reading greatly moved and awakened me. It made me realize that both in the area of work and in the area of relationships, I was unhappy and out of balance. I could admit to myself that I was in a dead end street. I had these surges of creative energy, I had dreams and visions for the future, but meanwhile I was simply holding on to a relationship and a working environment that were preventing me from truly expressing myself. I was afraid to be on my own again. A few months after I met this spiritual therapist, I started a course in intuitive development and aura reading with her and I quit my stressful, unsatisfying job. I started another easier part-time job (which would not last long either).

Self exploration

In the fall of that year 2000, I felt drawn to investigate my past lives through regression therapy. This proved to be an amazing adventure. I had already started to spontaneously view past life images, which evoked strong emotions in me and gave me the sense of being a much larger identity than just my current personality. In the past life regression therapy, I investigated many lifetimes, which explained to me a lot about why I had always felt certain ways. The one that perhaps impacted me most was the most recent lifetime in which I died as a Holocaust victim in the concentration camp of Auschwitz-Birkenau. Reliving this experience made me understand the inexplicable sadness that I had always sensed deep inside, and the resistance I had felt towards life. Other lifetimes, ranging from spiritually focused ones to very disempowered ones *and* ones in which I had misused my power, opened up such a new range of awareness, that I felt a great desire to share my experiences with someone who would understand. By then my boyfriend had started to think I was going slightly mad…

Meeting Gerrit

I had just gotten acquainted with the Internet then and browsing around, I stumbled on Gerrit's web site about reincarnation, time and spirituality. Immediately, I was struck by the energy it emitted and by the shared interests we had. I had the strangest feeling that either he was someone incredibly familiar to me, or I was really going mad and making things up. I decided to write to him anyway and a lively correspondence ensued. Three months later we met in person. I had by then broken up with my partner. When I met Gerrit, I had the sensation that I knew him very well, only not as this particular 20th century appearance! It was inexplicable and mysterious. I was immediately drawn to him and, as it happened, he to me!

I moved in with him a few months later, got pregnant right away and before the year was over we were married! In 2002, our daughter Laura was born. The period in which I thoroughly investigated my past lives, got to know Gerrit and moved to another part of The Netherlands where Gerrit lived felt to me like a period of deep transition, even dying. I felt like I was emerging from my previous personality as a new me, but more of me than I had ever been before! I felt like I was entering an altogether new way of being, in which, finally, things made sense, fit together and paved the way for long held dreams to come true.

Starting up my practice

After my daughter was born, I started my spiritual practice of aura reading and healing, and clients started to come to me from the middle of 2002 onward. Things just went naturally and smoothly, without having to put too much effort into it. I had finally found the work that I could truly express myself in. I did have to deal with a lot of fears that I had not anticipated. Now that I was doing the work I loved, I discovered I had fears about really expressing myself, about being different, being strong and self confident. I felt vulnerable, because for the first time I was truly expressing myself, withholding nothing, and the risk of being rejected or criticized frightened me. I could do only a few consultations a week.

Meeting Jeshua

Meanwhile, Gerrit and I often held sessions for ourselves, exploring our inner worlds, the emotional scars and wounds from this and other lifetimes and other subjects such as astrology and the changes in the world. One night, I felt a presence near me whose energy was different from what I was used to. It felt serious and solemn and it made me slightly nervous. I was used to making contact with spiritual guides, my own or other people's guides. But this felt different.

I decided to investigate who this was, with the help of Gerrit, and when I got into the trance state and connected to the energy, I saw the name *Jeshua ben Joseph* in front of my inner eye and I immediately felt it was true. In a split second, just before my intellect started to raise doubts and questions, I recognized Jeshua as a deeply familiar presence that it was very natural to feel close to. There was an inner recognition and therefore I accepted the connection. The fact that he presented himself as Jeshua ben Joseph and not as Jesus showed me that he wanted to make clear from the start that he was not the personality manufactured by the Bible and by tradition.

I started to explore the connection with Jeshua in the coming weeks and months. I told no one, only Gerrit knew. It felt authentic and right, even though I had to get used to the energy I felt entering my aura and body when I connected to Jeshua. His energy was very centering and grounding and it gave me a clear focus, devoid of sentimentality and drama. It was quite direct and powerful. What frightened me was the power in it! It offered me a level of consciousness in which one sees things very clearly, but also in a way that might be upsetting or unsettling to others. It was part of my personality that I tried to be nice and sweet, avoiding confrontations, and I thought I had already become quite independent and assertive. But Jeshua's energy showed me I had a ways to go yet! Especially working as a reader and healer, I had to balance my sensitive and empathic side with a male energy that would allow me to be up front, protect my boundaries and help me stay balanced and centered amidst heavy emotional energies. Jeshua offered me guidance in my work as a therapist, not only by giving me information in words or phrases, but by actually conveying his energy to me, making me understand what it is like to see things through his eyes, or perhaps better put: through the eyes of the Christ energy which is in all of us. By channeling his energy, literally by allowing it into my body and aura, I could grow personally and understand more.

After a while, Jeshua also started giving information to Gerrit and me that was more universal in nature. I would go into a trance state, guided by Gerrit, and then Jeshua would give me messages which came to me in the form of words or feelings which I had to translate into words. Perhaps the best way to put it is that he conveys *insights* to me (which make me feel like: Oh, now I see!) and that it is my task to translate these into the appropriate words, phrases and sentences. Sometimes the words roll easily out of my mouth, like they are given to me. At other times I have to look for formulations that match the energy I feel and it's more of a struggle. Also, the energy that comes forth in a channeling is sometimes difficult to put into words, for it is not just the literal information that comes through but also an energy of healing, love and clarity.

The first series of messages that came through was the Lightworker Series (part I of this book). It contains messages about the history of the lightworker souls, the coming of a new era and the transition from ego based consciousness to heart based consciousness. Jeshua told us this series of messages was meant especially for lightworkers. He said it was important that they wake up and realize who they are. It is when they have awakened that they will help other portions of humanity on their way towards a heart based consciousness.

Going public

I still had told no one about my connection with Jeshua, being afraid of ridicule and disbelief. It seemed quite impossible to me to say the words: "I am channeling Jeshua or Jesus" out loud to anyone. There was this skeptical philosopher lingering in the back of my mind, explaining to me I was about to have myself declared pretentious, confused, insane or worse. Nevertheless, I confided in some close friends and we had some small sessions together which worked out well. Also, we published the first series of channelings on my web site (in Dutch). Then, more than a year after I had "met" Jeshua, I got an invitation from a Belgian spiritual center to come and give a public channeling. I was shocked at the mere thought of it, but on the other hand I knew I should not refuse, that I had to go through this fear, and that Jeshua would not lead me astray. I was nervous for weeks and sick and sleepless the days before, but then the first public channeling took place and it had a great positive impact on me. It was a short channeling and Q&A session (the first one of the Healing Series, see part II of this book) but I felt Jeshua's presence pouring though me very clearly. People were warm and enthusiast in their reactions and the public hanging failed to occur.

I was on such a high after that first public channeling that I immediately decided to organize meetings at our own house and so we did. But the fears were not over yet. Every time I had to channel in front of an audience I felt great resistance, fear and even anger! I was never one who felt comfortable speaking in public, being shy and withdrawn. Why put myself in such a vulnerable spot, not sure whether anything coherent would come out my mouth or whether Jeshua was going to be there in the first place?! Of course, he was always "there" for me. My persistent insecurity, fear and indignation that "I had to do this" was simply my ego fighting to the last to put an end to this wildly irresponsible undertaking.

Having Jeshua speak through me went against all my safety mechanisms. It flaunted all my acquired habits of being cautious, reserved and on the sidelines. I had been a bit of a misanthrope for long, not trusting people easily. Now here was this energy presence, telling people through me how he loved and cherished them, encouraging them to embrace their own inner knowing and power, even scolding them humorously about their stubbornness or resistance. This could not be me!

I was amazed at the reactions we received. First, we put all the channelings on our Dutch web site, which started to attract a growing audience. We got hundreds of e-mails in the years that followed from people telling us they were very moved by the messages and that it was almost like Jeshua was speaking to them directly! After a while, I translated the channelings into English and we made an English web site as well. It didn't attract many readers at first but Jeshua told us to simply let it be and wait. Indeed, after more than a year we started to receive messages from English speaking readers and we started to offer long distance readings to people abroad as well. Things were getting busy.

Expansion

Several people from different countries then contacted us through e-mail and volunteered to translate the Jeshua messages. They manifested out of nothing to us, able translators and kindred spirits who felt like family and who simply offered their services because they were inspired by the Jeshua material. It's amazing. Translations into Spanish, Hebrew, French, Portuguese, German and Finnish are now available on the Internet. We got befriended by people around the world, sharing a common interest and desire which seems to transcend cultural boundaries. Jeshua had told me that I just had to write the material and then let go. It would find its own way and it truly did.

The Internet has been a major medium for this. One of the synchronicities in our story was that Gerrit works as an IT consultant and is able to design and maintain web sites. I also feel that my background as a philosopher has helped me a lot to translate the energy of Jeshua into words and concepts. Also, I had always loved to write and I had been trained to write in English as a student of philosophy. I feel that in creating the channelings and doing readings for clients, I am finally "doing my thing," the thing that I was born to do. It gives me a deep sense of fulfillment to receive so many warm and kind responses from people all over the world, and I also feel grateful that I can now make a living out of the thing that I love to do most.

Channeling – a bit of debunking

In conclusion, I would like to make some general remarks on the phenomenon of channeling. Perhaps being Dutch (they are considered to be a very down-to-earth people!) and still quite sceptical about some of the new age stuff I encounter, I would like to put some things about channeling into perspective.

The relationship between channeler and channeled entity

I think of channeling as a cooperation between a human being and a non-physical entity who acts as a teacher. The teacher offers inspiration and a larger perspective to the human being, and the human being translates the energy of the spiritual entity into the words and concepts that the human being is acquainted with through their upbringing, education and culture. I do not believe that it is possible, or even desirable, that human channels should completely set themselves aside in order to purely channel the non-physical entity's energy. I think it is inevitable that the channel's mind set, awareness and vocabulary greatly influence what comes through. Even if the channel goes into a deep trance state, the channel is the receiver, the vessel and therefore co-creator of the material. I think it is naive to presume that a channeler can receive a message totally from without, taking no part in it. I believe the messages come from within, through the channel's consciousness, *enlarged* by the spiritual teacher's consciousness, and that the quality of the channeling does not so much depend on the extent to which channelers can eliminate themselves as on the level of consciousness that both the channeler and the channeled entity posses. Channeling is essentially a co-creation.

How to judge the quality of channeled information

Channeling can be beautiful and inspiring. But it can also lead to nonsense, hollow phrases, or fearful, moralistic tales of woe. At its worst, it leads to the worship of authorities who have nothing going for them except their name or rank in some invisible spiritual hierarchy. Looking up to elusive authorities outside of us – isn't that precisely what all spiritual teachers have warned us against?

The fact that information is channeled says absolutely nothing about the quality of it. In the philosophy of science, the branch of philosophy that investigates what makes scientific theories scientific or trustworthy, a useful distinction is made between the "context of discovery" and "the context of justification." What leads to the *discovery* of a scientific theory has no bearing on whether it can be *justified*. Scientists can make up any theory they want, relying on personal dreams, associations, or reveries, but once they have formulated the theory, it will be judged by their peers on the basis of generally acknowledged criteria such as empirical confirmation, coherence, explanatory power, etc. So in the context of discovery, *anything goes*, whereas in the context of justification, the theory has to live up to certain standards of quality in order to be valued by the scientific community.

I think the same goes for channeled material. Channeled messages should be judged by the same standards as spiritual texts from "mere humans:" is the information clear, does it add new insights to your knowledge, does it inspire you to love yourself more, do you feel enlightened and uplifted by the message? I think if the answer is yes, the question of who channeled it and how it came about (the context of discovery) is relatively unimportant. The proof is in the pudding, not in the alleged rank or status of the cook who prepared it.

My own experience as a channeler

When I channel Jeshua, I feel myself getting larger instead of smaller. I feel his energy helping me rise to the greatness of my own greater Self. I think he is in fact mediating between the small everyday me and the larger Me, helping me to embody Me a little more. Every time he does this and I allow it, I am expanding my consciousness a little more, and it affects my own growth and empowerment. One time, I did a channeling ("Relationships in the New Era") in which I so strongly felt the presence of my own higher or greater self (who I call Aurelia), that I doubted whether I was still channeling Jeshua. I asked him that evening before I went to sleep, and then he said something very endearing to me: "Remember always: *I am there for you, you are not there for me.*" This made it very clear to me. We are all meant to fully embody and manifest our greater Selves here on earth. Teachers come along to help us on our path and if it's a true teacher, he or she will help you as long as you need it, and then get out of the way.

Jeshua is still with me, although I feel I am not "chatting" with him as much as I used to in the beginning. Often nowadays when I ask him a personal question, he asks me: what do you truly feel about it? And when I focus on that, the answer is there, from my own inner knowing and intuition. So Jeshua encourages us all to take up our own power and to see channeling as a means and not as an end. Perhaps one day I will be able to channel my own higher or Christ self, and not rely on Jeshua anymore. I am sure he would be the first to applaud me!

Jeshua on channeling

I will conclude with a "channeling on channeling," a few words from Jeshua on his relationship with me as channeler.

Channeling is a way of getting closer to yourself with the help of another – non-physical – being. This being temporarily plays the role of a teacher. The energy of the teacher helps you get to a deeper level of yourself. The teacher's energy lifts you out of the fears that keep your own light veiled.

A teacher shows you your own light. The teacher is more aware of your light than you are. As soon as this light, your inner knowing, is accessible to yourself, the teacher becomes superfluous. You are then able to channel your own light. The teacher does not have to act as a bridge any more between you and your higher self.

I am reminding you for a while of your own light. I mirror your greatness to you in the shape of Jeshua ben Joseph. In me you see yourself, your Christ self, but you do not realize this fully yet. I am like a frame of reference to you; my energy serves as a beacon. I help you get more deeply acquainted with your own Christ self. It will slowly move to the foreground and I will move to the background. This is all right. It is as it should be. Don't forget: in this relationship, I am there for you, you are not there for me. I am not the aim, but the means. The rebirth of Christ is the awakening of your Christ self, not mine.

I act according to what serves your greater Self. My aim is that you make me superfluous. When you channel me, do not try to make yourself small or invisible. I wish that you make yourself bigger, that you feel your true strength flow out of you and shine upon the world.

A teacher points at the road but it is you who walk it. After a while, you find yourself walking alone, having left the teacher behind. This is a grand and sacred moment. The teacher will stay with you, will live on in your heart as an inner presence, but the separate figure will disappear.

We stay connected, but as you grow, you will see me less and less, or want to call upon me as a separate being. I will slowly become part of your own energy. And at some point, you will not know me as separate from you anymore. This will show that you have truly heard and seen me.

Contact information

Pamela Kribbe and her husband Gerrit Gielen live and work in The Netherlands (Europe). They have their own spiritual practice and together they offer workshops and meetings, working closely with the energy of Jeshua. For more information on their work, as well as more channeled material, see their website www.jeshua.net

Pamela and Gerrit can be contacted at aurelia@jeshua.net

To order a copy of "The Jeshua channelings", go to www.jeshua.net/book

CPSIA information can be obtained at www.ICGtesting.com
Printed in the USA
LVOW051919060613

337393LV00002B/324/P